CREATING PROSPERITY

ABOUT THE INSTITUTE FOR PUBLIC POLICY RESEARCH

The Institute for Public Policy Research is an independent charity whose purpose is to contribute to public understanding of social, economic and political questions through research, discussion and publication. It was established in 1988 by leading figures in the academic, business and trade-union community to provide an alternative to the free market think tanks.

IPPR's research agenda covers the areas of economic and industrial policy, defence, governmental reform, human rights, social policy, the environment and media issues. It also publishes a quarterly journal *New Economy* (launched in 1993 and already a leader in its field) and a twice yearly newsletter, *In Progress*. Those with access to the Internet can visit IPPR and the CPPBB at: http://www.ippr.org.uk.

If you would like to support IPPR and receive up-to-date reports from the cutting edge of public-policy research, you can contact us at the address below. We also plan to follow on our work in this report and further develop some of the policy ideas. If you wish to receive information about this or would like to participate in future discussions, please write to or telephone:

Commission on Public Policy and British Business
IPPR
30–32 Southampton Street
London WC2E 7RA

Telephone: 0171 470 6100
Fax: 0171 470 6111

PROMOTING PROSPERITY

A Business Agenda for Britain

REPORT OF THE COMMISSION
ON PUBLIC POLICY AND
BRITISH BUSINESS

VINTAGE

Published by Vintage 1997

2 4 6 8 10 9 7 5 3 1

Copyright © 1997 The Commission on Public Policy and British
Business/Institute for Public Policy Research

Vintage
Random House, 20 Vauxhall Bridge Road,
London SW1V 2SA

Random House Australia (Pty) Limited
20 Alfred Street, Milsons Point, Sydney
New South Wales 2061, Australia

Random House New Zealand Limited
18 Poland Road, Glenfield,
Auckland 10, New Zealand

Random House South Africa (Pty) Limited
Endulini, 5A Jubilee Road, Parktown 2193,
South Africa

Random House UK Limited Reg. No. 954009

A CIP catalogue record for this book
is available from the British Library

ISBN 0 09 974761 8

Papers used by Random House UK Ltd are
natural, recyclable products made from wood grown in
sustainable forests. The manufacturing processes conform
to the environmental regulations of the country of origin

Printed and bound in Great Britain by
Cox & Wyman, Reading, Berkshire

Designed by Roger Walker

A VINTAGE ORIGINAL

CONTENTS

Part Three: Framework

LIST OF FIGURES, TABLES AND DIAGRAMS

Figures

Tables

Diagrams

CHAIRMAN'S FOREWORD

The Commission on Public Policy and British Business was set up in April 1995 at the instigation of Baroness Blackstone and Lord Hollick. Their aim was to build on the success of John Smith's Commission on Social Justice, which set the agenda for reform of the welfare state and education when it was published in the autumn of 1994. While its remit was to investigate the allocation of wealth and opportunity, ours has been to investigate the competitive position of the UK economy and the role that public policy should play in improving it. As Lord Hollick remarked at our launch, 'If that Commission was on how to spend it, this one is on how to make it.'

Perhaps the most remarkable feature of this Commission is its broad appeal in terms both of its own membership and the conclusions it draws. The Commissioners themselves cover a wide range of the political spectrum. They include both business practitioners from a variety of sectors including manufacturing, services, retailing, finance and consultancy, and academics with expertise in different areas. Their one common attribute is that they are all leaders in their own fields and, indeed, are nationally respected figures. As a result, their deliberations and conclusions have transcended narrow business or political interests, and their conclusions are based on a genuine common interest in promoting a prosperous future for Britain.

This book constitutes the final report of the Commission, which was unanimously agreed at our last meeting on 14 October 1996. It provides an agenda for promoting prosperity in Britain. After identifying the problems that need fixing and summarising the potential role of government, we establish four policy themes which we believe should guide any government wishing to promote prosperity. In our view the government of the United Kingdom should act to promote competition and co-operation, foster far-sighted companies, mobilise people's potential and ensure consistency in public policy. These four themes underpin all the policy considerations and recommendations we make in the report.

The Commission's base was the Institute for Public Policy Research, the independent, centre-left think tank in London. The scope and scale of its investigations have been very broad. During its lifetime the Commission met fourteen times and detailed investigations were carried out by working groups in nine areas. We also hosted two consultative conferences: on finance–industry relations in October 1995 and on corporate governance in February 1996. Finally, in addition to this report we published six 'issue papers' on topics as diverse as competition policy and globalisation. These greatly helped to stimulate our thinking and our thanks go to the people who took the time and effort to write these papers. In addition, numerous organisations and individuals submitted evidence, either in writing or orally, to our investigation. Their willingness to come forward and offer their opinions is in itself testimony both to the need for change and the widespread acceptance of the Commission and its work.

The Commission was staffed by its Secretary, Dr Simon Milner; a Research Fellow, Andrea Westall; and two Administrators, Joanne Bailey (until December 1995) and Ella Truscott (January to September 1996). We are most grateful to our staff for their creativity, consistent hard work and superb organisation. We are also grateful to The Gatsby Charitable Foundation for its grant to the IPPR, which made the Commission possible.

Professor George Bain
18 October 1996

THE COMMISSIONERS

Professor George Bain (Chairman)
Principal, London Business School

Bob Bauman
Chairman, British Aerospace

Bob Bischof
Chairman, Boss Group Ltd

James Hall
Managing Partner, Andersen Consulting

Jan Hall
European Chief Executive, GGT Group

Sir Christopher Harding
Chairman, Legal & General

Lucy Heller
Chairman, Verso

Lord Hollick
Chief Executive, United News and Media

Gerald Holtham
Director, Institute for Public Policy Research

Alan Hughes
Director, ESRC Centre for Business Research, University of Cambridge

Professor John Kay
Chairman, London Economics, and Director of the School of Management
Studies, University of Oxford

Professor Richard Layard
Director, Centre for Economic Performance, London School of Economics

John Monks
General Secretary, Trades Union Congress

David Sainsbury
Chairman, J Sainsbury plc

George Simpson
Managing Director, The General Electric Company plc

ACKNOWLEDGEMENTS

In addition to the many people who wrote papers and answered queries, the Commission is indebted to a number of people who were especially helpful during the course of the Commission's work. Among IPPR staff we would like to thank senior economist Dan Corry, the press and publications team of Joanne Bailey, Rosaleen Hughes and Helena Scott, research fellows Chris Hewett, Josh Hillman, Cristina Murroni and Stephen Tindale, and members of the administrative team including Lucy Delap, Judith Edwards and Melanie Vincent and our graphic designer James Sparling of Emphasis. We have also been helped by a number of interns and occasional researchers: Sarah Franklin, Ben Jones, Ranjita Rajan, Anand Shukla and Joanne Yoon.

Of the many people who provided oral and written evidence, listed at the end of the report, a number were particularly helpful in responding to our many questions. These include Robin Aaronson, Stephen Bond, David Charles, Nigel Collard, Simon Deakin, Malcolm Gammie, Mark Goyder, Kirsty Hughes, Stephen Joseph, Colin Mayer, John Mulvey, Kate Oakley, Nick Oulton, John Parkinson, Keith Pavitt, Peter Robinson, Chris Savage and Giles Slinger.

We would like to thank the management and staff of the Hawkwell House Hotel, Iffley, for providing a 'lively' venue for our weekend retreat in September 1996.

Finally, many thanks to Morgan Witzel for his valuable help in editing the manuscript and to the publishing team at Vintage, particularly Will Sulkin and Rowena Skelton-Wallace, for keeping us on our toes.

ABBREVIATIONS

ABI	Association of British Insurers
ACE	Allowance for Corporate Equity
ACT	Advance Corporation Tax
AIM	Alternative Investment Market
BCC	British Chamber of Commerce
BVCA	British Venture Capital Association
CBI	Confederation of British Industry
CEO	Chief Executive Officer
CEST	Centre for Exploitation of Science and Technology
CGT	Capital Gains Tax
CII	Council of Institutional Investors
DfEE	Department for Education and Employment
DGFT	Director-General of Fair Trading
DTI	Department of Trade and Industry
EMU	European Monetary Union
ERM	Exchange Rate Mechanism
ERVET	Agency for Economic Development for the Region of Emilia-Romagna
ESOP	Employee Share Ownership Plan
EU	European Union
EWC	European Works Council
FMC	Financial Management Certificate
FTA	Fair Trading Act, 1973
GDP	Gross Domestic Product
GGFD	General Government Financial Deficit
GNVQ	General National Vocational Qualification
IBM	International Business Machines
IFS	Institute for Fiscal Studies
IiP	Investors in People

ABBREVIATIONS

IMF	International Monetary Fund
IoD	Institute of Directors
ION	Investment Opportunity Network
IPPR	Institute for Public Policy Research
IRR	Internal Rates of Return
LBS	London Business School
MMC	Monopolies and Mergers Commission
MGS	Mutual Guarantee Scheme
NACETT	National Advisory Council on Education and Training Targets
NAIRU	Non-Accelerating Inflation Rate of Unemployment
NAO	National Audit Office
NAPF	National Association of Pension Funds
NASDAQ	National Association of Securities Dealers Automated Quotations
NCE	National Commission on Education
NED	Non-Executive Director
NIC	National Insurance Contribution
NIESR	National Institute of Economic and Social Research
NTBF	New Technology-Based Firm
NVQ	National Vocational Qualification
OECD	Organisation for Economic Co-operation and Development
OFT	Office of Fair Trading
OLA	Open Learning Agency
ONS	Office of National Statistics
OST	Office of Science and Technology
PFI	Private Finance Initiative
PSBR	Public Sector Borrowing Requirement
QMV	Qualified Majority Voting
R&D	Research and Development
RCEP	Royal Commission on Environmental Pollution
RSA	Royal Society for the Encouragement of Arts, Manufacture and Commerce
SACTRA	Standing Advisory Committee on Trunk Road Assessment
SBI	Small Business Initiative
SEA	Single European Act
SFA	Shareholders' Fund Account
SME	Small and Medium-Sized Enterprises
TEC	Training and Enterprise Council
TUC	Trades Union Congress

EXECUTIVE SUMMARY

Promoting Prosperity is a public policy agenda for a more prosperous Britain – an aim that calls for progress in business competitiveness and performance. Better businesses will improve productivity, increase investment, and yield gains for the whole country in the form of rising real incomes, employment and morale.

In order to achieve this ambition we must tackle the economic underperformance of many British companies. The causes of underperformance are various and interrelated; we identify four in particular. We offer no panacea to correct them, but set out four broad policy themes, while stressing that improved performance requires the patient application of numerous specific measures. Our policy recommendations cover three main areas:

- companies and management;
- people or 'human resources';
- the national economic framework.

Chapter 1: What Needs Fixing?

The United Kingdom is a wealthy country with a great commercial tradition, but for most of this century it has been sliding down the international league table of prosperity. We trace this relative underperformance to four related characteristics of the national economy:

- too many inefficient and poorly run companies;
- too many underachieving people;

- too little investment in research, innovation and physical capital;
- too frequent shifts in government policy.

To tackle these problems would be hard at any time. The challenge is greater and more urgent today because change and uncertainty are accelerating, driven by the globalisation of the world economy and by the information revolution.

Chapter 2: Role of Government

In a market economy, companies are the engine of wealth creation, but government has a supportive and collaborative role to play and its impact in the UK should be focused more sharply and energised more powerfully by concentrating on four themes:

Competition and co-operation. Strong economies combine shrewd and demanding consumers with highly competitive product markets and co-operative inter-firm structures (such as production networks or supplier groups) to disseminate best practice or share key human or organisational resources. Government must monitor and maintain competition, and should also seek ways to keep consumers better informed and to facilitate co-operation among companies.

Far-sighted companies. Managerial short-termism is a common UK problem. Government should foster far-sighted management by removing obstacles to, and providing incentives for a long-term perspective.

Human potential. In raising the standards of education, training and skills among our current and future workforce, government plays a central role. Long-term unemployment and welfare dependency are not only social evils in themselves, they also hobble and hold back the economy.

Consistency in government policy. In order to provide a stable and fruitful environment for business, the various arms of government policy that affect it should be consistent, both with each other and over time.

We believe that the agenda of market liberalisation has largely run its course. More than that, it has cleared an arena in which government must now consult and work with the business community to improve corporate and national economic performance. While the European Single Market offers an essential institutional framework for this partnership, there are ways in which it constrains British policy and poses awkward choices. If this country, and Europe as a whole, are to thrive in the global economy, Britain must confront these choices and work for an open, competitive, and lightly but clearly regulated system.

Chapter 3: Competitive Product Markets

Vigorous competition in domestic markets must be central to any initiative to strengthen UK competitiveness. Government has an important role in sustaining competition, directly through reformed competition policy and indirectly by raising the quality of domestic demand. Current competition policy is feeble. Anti-competitive practices may be banned, once identified, but there is little other penalty. Actions, affiliations and arrangements aimed at undermining competition should be specifically outlawed, with the possibility of substantial fines for breaches. The responsibilities of the regulatory authorities, the Office of Fair Trading (OFT) and the Monopolies and Mergers Commission (MMC), should be extended and reallocated to underpin a tougher régime. The government should also have an explicit bias towards publicly disclosing any information it has which will help consumers to make informed choices.

Chapter 4: Far-Sighted Management

It is not just the inefficient companies, the long tail of underperformers, which suffer from short-termism. The problem is also present in some otherwise competent companies. The UK's economy would be sounder if more companies followed best practice in dealing with customers, investors, employees, suppliers – all those groups that have a common interest in the company's performance – and if more companies operated with a far-sighted business ethos. Although short-termism is pervasive in the UK's corporate culture, it should not be blamed solely on the financial sector. Nevertheless, there is room for improvement in the communications between companies and the financial institutions that represent their shareholders.

Two policies in particular would help to overcome the inertia of corporate culture. They are, first, a freer formulation of directors' duties, and, second, enhanced requirements for company reporting of non-financial performance measures. Enhanced reporting would focus attention on those elements of a company's practice that are relevant to its longer-term performance, and so would augment short-term financial measures. We also recommend establishing a Council of Institutional Investors, which would monitor underperforming firms and make public its assessments, without impairing the ability of individual fund managers to trade on their own judgements. This would act to improve communications between managers and investors, and would be a source of discipline on managers, perhaps reducing the need for hostile takeovers. Relationships with employees should be reinforced by further opportunities for share ownership, and enhanced rights to information and to redundancy compensation immediately after a takeover.

Chapter 5: World-Class SMEs

Small and medium-sized enterprises (SMEs) share most of the problems of larger companies. They also face problems of their own. Government policy already targets SMEs for substantial assistance through a miscellany of supporting bodies and schemes. These need to be rationalised. The present system gives rise to duplication and turf battles, and the existing agencies are too geared to providing standardised support services. They do not do enough to stimulate SMEs to analyse their own requirements and to help themselves through creating networks or co-operative associations. We recommend an alternative strategy for SME policy based on the encouragement of self-help networks. A basic example would be improving SME access to finance through mutual guarantee schemes. The measures we recommend to reduce the reliance of SMEs on short-term debt include establishing a Financial Management Certificate and liberalising rules on the issuance of non-voting shares.

Chapter 6: Improving Skills

Competitiveness depends crucially on a motivated force of skilled and adaptable workers. Despite some recent improvements, Britain's education and training system continues to fail people and business alike. The United Kingdom still generates a higher proportion of underachieving people than its competitors. Many children specialise too early, with the result that school and college graduates have too narrow a range of competence and many lack basic skills. The problem is compounded by adults having too few opportunities for first-class learning, particularly to acquire new general skills. We recommend specific improvements in schools, increased funding for early learning, and reform of A Levels. We also propose a national training requirement for 16- to 19-year-olds leaving school, and equality of finance between further and sixth-form education and between full- and part-time learners in higher education. Government can also facilitate training by broadening the role of training and enterprise councils (TECs) and through certain small-firm initiatives which exploit new technology.

Chapter 7: Effective Labour Markets

Underperformance and underachievement can lapse too easily into failure and decay. Low productivity starts up the vicious circle of months and then years of unemployment, and eventually welfare dependency. The long-term unemployed struggle to find jobs, skills erode, and as the fiscal burden on the state increases it hampers competitiveness. Good training succeeds in the long run, but in the meantime we must ensure that those with fewer skills can still find work. We propose to extricate the short-term unemployed from the cycle of unemployment by using benefit money as a wage subsidy, with a fall-back scheme for part-time work organised through local government. In order for schemes like this to work, we have to eliminate unemployment traps created by the tax and benefit system. That entails preserving and extending the present policy, which pays benefits to low-income workers as well as to the unemployed. A minimum wage prevents unscrupulous employers from substituting benefits for wages, and acts to limit costs to the taxpayer. The provisions of the European Social Chapter are currently innocuous, though signing it does carry potential risks. Nevertheless, the UK's position and continued influence in the Single Market require that we opt in.

Chapter 8: Strengthening Science, Transport and Public Procurement

Companies operate within a national framework of law and practice that also includes the physical infrastructure and the sphere of publicly funded research. By its management and upkeep of that framework, government exerts a vital influence, both direct and indirect, over the national economy. In many areas of infrastructure provision the UK is relatively well served. In basic scientific research, transport and public procurement, however, there is scope for changes that would enhance business competitiveness. Without a solid science base, innovation can only decline, yet finance for pure scientific research has been run down. It is right to encourage practical development of scientific advances, but it is misguided to do so at the expense of pure research.

A piecemeal physical infrastructure, especially transport, can only impede competitiveness. The government cannot leave the future of transport infrastructure entirely to the market; it needs a broader strategy involving some rationalisation of road use through pricing and improved public transport. Finally, a far-sighted approach to public procurement can promote innovation and best practice in the private sector. This is worth attempting, despite some risk to procurement costs.

Chapter 9: Even-Handed Business Taxation

Two themes draw our attention to the corporate tax system. We want to promote far-sighted companies and to counteract underinvestment. The desirable attributes of a tax system are stability, simplicity and neutrality, but the present UK system fails on the last two. We recommend changing the system of corporate taxation to lower the cost of capital after tax, and to restore neutrality among types of investment and finance, and between profit retention and dividend distribution. Among various ways to reform corporation tax to achieve these aims, the system of allowing a normal return on corporate equity against corporation tax, known as ACE, is one of the more promising. It would put an end to tax imputation for dividends, and to the complicated advance corporation tax (ACT) system. But since we are also concerned with policy stability, we recommend that any changes be phased in gradually.

Chapter 10: Macroeconomic Stability

Business requires a stable financial environment, yet relatively unstable inflation and a more fluctuating business cycle have placed British-based companies at a severe disadvantage in recent decades. Macroeconomic policy bears part of the blame, and here we need a disciplined steadiness. The government should adopt a new and tighter framework for fiscal policy, backed by a proper system of accounts on an accruals basis which would allow more productive investment by public corporations. The government should also set a nominal GDP growth target, encompassing the paramount need to control inflation and the objective of maintaining stability. With such a target set by politicians, the Bank of England can be given autonomy to control interest rates. Whatever the decision over the single European currency – in or out – there will be risks. Business can cope with the economic pressures in either event. There is also a crucial political dimension. The United Kingdom must retain its place in the Single Market and its influence over EU legislation. If entry to EMU is necessary to maintain that place and influence, then we should take part. In practice, much may depend on how many other countries join EMU.

Recommendations

PART ONE: COMPANIES

Chapter 3: Competitive Product Markets

1 The government should adopt a prohibition approach to restrictive agreements and abuse of market power with stiffer penalties for anti-competitive behaviour, including fines up to, say, a maximum of 10 per cent of turnover in the market concerned.

2 There should be a substantial increase in the powers of the Director-General of Fair Trading and his staff to investigate suspected anti-competitive behaviour.

3 The Secretary of State's role in competition policy should be made transparent through the publication of a report with reasons for his decisions.

4 The responsibilities of the OFT and MMC should be realigned to make the OFT the principal agent of investigation and prosecution with the MMC concentrating on adjudication.

5 The government should be predisposed to public disclosure of the information it has about companies where that would enable consumers to make more informed choices.

Chapter 4: Far-Sighted Management

1 The government should clarify directors' duties as currently stated in the Companies Act to enable directors to take a broader view of their responsibilities.

2 Trust law should be simplified to allow blocks of shares to be assigned to employees collectively and held for them indefinitely, and current practices limiting the issuance of non-voting shares should be liberalised.

3 There should be no new administrative restraints on takeovers, but contracts between management and individual employees should be binding and redundancy rights should be extended for a period after an acquisition.

4 There should be an extension of individual employee rights to information and consultation.

5 There should be extended reporting requirements under the Companies Act and companies should be encouraged, through the development of 'best practice' codes, to state their objectives more fully and to report on non-financial performance measures.

6 A Council of Institutional Investors should be set up to monitor and research underperforming companies. It should publish a list of those in which it lacks confidence. The government should make subscription to this body mandatory for any investment fund wanting to trade in the UK.

Chapter 5: World-Class SMEs

1 Business Links should become predominantly sign-posting bodies to public- and private-sector service providers. They should no longer be required to become self-financing.

2 The government should initiate an information campaign about the value of SME networks and investigate the most appropriate means for encouraging their formation, perhaps involving financial bursaries for successful proposals.

3 Information flows between banks and new, especially high-tech, borrowers should be improved, with mutual guarantee schemes employed to reduce uncertainty. These should receive some seedcorn money which should be conditional on the mutual guarantee scheme not operating to restrict competition.

4 Action should be taken to improve the market in equity capital, including the establishment of an Investment Opportunity

Network and the relaxation of restrictions on the issuance of non-voting equity.

5 The government should help to establish a Financial Management Certificate specifically designed for SME owner-managers.

PART TWO: PEOPLE

Chapter 6 : Improving Skills

1 The top priority in education should be to improve the quality of teaching and learning in schools. As well as reform of teacher training and assessment, this will require increased spending.

2 The government should fund high-quality nursery education for all three- and four-year-olds whose parents want it.

3 Class sizes in all primary schools should be reduced to thirty or under.

4 Mandatory traineeships should be introduced for all young workers to ensure that they are not lost to the education and training system at the age of sixteen.

5 The long term objective of phasing out A Levels should be pursued by broadening university entrance requirements.

6 Funding biases in adult education should be eliminated by making all sub-degree courses free and charging partial fees for all part- and full-time degree courses.

7 TEC funding should be made more flexible to enable them to promote employee training.

8 The government should encourage a business angel approach to training for SME managers.

9 The government should actively promote the use of advanced information networks in adult education and training.

Chapter 7: Effective Labour Markets

1 An effort should be made to prevent people remaining unemployed for more than a year by using the money saved by not paying their benefits to subsidise job opportunities. A back-up scheme should provide part-time work at a local level for the long-term unemployed.

2 The government should extend in-work benefits for low-income workers to combat the unemployment-benefit trap, but a minimum wage should be introduced to prevent this being exploited by unscrupulous employers at the taxpayers' expense. The minimum wage should not be set too high since it could destroy jobs in some sectors.

3 In order to preserve the EU Single Market and to influence the future development of European social policy, the UK should opt in to the Social Chapter.

PART THREE: FRAMEWORK

Chapter 8: Strengthening Science, Transport and Public Procurement

1 The government should increase spending on the public science base to the average of the UK's main competitors.

2 The government should set out a coherent statement of the principles and targets of its transport strategy.

3 The management of demand for road use in some urban areas should involve road pricing.

4 There should be increased emphasis on inter-modal linkages for freight and passenger transport.

5 The government should implement a new approach to public procurement that promotes innovation and best practice in the private sector without forsaking long-term value for money.

Chapter 9: Even-Handed Business Taxation

1 The government should aim to restructure the system of corporate taxation to achieve neutrality and, in particular, to remove biases which favour distribution rather than retention of profits. Any reform should be self-financing.

2 The Inland Revenue should relax rules about the types of business loans on which interest payments are tax deductible.

3 Tax legislation should include a preamble indicating the purpose of the legislation in order to assist the courts' interpretation in disputes.

4 Eligibility for the lower rate of small company taxation should be based on company results, or perhaps turnover, averaged over three years.
5 After consultation about the change, the government should introduce a new, lower rate of capital gains tax for assets held for the very long term, meaning at least ten years.

Chapter 10: Macroeconomic Stability

1 Fiscal policy should be supported by a proper system of accounts on an accruals basis.
2 The government should adopt a new, tighter framework for fiscal policy but one which would also allow more investment by self-financing public corporations.
3 The government should set a nominal GDP growth target and give independence to the Bank of England to achieve the target through control of interest rates.
4 The government should decide about EMU on the basis of a political judgement. If a substantial majority of EU economies choose to enter in the first wave, then the United Kingdom should join them.

1

WHAT NEEDS FIXING?

Promoting Prosperity *is an agenda for public policy designed to help realise a vision of a more prosperous Britain. In this chapter we first set out what we mean by prosperity and its foundation in business competitiveness. Britain is a wealthy country with much business success to its name. But for over a century it has lost ground relative to the most competitive countries; the bulk of the chapter examines the problems of the British economy and provides a diagnosis of their causes. We also analyse two important developments which are shaping progress in this country and elsewhere and will continue to do so: globalisation and the information revolution.*

At the heart of this report is a vision of a more prosperous Britain. Its central element is high and rising income per head, secured by rising productivity of both capital and labour; sustaining these are an adequate level of savings and investment, a reasonable distribution of economic activity across regions and people, and the preservation and maintenance of the natural environment.

This vision is within our grasp, but it requires the reversal of a manifest tendency to underperform. For most of the last century we have slid steadily down the league tables of national competitiveness. While this underperformance is relative and as a nation we are richer than ever before, the stark fact remains that over the long term our main competitors have been outperforming us. We know it is possible to do better.

In looking at British business, we are immediately struck by a disparity. The best of British firms are equal to the best in the world, but at the same time we have a large number of underperforming firms, a 'long tail' that drags down average business performance. The 'long tail' stems from a failure to adopt best practice and is linked to a further problem of underinvestment in innovation, research and physical capital. There is a 'long tail' not only of firms but also of people. A poor record of education and training, when compared with our rivals, has left us a legacy of underachieving people, too many of whom are long-term, even permanently, unemployed. Failure to mobilise people's potential has not only denied us the use of valuable human resources; it has also created an economic 'drag anchor' on competitiveness and prosperity. Finally, British firms have been hindered for decades by instability and uncertainty in the economic environment. In areas such as transport, taxation and investment in the science base, changeable government policy has let business down. The most damaging feature of all has been macroeconomic instability, which has been exacerbated by government policy errors.

What needs fixing? We concentrate on three areas. First, we need to look hard at firms, how they are managed and how they prepare for the future. Second, we must tackle the problem of personal underachievement and help people to fulfil their potential. Third, we must examine the climate in which businesses operate and ensure that they are supported, not hindered, in their efforts to compete and to promote prosperity.

Our Objective: Growing Prosperity

High and growing prosperity is our principal objective for Britain. No single economic indicator can adequately measure prosperity, but let us begin with the conventional measure, GDP per person or domestic output per head. GDP is the total output of the national economy, minus depreciation, over a period of time. *Sustained and vigorous growth in GDP per head*, as well as a relatively high overall level of GDP, is the first element in our vision of a prosperous Britain.

But this goal must be qualified. GDP per head has well-known limitations as a measure of welfare or prosperity. Two countries could have similar GDPs, but in one the workforce might work an average of fifty hours per week while in the second the average might be only thirty-five. Most would agree that the citizens of the second country would be better off since they would have more time for leisure and social activities. Therefore, *productivity growth*, and not simply longer hours, should be at the heart of growth in GDP.

Growth can also be increased if people work the same number of hours but consume less and save more. If the savings are then used for investment in capital, the increased automation or capital intensity of production can also boost growth. This may be desirable, but only up to a point. Consumption is the main purpose of economic activity, and to sacrifice it unduly to force investment does not raise welfare. The most desirable forms of growth maintain or increase the productivity of capital as well as increasing the productivity of labour. Therefore, we need to *increase the productivity of both people and capital* if we are all to enjoy the fruits of growth.

High and rising productivity of people and capital will create income and wealth. While wealth creation is the primary objective and public policy should seek to promote it, we cannot ignore the distribution of economic activity and what it implies for employment. If two countries have the same GDP per head but in one everyone is employed while in the second there is high unemployment, we would presumably regard the first as better off; it would probably be a calmer place, where political stability and economic success were more robust and assured. In the second country, some of the GDP of the employed 80 per cent would probably be required to police higher levels of crime and administer social services for the unemployed. Hence, *high levels of employment* and *a reasonable personal and regional distribution of economic activity* are also components of our vision.

Finally, growth must be ecologically sustainable. The use of natural resources as raw materials, as energy sources or as repositories for waste should be limited within the regenerative capacity of natural systems. A pleasant environment is among the good things which people typically wish to enjoy as they get richer. Moreover, we should not underestimate the value of a pleasant urban and rural environment in continuing to attract foreign investment to the United Kingdom.

In sum, prosperity involves a high and growing level of income per head, secured by rising productivity of people and capital. For this to be sustainable, we need a reasonable regional and personal distribution of economic activity, an adequate saving and investment rate and sufficient attention and resources devoted to the preservation of the natural environment.

Few, we hope, would disagree that this is a desirable vision for the United Kingdom. In a predominantly private enterprise economy, only business success can make this vision a reality. Business success alone will not ensure environmental preservation or full employment, but it is an indispensable precondition if those things are to be combined with material prosperity. Fortunately, there is a more widespread understanding of this principle today in the UK than there has been for many years. Our culture has always had certain anti-commercial elements, but in recent times these seem to have declined; now it is more generally accepted that the material fortunes of us all, the schoolteacher and the artist as much as the employee and shareholder, depend on the success of British business.

UK Prosperity in Perspective

In absolute terms British prosperity has continuously increased – we are richer now than at any other time in history – but in relative terms British prosperity has declined for much of this century. Most of our competitors have grown richer more rapidly than us.

Worrying about British economic underperformance has become a tradition. In the middle of the nineteenth century, Prince Albert, concerned that Germany was threatening UK pre-eminence in technically advanced manufacturing industries, initiated the Great Exhibition of 1851 and built the original Crystal Palace as a showcase for the commercial threats that lay across the Channel. The proceeds of the exhibition were used to establish the Imperial College of Science and Technology and the

Victoria and Albert Museum, which were to inform artisans of the best designs and technologies being employed elsewhere.

Three decades later, the Royal Commission on the Depression of Trade and Industry reported on the damaging effects of foreign competition in markets where British firms had formerly enjoyed a monopoly. Since that time, as the threat became more serious and our standing in the world prosperity league continued to fall, there has been a plethora of books, articles and reports trying to explain and prescribe for the UK's decline. These have ranged from all-encompassing tomes on economic history (Caves, 1968; Maddison, 1991) to single-issue explanations, such as Wiener's thesis that Britain has always had a much more virulent anti-industrial culture than our main competitors (Wiener, 1981).

The UK's fall from the top of the world prosperity league near the turn of the century, as we were overtaken by the United States, was understandable. It was always likely that countries with greater natural resources would overhaul our early lead in industrialisation. More disturbing has been our tumble since the Second World War, first out of the group of the top three or four most prosperous developed nations, and then out of the top ten. In 1950 we were second in Europe in terms of income per head (behind Switzerland, with the United States far ahead). By 1970 we had dropped out of the top ten, and by the end of that decade we had slipped to sixteenth place. The relative decline may be bottoming out since we are roughly in the same position now as we were twenty years ago (Table 1.1). This is partly due, how-

Table 1.1: UK's Position in the World Prosperity League, 1900–95

Year	Position
1900	1st
1950	3rd
1970	10th
1975	15th
1985	19th
1995	16th

Source: Cabinet Office (1996a), Chart 2.9 and Maddison (1991).

Figure 1.1: GDP Per Capita, 1995 (UK = 100; *at purchasing power parities*)

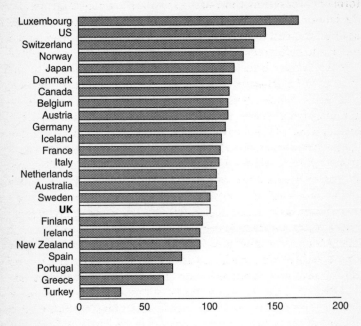

Source: Cabinet Office (1996a), Chart 2.7.

ever, to a general slowing of growth in Europe; moreover, some east Asian countries are growing fast. Figure 1.1 shows the magnitude of the gap in prosperity between the UK and other OECD countries in 1995.

The Thatcher Revolution

In response to this decline in relative prosperity, nearly every government since the Second World War has come to power with a programme for the economic regeneration of Britain. The Conservative government elected in 1979 was a particularly striking example. It believed that most of the postwar programmes for renewal had been not just poorly effected, but were also misguided. Its leaders claimed that they had a new answer. Their agenda of *market liberalisation* involved the rejection of any form of corporatism, thorough reform of industrial relations and the labour market, the privatisation of public corporations and utilities, the deregulation of financial and other markets, and a tough anti-inflation stance.

It is impossible to know what would have happened in the absence of Thatcherism, and arguments about its successes or failures will continue. It is widely accepted, however, that a programme of market liberalisation was necessary in the UK, and that at least some of the measures taken were salutary, although it is hard to believe that all of the high social costs associated with these changes were inevitable. Certainly this period saw a much greater appreciation of the role of business. While market liberalisation and some deregulation were appropriate, even the strongest devotees of these policies do not claim that they alone were, or are, sufficient to resolve Britain's economic problems. The UK is still languishing in a low position in the prosperity league, and although there are some indications of bottoming out, clear signs of relative improvement have yet to emerge. Nor is there evidence that Britain's long-term trend rate of GDP growth – fractionally over 2 per cent a year – has been increased (although in the absence of some liberalisation it might well have fallen further). Certainly the current conduct of macroeconomic policy, not to mention the advice of the Bank of England, indicates that the government itself has no belief that trend growth is faster.

Whatever the situation two decades ago, clearly the most serious problems facing Britain today are not over-regulated labour, product or financial markets or an excessively large nationalised sector. The key to future policy must be to move beyond the confines of the deregulation agenda and diagnose the most immediate impediments to higher growth. We believe that four inter-related difficulties explain why UK prosperity growth is still languishing behind that of many of our close competitors: a long tail of underperforming firms; underinvestment in innovation, research and physical capital; a long tail of low-skilled, underachieving people; and unsteady government policy (Diagram 1.1).

Diagram 1.1: What's
Holding the UK Back?

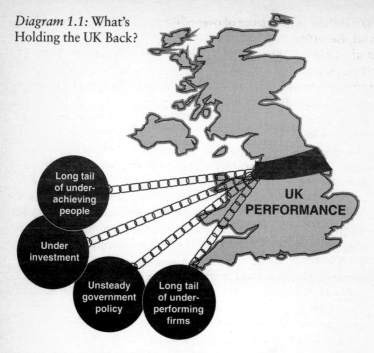

Long Tail of Underperforming Firms

Britain has some of the best companies in the world, and in a few sectors UK-based firms are outstandingly successful: pharmaceuticals, business and financial services and the media stand out. The British malaise is one of a low average, caused by our substandard firms being more numerous – and more sub-standard – than those found elsewhere. This is not a new problem. As long ago as the 1960s, the wide variation in labour productivity between plants and companies was spotted as a major cause of low UK competitiveness (Salter, 1966). Identification of the problem has not led to solutions, however, and the problem of the long tail has persisted into the 1990s.

Perhaps the best recent evidence on the scale of the problem comes from the IBM/London Business School study of manufacturing in a number of European countries. In 1994 Chris Voss and his colleagues examined the management production practices and the performance of over 650 manufacturing sites in Finland, Germany, the Netherlands and the United Kingdom (Voss *et al.*, 1995). The survey amassed information on comparative organisation, product quality, product development, manufacturing systems, logistics, market share, productivity and financial performance. The individual measures were then collated into various indices, including an overall index of practice and performance, calibrated against best practice worldwide.

Among the findings from this study, the most pertinent for the United Kingdom is that the best UK manufacturing sites are as good as those anywhere in the world, but that the UK differs by having far more poor performers. When all the companies in the sample are categorised into the top 10 per cent ('leaders') and bottom 10 per cent ('laggers'), the United Kingdom has a similar proportion of leaders as the other four countries, but many more

Figure 1.2: Percentage of Companies in Each Country Which Are Leaders and Laggers

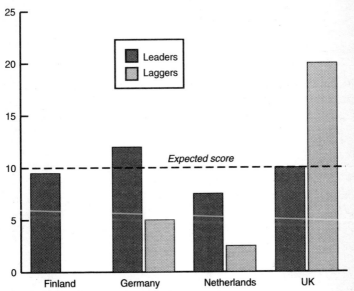

Source: Voss *et al.* (1995), Figure 7.
Note: See text for definition of leaders and laggers.

21

Figure 1.3: Distribution of Practice-Performance Index Scores

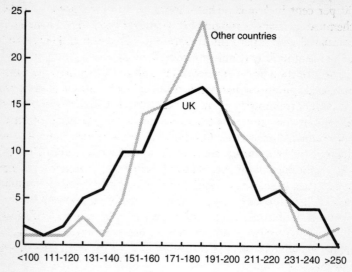

Source: Voss *et al.* (1995), Figure 8.
Note: See text for an explanation of practice-performance index score.

laggers than the other three countries put together. Around 20 per cent of UK firms in the sample are laggers compared with only 5 per cent of German companies, 2 per cent of Dutch companies and none of the Finnish companies (Figure 1.2). Alternatively, when the spread of scores of the combined practice-performance index are compared, the UK has a much longer 'tail' of companies (Figure 1.3).

This study's findings are not unique. The third Competitiveness White Paper, *Creating the Enterprise Centre of Europe*, provides further evidence of the long tail based on data from two manufacturing industries (the office machinery/computer industry and the chemical industry). Analysis of these two industries by the DTI's economists, using data from 1993 and dividing firms into low, medium and high productivity categories, reveals that in both cases the UK has a much higher proportion of poor performers than Germany, France or Italy. Around three-quarters of UK companies in office machinery are poor performers compared with only about 10 per cent in Germany and Italy and 20 per cent in France. The number of poor performers in the chemical industry is roughly 40 per cent of the total in the UK, compared with 2 per cent in Germany, 7 per cent in France and 15 per cent in Italy (Cabinet Office, 1996a).

Most of the studies of performance across companies use samples based purely on manufacturing, mainly because it is easier to measure productivity in manufacturing firms than in service firms. But this should not lead us to assume that the problem does not exist in services. On the contrary, a recent study of productivity in 140,000 UK companies over the period from 1989 to 1993, conducted by the National Institute of Economic and Social Research and covering both manufacturing and services, reveals that the long-tail problem is actually *worse* in services than in manufacturing (Oulton, 1996). The author puts this down to the 'fuller blast' of international competition in manufacturing which essentially stops many poor performers from trading.

So far, so bad. But the situation is aggravated by many of these underperforming companies being ignorant of their own uncompetitiveness. The complacency of much of British management was illustrated in the findings of the RSA's *Tomorrow's Company Inquiry* (RSA, 1995), and the IBM/LBS study reported that while 70 per cent of UK companies thought they performed at world-class levels, only 2.3 per cent actually did so. In lack of self-awareness, however, UK management differs little from the rest of Europe. Most of the managers surveyed by Voss and his colleagues were very optimistic about the performance of their own companies.

Underinvestment

Bond and Jenkinson (1996:1) have pointed out that 'investment is the critical determinant of long-run economic performance'. A major reason for the UK's failure to climb back towards the top of the prosperity league has been our persistent failure, relative to most of our competitors, to invest sufficiently and sensibly in research and development (R&D) and in physical capital. We believe that low investment is largely a result of the problem of *managerial short-termism* though it is also connected with the problem of macroeconomic instability discussed below. Many managers, both in large firms and in SMEs, appear to behave reactively and to focus on short-run financial performance rather than to plan for the long term.

This conclusion is widely accepted by many business leaders and politicians, but it remains controversial among academic economists, who are fastidious in distinguishing symptoms from true underlying causes. They are aware that high growth may lead to high investment in equipment and research, and growth may be inhibited for reasons other than low investment, which could then occur as a symptom rather than a cause. We believe nevertheless that underinvestment is a major contributor to slow growth and is connected to the long tail of underperforming firms. In any case, analysing underinvestment may lead us to a better assessment of the underlying problems and to measures for tackling them.

Innovation is essential to success. Research is an important factor behind successful innovation, and will become even more important in the context of rapidly changing product markets and globalisation. Yet, just as the significance of innovation has become widely recognised, the UK has begun to lose its pre-eminence in pure research. The proportion of GDP spent on R&D has declined quite markedly since the early 1980s in the UK, whereas it has increased in most of our competitors (Figure 1.4) and a number of experts on economic performance have identified the UK's underinvestment in research and innovation as a significant contributor to the decline in our relative prosperity (Greenhalgh, 1990; Crafts, 1996a).

As for physical investment, a recent government paper claimed that UK investment levels have been no worse than those of our major competitors, and that even if they were lower, this would not necessarily have had any impact on economic growth (Cabinet Office, 1996b). This claim is contradicted by the data in Table 1.2, which shows that the aggregate level of physical investment in the UK has been lower than that of our major competitors in recent decades. The United States is the only other developed

Figure 1.4: Gross Expenditure on R&D as a Percentage of GDP, 1981–93

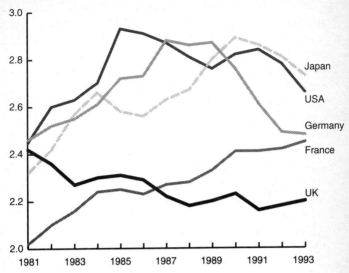

Source: OECD, in correspondence.

country to have had an investment rate below 20 per cent, and even its rate is slightly higher than that of the United Kingdom. The government's response to these numbers is to argue that they are explained by low housing investment rather than low business investment. It claims that 'since 1979, the UK business sector has invested a greater proportion of GDP than in France, Germany, Italy and the US' (Cabinet Office, 1996b:9).

In their thorough study of investment performance, however, Bond and Jenkinson (1996) reject this explanation and question the data for comparative business investment on the grounds that it excludes public investment in infrastructure such as transport and education. Given that privatisation has gone much further in the UK than in most other developed countries, the United Kingdom could be expected to have a higher level of business sector investment than other countries, and certainly there should have been an increase as important activities were transferred to the private sector. In fact, as Table 1.2 shows, UK investment,

25

Table 1.2: Investment as a Share of GDP in Six OECD Countries, 1960–93

Investment measure	Japan	Italy	Germany	France	US	UK
1980–93						
Gross fixed capital formation	29.7	20.6	20.5	20.5	18.2	17.3
Gross fixed capital formation excl. residential construction	24.1	14.8	14.6	14.9	13.9	13.7
Gross fixed capital formation: machinery and equipment	11.5	9.7	8.6	8.8	8.0	8.0
1960–93						
Gross fixed capital formation	31.3	22.8	22.4	22.4	18.4	18.1
Gross fixed capital formation excl. residential construction	25.1	15.9	15.9	15.5	13.8	14.4
Gross fixed capital formation: machinery and equipment	12.4	9.8	8.7	8.9	7.6	8.4

Source: Bond and Jenkinson (1996), Table 1.
Note: All figures for Germany refer to West Germany.

excluding residential construction, has been *lower* than that of all our major competitors except the United States. In further analysis of the data, Bond and Jenkinson conclude that the persistently low level of investment in the UK, particularly in manufacturing, has resulted in a relatively low level of capital stock and equipment per worker; UK industry is much less capital-intensive than industry elsewhere.

The government's second line of argument is that underinvestment has not been a problem. It maintains that the quality of investment is at least as important as quantity in determining growth. Few would dispute this. As is demonstrated in former Communist countries, it is possible to make investments in so wasteful a fashion that even a high rate of investment does nothing for growth. The contribution of aggregate investment to growth is the subject of a major theoretical and empirical debate among academics (for a summary, see Bond and Jenkinson, 1996; Crafts, 1996b). This debate is beset with problems of inadequate data (for instance, investment in computer hardware and software is generally not counted as investment) and complex statistical difficulties. After reviewing the debate and consulting some of the experts involved, we conclude that even though a low rate of physical investment is not the *primary* reason for UK underperformance, it is none the less a factor. Other things being equal, increased investment should improve the UK's economic performance. It is also true, however, that increased investment will follow improved performance. Our objective must be to enter a virtuous circle of performance and investment.

Long Tail of Underachieving People

Britain's underinvestment in education and training is among the most regrettable aspects of our economic record, particularly as it also has significant social and cultural effects. In statistical terms, there is a positive correlation between national prosperity and the educational attainments of populations, and there is evidence that the rapid growth of Japan and, more recently, Singapore and South Korea has much to do with the investments these countries have made in their people (Cabinet Office, 1996a).

There is now an unprecedented consensus among politicians and business leaders that Britain must make a significant effort to catch up in the skills stakes, and that this is vital for future competitiveness and performance. In 1995 the current government demonstrated its concern by commissioning a skills audit, comparing our performance with that of four of our major competitors (the United States, France, Germany and Singapore). Each of the Competitiveness White Papers has also included a range of initiatives designed to tackle the skills problem, and both the main opposition parties have put education and training at the forefront of their draft manifestos.

The results of comparative studies are unequivocal. Just as we have a higher than average proportion of underperforming firms, so we also have a higher proportion of underachieving people. Britain is educating and training a larger proportion of its current and future workforce to higher levels than ever before; but there remains an uncomfortably large group of children, young people and adults who lack the basic skills required for them to be employable, or even to function properly as citizens in society (see Figure 1.5).

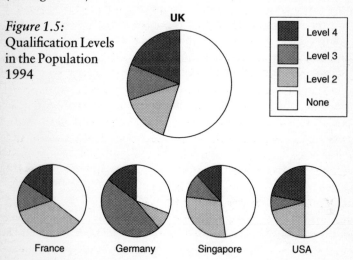

Figure 1.5:
Qualification Levels
in the Population
1994

Source: DfEE (1996), Table A8.16.

28

The latest CBI policy document on education and training states that 'although the best in the UK is world-class, the tail of education and training underperformance is striking' (CBI, 1996a:13). Similarly, Sig Prais, the doyen of empirical researchers into the impact of education and training on industrial and economic performance, concluded, in a lecture to the British Academy in 1993, that 'there needs now to be greater concern with the schooling attainments of average and below-average school-leavers than simply with those top-attainers who are to join the ranks of university graduates' (Prais, 1993:167).

A particular consequence of the long-tail problem is that part of the tail ultimately becomes detached altogether. Underperformance turns into decay and some of the less skilled become more or less permanently unemployed. High levels of welfare dependency associated with long-term unemployment and economic inactivity then create an economic drag anchor on the rest of society.

Some argue that these are purely social and labour market problems, not business problems at all. We disagree. The problems of poverty and the distribution of employment and national income can have massive fiscal implications. If levels of welfare dependency are allowed to rise too high, then inevitably there will be a significant impact on business as well, particularly on taxes and incentives. One theoretical solution is, of course, to cut welfare benefits in order to reduce the fiscal burden. The current government has already gone down this route, limiting increases in most benefits and access to unemployment benefit, but the cost of transfer payments has still continued to rise. Public investment has had to be slashed to stop taxes rising, and some of that lost investment, particularly in infrastructure, would have helped business. Moreover, high unemployment and pressure on income-maintenance transfers tend to be associated with high crime rates, which makes life more difficult for everyone. Clearly, high unemployment is not purely a social problem, and a government interested in permanently boosting British economic performance must try to pull up this drag anchor.

Unsteady Government Policy

The fourth over-arching explanation for UK underperformance is unsteady government policy. The most damaging effects of this unsteadiness have been felt in the sharp ups and downs of the macroeconomy over recent decades. Changes of strategy and policy reversals have also been prevalent in areas such as infrastructure, especially transport, and in science policy and public procurement; but without doubt, the key issue for most businesses is macroeconomic instability. Seventy-two per cent of the 501 companies responding to the 1994 *Middle Market Survey* identified 'our roller-coaster economy' as a factor contributing to the decline of British industry, second only to 'short-termism in the City' (Coopers and Lybrand, 1994).

Excessive macroeconomic volatility damages both business confidence and business performance. It acts as a major disincentive to long-term investment by companies, particularly in physical capital, since firms cannot be sure of reasonable real returns. Surveys of business confidence and investment plans regularly show that the single most important constraint on investment is 'demand conditions' or 'uncertainty about future demand'.

A promise to end the boom–bust economic cycle has been repeated at every election since the 1960s. A government which could actually deliver this objective would be warmly applauded by the business community, but this is an area in which it is far easier to promise than to deliver. Our history of instability is a millstone around the neck of British business, and forecasts of stability in the years ahead are not going to reassure British companies. Only experience of long-term stability – the slow wearing away of the millstone – will do the trick.

The current government and its officials recognise the problem. At our consultative conference on City–industry relations in October 1995, a leading Treasury official stated that 'short-termism is pervasive in the UK by comparison with a number of other countries' and 'the primary fault lies with the UK Treasury' for its failure to manage the macroeconomy adequately (Robson, 1996). More detailed evidence comes in a comprehensive study, conducted by the National Institute of Economic and Social

Research (Oulton, 1995), on the impact of macroeconomic volatility on economic growth in developed economies. This study examined macroeconomic performance over the period 1970 to 1994 and found that:

- The UK's growth rate has been more volatile than that of most other countries. The UK ranks third out of eleven countries, behind Austria and Australia, in the variance of its quarterly GDP growth rate between 1970 and 1994. Our economy has been twice as unstable as that of Germany over this period, and one and one-half times more unstable than the economies of the United States, Japan and Italy.

- The UK has spent longer in recession – defined as a period during which output remains below its previous peak – than most other developed countries. Figure 1.6 demonstrates that in terms of time spent in recession (labelled 'bust' as opposed to 'boom') since 1970, the UK is second only to Switzerland. We have spent nearly 50 per cent of this period in recession. This is in sharp contrast to the United States, which has been in recession for 20 per cent of the time, and also to other European countries such as France (12 per cent) and Germany (21 per cent).

- UK performance has been characterised by short, sharp booms and long, shallow recessions. The United Kingdom performs worst out of eleven countries on a composite measure of skewness (how much the economy deviates from its mean growth rate and the extent to which the deviations are up or down). This is a useful measure, given the general view that deviations above the mean are preferable to those beneath it, since extended recessions mean excessive scrapping of plant and machinery and long-term unemployment.

- The pattern of instability in the United Kingdom has led to lower growth. Comparisons of overall growth performance and the pattern of booms and recessions in thirteen countries reveal that the UK has had the worst pattern. The report concludes that 'a cyclical pattern like the UK's is associated with a lower trend growth rate. If the UK had had the average skew-

Figure 1.6: Boom and Bust in the OECD, 1970–94

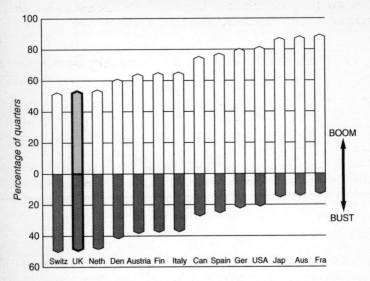

Source: Oulton (1995), Table 12.
Notes: All data are for 1970–94 except Denmark (1977–94), Finland (1975–94), Netherlands (1977–94) and USA (1970–95). See text for definition of 'boom' and 'bust'.

ness of this sample, its annual growth rate would be predicted to have been 0.57 percentage points higher' (Oulton, 1995:65).

Stability is essentially about smoothing the economic cycle rather than eliminating it. No country has succeeded in eliminating cycles; trying to do so leads to attempts to 'fine tune' the economy, with frequent policy changes that are likely to lead to further destabilisation, exacerbating rather than eliminating the problem. Economic stability requires steadiness in macroeconomic policy.

The strong connection between macroeconomic instability and short-termism has already been noted. The consequent low investment and instability are mutually reinforcing. Instability discourages long-term planning, causing low investment, and low investment contributes to instability since it limits the supply response to increased demand in an upswing.

Britain's Prosperity in a Changing World

The four broad causes of British underperformance highlighted above – the long tail of underperforming companies, underinvestment, the long tail of underachieving people and unsteady government policy – are not new. But we are faced with the prospect of mastering them in rapidly changing circumstances. Two specific developments in the economic environment – globalisation and the information revolution – require particular consideration.

Globalisation

Ask groups of politicians, business leaders or commentators to draw up a list of the most important influences on British prosperity now and in the immediate future, and 'globalisation' would probably come somewhere near the top of every list. Moreover, most respondents would also describe globalisation as a threat to our prosperity. The rapid growth in world trade and capital flows and the pace of industrialisation in many developing economies has been blamed for our high unemployment, the decline of our manufacturing industry and the marked increase in income inequality between skilled and unskilled workers; and globalisation itself is widely cited as an obstacle to effective national economic policies to combat these problems. These views are not universally held, however, and some commentators have argued that globalisation is actually an overrated phenomenon; for example, Paul Krugman, the eminent American economist, has dubbed it 'globaloney'. Others claim that far from being a threat to prosperity, globalisation offers an exceptional opportunity for developed countries.

We commissioned Marina Wes of the Centre for Economic Performance at the London School of Economics to review the evidence for and against these propositions. She offers three main conclusions (Wes, 1996):

- Globalisation is more than, as some have argued, just a return to a world trading economy such as existed at the beginning of this century. The share of trade in world GDP is considerably higher now than then, and the number of trading countries is much greater. New communications and transport technology mean that markets can change more swiftly.

- Globalisation produces both winners and losers in developed economies such as the UK, although the magnitude of both gains and losses has been exaggerated. Skilled workers benefit both from cheap imports of goods and services, produced by unskilled workers elsewhere, and from increased demand for high-skill content products in developing countries. Unskilled workers lose out, however, since either their wages tend to fall as a result of increased competition from developing countries or their jobs are lost altogether.

- Globalisation may be reversible, since economic integration has been partly a product of political change. The broadening and deepening of the European Single Market, the transition of former Communist countries to market economies and the opening up of China to Western trade and foreign investment have all been significant push factors. There is no sign of a radical change in the political scene, but there is a possibility that politics could become more parochial or protectionist at some point in the future.

With regard to Wes's third conclusion, we believe that several of the non-political forces contributing to globalisation, such as the speed and convenience of global communications, cannot be undone. We recognise, however, the danger that politicians might offer the promise of protection from globalisation to those suffering from it, perhaps in the context of a so-called 'fortress Europe' scenario. Such a programme would be dangerous. Other trading blocks would probably retaliate, and we would lose the many gains from globalisation that most citizens in developed countries have been enjoying in recent years.

On the basis of the Wes report plus our reading of other evidence (Hirst and Thompson, 1996; OECD, 1996; Thurow, 1996; Krugman, 1995), we conclude that globalisation offers more opportunities than threats for British business, people and government. It will, however, exacerbate problems stemming from the long tail of personal underachievement, particularly the plight of the low-skill unemployed. Attention to these problems is therefore all the more urgent. We do not subscribe to the view that individual governments have lost their power to determine the economic fortunes of their nation, but we accept that government power is more limited than in the past because of the influence of international financial markets, faster communications and greater capital and labour mobility. It is therefore all the more important that government policies work with the grain of the market rather than seek to override it.

In this context, the growth and development of the European Union is of central importance. The European economic area will create in microcosm many of the conditions associated with globalisation. Within that area, goods and capital will move increasingly freely and companies will become increasingly ready to locate anywhere on the basis of purely economic factors. The governance and international co-operation structures of the European Union represent an attempt to get around the reduced capacity of national governments to manage economic life. Many British government policies must be pursued at EU level, either because we are constrained by international agreement or because they will not work at any lower level. The impact of our policies on other European countries and our relations with them must always be borne in mind. We can perhaps seek to opt in or out of particular initiatives in a 'variable geometry' Europe, but we cannot escape the need to work closely with our European partners and assist them in building a new sort of political and economic union which is acceptable to all its members.

The information revolution

Information is the lifeblood of every economic system, and any innovation which greatly enhances our ability to access, process or transmit information is likely to have a significant bearing on the efficiency and organisation of the system itself. At the heart of the information revolution is digital technology, which enables the global convergence of telecommunications, information technology, broadcasting and publishing (Jameson, 1995). Even if the magnitude and impact of the revolution is sometimes exaggerated, we cannot doubt that it will continue to act as a major influence on the prosperity of this nation, and indeed every nation, and the way in which every individual will live and work.

From the policy perspective, the central characteristic of the information revolution is its ubiquity. Information is not simply a new industry which will have a big impact on the economy; it is a genuine revolution that is changing the potential and production methods of many, perhaps all, other industries. No business can afford not to know how information technology is affecting its market and way of doing things. This in turn enormously reinforces the importance of training, since it means almost everyone must have the basic skills necessary to work with computers and information systems. It also increases the demand for specialists, able to combine knowledge of a wide range of business sectors with skill in the use of new technologies, so as to adapt the latter to new applications.

There is also a link between the information revolution and globalisation. By reducing costs of transmission of many services, the information revolution has already given a great boost to the globalisation process. Business services that once had to be performed at home can now be obtained from anywhere in the world. European airline bookings can be handled from India; German banks can have their books kept in Ireland. Cross-border transactions of this type are likely to become increasingly common.

In the near future, the wealth of a nation will not simply be indicated by the size of its capital stock, its great buildings, bridges, factories and power stations; it will also be indicated by the range and quality of its computer programs. The new labourer will be a computer programmer, the new architect will be the person who designs the program and the new entrepreneur will be the person who sees which new programs and applications are both possible and necessary.

Conclusion

We have identified four inter-related characteristics associated with British underperformance: a long tail of underperforming companies, underinvestment, a long tail of personal under-achievement and unsteady government policy. We have also noted two of the most marked trends in the world economy today, globalisation and the information revolution, and how these trends are interlinked. It is probable that both trends, which are full of opportunities for enhanced prosperity, will also exacerbate two of Britain's existing problems. Globalisation may widen the divide between economic successes and the also-rans, and may worsen the plight of the least skilled. The information revolution is also likely to reinforce that widening and will certainly increase the premium on training and education. We do not believe that these trends in the world economy should be feared, but they do make it all the more urgent that we deal with Britain's problems.

2

ROLE OF GOVERNMENT

In this chapter we identify the appropriate functions of government in a predominantly private enterprise economy, and review what government can do to foster competitive companies and promote buoyant economic activity. Then, in view of the particular problems identified in Chapter 1, we draw out a number of policy themes which run through the specific policy discussions in succeeding chapters. Competition is the primary spur to business performance. At the same time, gains in productivity can be achieved from co-operative networks. Government must strengthen competition policy while stimulating producer networks, especially for SMEs, hence our theme of competition and co-operation. Government should also foster far-sighted companies as an antidote to management short-termism and underinvestment. This requires attention to the legal and fiscal framework rather than ad hoc *interventions or subsidies. Another important policy goal must be to mobilise the potential of our people. Government must do what business cannot do in terms of general education, shifting resources to address the problem of the low average and the long tail of underachievement. Finally, consistency in government policy is essential in all areas, most importantly in macroeconomic policy. Government must do its utmost to ensure a stable environment for business.*

Policy must not swing from one extreme to another. Just because a philosophy of minimising government and scaling back its role in economic life has not been sufficient to solve Britain's problems, it does not follow that we should replace that régime with one of *ad hoc* intervention based on 'the squeaking wheel gets the grease'. A return to former industrial policies, involving substantial state assistance to ailing companies or favoured treatment for 'national champions', will certainly not rectify Britain's remaining deficiencies. It is important that we chart a new way forward. Central to that way is a partnership for prosperity, involving both the public and private sectors, with a clear vision of the appropriate role of government in the economy.

Government in a Modern Economy

Economic orthodoxy says that, in a predominantly private enterprise economy, the government's role is primarily one of co-ordination. One aspect of this role is macroeconomic co-ordination. Ungoverned economies can display extreme cyclical behaviour, and regulation of the cost of short-term credit with a view to limiting cycles is an accepted government function in all countries. Another wider and more important form of co-ordination is the setting, maintenance and enforcement of laws or rules which define property rights and provide a framework in which companies and markets can operate. It is important that those laws and rules (including codes of taxation) should provide the right incentives to private persons and companies – that is incentives to behave in ways which are aligned as far as possible with the public interest.

It is widely understood that, even with a framework of effective rules in place, special circumstances can result in market failure. People acting intelligently in their own interests can and sometimes do create results which are not beneficial to the economy or society as a whole. Government's co-ordinating role must include monitoring such market failures and considering whether anything can be done to remove them or lessen their effects. The government must always be aware, however, that its actions can have unintended side effects and that the cure may be worse than the disease.

The main sources of market failure are familiar in economic theory: monopoly (where market dominance leads to a restriction in output or excessive pricing), information failures (where, for example, potential buyers find it so difficult to gauge the credibility of a seller or product that they fail to purchase or make purchasing mistakes), externalities (where the cost or price of some good or service is not entirely met or appropriated by the consumer or producer, and costs or benefits spill over to others), and public goods (where externalities are so great that only the public sector has an incentive to supply the service). Examples of government activity connected to each of these failures include regulation of utilities, setting and enforcing competition law (against monopolies), regulation of the pensions industry to prevent bad advice (information failure), introduction of pollution controls and taxes on cigarettes (against externalities) and the provision of police and schools (to supply public goods).

The role of government as outlined so far is fairly uncontroversial in principle. The interesting arguments come over how to implement the principles in particular cases. There is general agreement that government should provide a fiscal and legal framework, regulate monopoly, use taxes or regulation to internalise externalities, and provide those public goods that are necessary from general taxation. Doing so promotes welfare and helps business in general. But some would like to go further. They argue that the government has a particular responsibility for British-owned business, and also that it should identify and promote certain industrial sectors above others. Since industrial policy in the past, both in the United Kingdom and elsewhere, frequently embodied those views, it is worth considering them in more detail.

What Is British Business?

If we are primarily concerned with the prosperity of British citizens, which businesses should we seek to promote? What exactly is meant by *British* business? This is particularly pertinent since Britain is unrivalled in Europe today in its ability to attract investment from abroad. We have the highest ratio of inward (and also of outward) investment to GDP of any leading country. Few would question the value of foreign investment here for

British prosperity, but there are some who argue that it is second best, that we would be better off if these new factories and businesses were owned by British companies so that the profit, as well as the wages, belonged in Britain.

In his well-known book *The Work of Nations*, Robert Reich (1992) took the opposite tack and argued that ownership is irrelevant. International companies, he asserted, cannot afford sentiment and will always take decisions about the location of high value-added operations on strictly commercial considerations. Therefore, the only factor that matters is the scale of investment in the domestic operation, not the ownership of it. We believe that the issue is more complicated than Reich suggests. In our view, it comes down to two points: how profits are shared out and the right level of saving.

If the UK were to save nothing (for example, because private saving was all borrowed and spent by the government on current expenditure), any investment in the country would be courtesy of foreign borrowing. The citizens could remain quite prosperous, although eventually they would all be working for foreigners and the capital stock would be foreign-owned. Their incomes would grow faster if they were to save more and enjoy some return on capital as well as wage income. That would also be true, however, even if they were to use their savings to buy investments abroad. In that case domestic capital would still be foreign-owned but now some foreign capital stock would be British-owned. There is obviously a case for citizens saving adequately (and for government borrowing to be reasonable and restrained), but so far there is no argument that British-based companies need be British-owned.

Ideally, British factors of production, either labour or capital, should be employed for maximum returns, where the profits from their activities or value added are highest. In that case British capital should be invested where the profit rate is highest, so long as Britain continues to attract sufficient foreign investment to maintain a high level of domestic activity. The sort of foreign investment that is particularly desirable is in 'people' businesses where workers earn a high return; foreign capital coming in search of cheap labour to employ at rates competitive with the unskilled elsewhere in the world, and with the aim of repatriating 'supernormal profits', is not so attractive. (Such profits are those over and above the profits consistent with a normal rate of return on investment given a competitive product market.)

Nationality of ownership would therefore only be an issue if a large net export of capital went along with persistent unemployment, or if British investment overseas were in high value-added enterprises while foreign investment here were in low value-added assembly-type operations. At the moment there is no evidence that this is the case. That leaves only a nagging question: do companies have a nationality conferred by the loyalties of top managers? If companies are influenced by non-commercial elements, then it could be important to have enough 'British' companies biased towards locating core functions in the United Kingdom to offset the bias of foreign ones. That is not a dominant consideration at present, however, since the bias does not appear very great. The major concern, therefore, must be to foster *British-based business*, irrespective of ownership, noting that the most desirable businesses are those where labour adds high value.

Are there 'special' sectors?

A contentious issue in industrial policy is whether some sectors have a special place in the economy, and whether government should discriminate in their favour. Some argue that manufacturing is special; others that high-tech industries are what matter. A third group believes that high-value-added sectors are worthy of support (which implies backing, if not picking, winners). Each of these views has at one time or another influenced industrial policy-making in the UK.

Three features of an industry determine whether or not it has a special place in the economy: whether its output is traded internationally; the extent to which it generates 'external' effects on other industries or people who do not buy its products; and the degree to which it is a source of high pay and profits.

The first distinction is practical and uncontroversial. The products of some sectors are traded internationally, others are not. If a country were to specialise increasingly in the production of non-internationally traded products, the price of those goods would have to fall continuously relative to that of internationally traded goods. In other words, the price of much of the country's output would deteriorate relative to import prices, slowing down the growth of income and wealth. It may not matter what the country exports – goods or services – but it must be exporting something. Technical change is altering the boundary between traded and non-traded products all the time, but none the less many products (such as housing and many personal services) are not traded to any significant extent. Since the UK will continue to import many goods and services, it must also maintain and grow capacity in manufacturing and internationally traded services.

The second consideration is that some products may generate 'externalities' – that is, effects on people other than the consumer – which may be good or bad. That alters the social view of the value of those products relative to the price they command. For example, alcohol and cigarettes may be enjoyable, but if they stimulate anti-social behaviour or entail health costs the community may regard them as less valuable than their market price implies. Their production and consumption may be discouraged by, for example, the imposition of specific taxes. Other products (such as education) may be regarded as having positive spin-offs and be subsidised.

The third consideration is the extent to which a sector is a source of high pay and profits. Kay (1993) has demonstrated that for an individual company the best activity is supplying relatively scarce services or products. The relative scarcity gives high returns, especially if it persists or can be defended. The situation is no different for countries. A country is prosperous if its businesses are making high returns; they will achieve this by doing things other countries cannot do as well or at all.

This conclusion has led many politicians and commentators to favour high-technology sectors. The thinking is that a new technology, almost by definition, permits new things to be done, which automatically confers a scarcity value and the supernormal profits that go with it. But this argument is not as conclusive as it seems. High-technology processes or products may be more easily imitable than some other sources of competitive advantage, and the initial advantage may be short-lived. Nor is high technology a necessary prerequisite for scarcity value. French wine, perfume and haute couture, for example, have more secure competitive niches than the French aviation or space industries. Finally, technical progress in a sector may also reduce costs and increase potential output in that sector, leading to a decline in relative price. Specialisation in computer manufacture may have looked impeccably modern and high-tech a decade or two ago, but the supernormal profits made then have since been rapidly eroded.

A more subtle argument is that we should concentrate on sectors that have 'ripe' or 'pregnant' technologies, which are characterised by near-continuous advancement. Each advance can be quickly imitated so supernormal profits soon disappear, but each advance also spawns its own successor, generating another supernormal profit as soon as the previous one disappears. High returns are made by surfing the crest of the technological wave, always keeping just ahead of the competition.

This is a fine and exciting prospect, but its importance as a basis for policy is easily exaggerated. First, by definition, we don't know what we don't know. It is often very hard to tell which technologies are 'pregnant'; it is far from obvious that government in particular can identify them. Efforts made on these grounds to encourage activity in some sectors and not in others are hazardous. Second, the really big returns from technical advances may be made not in the sector that generates them but in other sectors that find ways to apply them. Third, of all the world's enduringly successful businesses, only a tiny minority base their success on continuous invention and technical advance of the type described. The great bulk of business and national success must therefore be based on something else.

Importance of the traded sector

It is possible to exaggerate the importance of high-tech and invention. In a changing and competitive world, however, businesses must be adaptable and looking relentlessly for improvement in both products and processes. Innovation in the broad sense, rather than in the sense of developing new technology, is crucial to business success, and policy should encourage it. Innovation depends in particular on having a skilled labour force, which is able to adapt to change and to make use of technologies developed elsewhere. While businesses may not need to be in 'high-tech sectors' to be successful, in an age of rapid technical change they must be able to employ people with up-to-date technical knowledge.

Within that framework, government should promote all business, regardless of sector. There should be no prejudice in favour of any particular sector, be it manufacturing or 'high technology' industries. None the less, tradable products are important and, for the foreseeable future, the structure of the tradable sector and therefore the balance of payments will be dominated by manufacturing (Cosh *et al.*, 1993). The goal must therefore be for the country to increase capacity and capability in a sufficient number of manufacturing sectors.

In the past, much damage to the traded goods sector has resulted from an inappropriate mix of macroeconomic policies, which have generated instability of the real exchange rate and periods of severe overvaluation. The performance of the traded sector in particular should therefore be boosted by macroeconomic stability and an appropriate policy mix. This will be insufficient to reverse completely the UK's weakness, but those policies which foster business as a whole will also help to improve the competitiveness of the traded sectors as well.

Government's Role and Britain's Symptoms

Given this perspective on the role of government, how can government policy deal with the symptoms of economic underperformance described in Chapter 1?

Shortening the long tail of underperforming firms

If a large number of firms are underperforming, as in the UK at present, it means that conditions are at once too easy and too difficult; too easy because competitive pressures are not eliminating underperformers or forcing them to improve, and too difficult because firms are not finding a way to achieve best practice which would make them more profitable. The slowness with which innovation in techniques and management practice diffuses through the system, particularly in comparison with our more dynamic competitors, is a well-documented characteristic of the UK economy.

This brings up our first policy theme, that of *competition and co-operation*. These two notions may seem contradictory but in fact they are not; successful economies tend to have more of both than less successful ones. Competition in domestic product markets needs to be increased, both for the benefit of consumers and for the long-run health of British companies, while at the same time there must be more co-operation in the diffusion of best practice. The need to introduce simultaneously more competition and co-operation is worth setting out in more detail.

Research has shown that competitive pressures cause companies to become more innovative and productive. Studies of individual countries reveal that sectors in which the domestic market is highly competitive tend to produce world-class companies. It is now well documented, for example, that the industries in which Japan is internationally competitive are those in which there is strong competition in the domestic market (Porter, 1990). The beneficial effects of competitive markets are reinforced in a country in which consumers are particularly discerning, demanding the best products and services from domestic and overseas producers. High-quality demand is a key spur to competition and business performance. One has only to consider the very low level of productivity achieved in Eastern Europe relative to Western Europe by the end of the Communist era to see what happens when competitive forces are repressed. After a thorough review of competitive advantage around the world, Porter (1990:117) concluded that 'among the strongest empirical findings in our research is the association between vigorous domestic rivalry and the creation and persistence of competitive advantage in an industry'.

If inadequate competition explains the failure of best practice to take root more widely, a complementary explanation is that information about best practice flows less quickly and easily than it might. This is related to a lack of four different forms of co-operation: co-operation among firms themselves, co-operation among firms and higher educational research institutions, co-operation between firms and government and co-operation within companies between management and employees.

Probably the most important form of co-operation is that among firms. This co-operation is related to the currently fashionable idea of 'social capital', the tendency for people and companies to be civically and economically active and to build up relationships. The potential role for social capital is clear in speeding up information flows, allowing people to learn from the experience and practice of their neighbours and associates, and generally promoting the diffusion of good ideas and the development of synergies. The influential study of the Italian economy by Robert Putnam (1993) found a strong correlation between economic success and the number of so-called intermediate organisations that exist. Where there are dense clusters of trade associations, chambers of commerce, political and civic organisations, and clubs for enthusiasts of technical hobbies such as computing or car maintenance, the economy tended to be more successful and prosperous. Another example is found in Japanese supplier organisations (*keiretsu*), through which large customers such as Mazda or Sony can influence the performance of their suppliers and the suppliers themselves also share information on best practice (Sako, 1992).

British companies, especially smaller ones, seem less inclined to engage in co-operative activity than, for example, their German, Italian or Japanese counterparts. Some British industries do combine fierce competition with a network of association and co-operation, however, and they are among the more successful. One example is the Scotch whisky industry, our fourth largest export earner, where there is fierce competition among brands but where blenders buy single malts from each other's distilleries and collaborate for certain purposes in a trade association. Another is the racing car industry. No industry has fiercer competition, but a successful racing car is the result of collaboration among numerous high-tech boutiques providing components. These boutiques can shift alliances, and staff frequently move back and forth between them (Aston and Williams, 1996).

Such networks or clusters are frequently the key to business success. The role of the state in promoting them directly is limited, but it should do what it can to encourage them.

The benefits of co-operation apply at least as much to relationships within companies as they do to relationships between companies. We share the view that companies which develop partnerships with their employees are more likely to secure the commitment of their people, and in particular to manage change effectively. In this area our theme of *fostering far-sighted companies* combines with the *competition and co-operation* theme, as we explain more fully below.

In terms of concrete policy prescriptions, our approach to competition is relatively straightforward. British competition law should be strengthened and applied more vigorously and the government should also try to raise the quality of demand (see Chapter 3). Encouraging co-operation is rather more difficult, and the German practice of obliging firms to join associations or chambers of commerce would not work in the United Kingdom. Rather, we need to reorient a number of different policies so that they encourage, or at least do not inhibit, co-operative networks or ventures. Some of our policy proposals designed to improve the management of large companies in Chapter 4 are influenced by the theme of competition and co-operation. The theme is developed further in Chapter 5 with proposals for improving small company performance.

Tackling underinvestment

Underinvestment in research and capital equipment largely results from managerial short-termism. Short-termism also results in not enough British companies developing productive, high-trust relationships with investors, customers, employees, suppliers and other groups involved in the success of the company. This problem motivates our second underlying policy theme, *fostering far-sighted companies*. We need to look again at the legal and fiscal framework governing companies and changes should encourage companies to take a longer, more strategic view. The notion of the far-sighted company has affinities with the 'inclusive company' described by the *Tomorrow's Company* report (RSA, 1995) and the 'stakeholder company' advocated by a number of authors (Hutton, 1995; Kay and Silberston, 1995).

Essentially, the 'far-sighted company' is one in which managers are encouraged to view their businesses as economic entities that are more than capital market vehicles. It does not imply that shareholders' interests are to be neglected or that firms should not seek to maximise profits. What it does imply is that firms should seek to maximise profits, and thereby further shareholder – and other stakeholder – interests over a long time horizon. To this end, management should seek to make key stakeholders, in particular the employees, feel involved in the company's fortunes. Recognising as much, many of Britain's leading companies have developed a partnership approach, involving commitment from management and employees to work for the benefit of all. Where possible, the government should encourage such an approach. Some of our proposed policy changes to encourage the long view are to be found in the field of City–industry relations and corporate governance (Chapter 4), while others are in the field of corporate taxation (Chapter 9). In both cases, the changes seek to alter the framework of incentives but to leave the initiative firmly in the hands of companies themselves to map out their own destinies undisturbed by *ad hoc* government intervention.

Ending personal underachievement

Tackling underperformance and underinvestment requires more than improving management incentives. It also requires the government to get certain aspects of the economic environment right. Companies will find it easier and more profitable to produce, and therefore more attractive to invest, if certain complementary factors which they find difficult to provide for themselves are readily available. By far the most important of these, especially in view of the impact of globalisation, is an adequately educated labour force.

Mobilising the potential of our people is therefore the third theme of this report. Basic education has the characteristics of a public good, since firms have little incentive to provide it; specific training may attach the worker more closely to the firm, enabling it to recoup its outlay on training, but general education will tend to make the worker more adaptable and mobile. General education must therefore be the responsibility of government.

At the same time, there is abundant evidence that it is the worst-educated workers who receive the least training. Companies are readier to invest in the skills of more educated workers who are seen to have the most potential. There is little doubt, therefore, that the process of increasing investment in both skills and capital must begin with improving the general education of the British people and we set out a number of recommendations to achieve this in Chapter 6.

An associated task facing government is pulling up the 'economic drag anchor' of high levels of long-term unemployment and inactivity. Doing nothing about these problems is unacceptable, since they are a social blight as well as a burden on our economy. Slashing welfare payments will do little to cut the burden on business or society, since lower taxes may be offset by higher costs of crime. A policy is required to reconnect the people concerned to the formal labour market, and such an approach is outlined in Chapter 7.

Countering unsteadiness in government policy

Chapter 1 identified short-term, reactive policies as contributing to the UK's problems, most evidently in the field of macroeconomic policy. This brings us to our fourth theme: *consistency in government policy*. Government policy should be relatively steady – without erratic shifts in direction in the short to medium term – and it should be internally consistent such that individual policies do not contradict one another. Although many factors have caused macroeconomic instability, the British economy has been much more volatile than others because government policy has not been consistent enough. If government cannot stabilise macroeconomic fluctuations, then it should at least refrain from contributing to them. Greater consistency is required, certainly in the philosophy of policy and, in some cases, in the actual setting of policy instruments. This issue is discussed in more detail in Chapter 10.

Government traditionally provides certain forms of economic infrastructure which business does not provide adequately for itself, including both physical infrastructure, such as roads and bridges, and more nebulous forms of 'soft' infrastructure such as basic science research or the provision of government information. Much British infrastructure is adequate and does not pose a problem for the economy. However, the government has been underinvesting in infrastructure because capital spending is the easiest sort to cut in times of fiscal stringency. In particular, the future provision of an adequate transport infrastructure could become a serious problem. A consistent long-term strategy is required. The same is true of government support for scientific research. A welcome emphasis on promoting diffusion of discoveries has been financed at the expense of pure research, but now there are questions over the continued adequacy of the pure science base.

Government procurement policies have in the past few years swung from a focus on detailed specification with inadequate attention to costs or competition to a focus on value for money. No one could quarrel with that approach but there are signs that a salutary change is being pushed too far, leading to a short-sighted approach which minimises immediate expenditures without considering long-term implications. A more co-operative relationship between government and firms in the area of procurement could be a valuable means of promoting innovation and diffusing best practice (though this would need careful monitoring to avoid too cosy relationships). Here the themes of consistency in government policy and competition and co-operation come together. All three of these issues, science, transport and public procurement, are discussed in Chapter 8.

Policy Themes and National Competitiveness

The themes of our report – promoting competition and co-operation, fostering far-sighted companies, mobilising people's potential, and consistency in government policy – can be related to seminal studies of why some countries have fared much better economically than others in the last half century. Michael Porter, for example, in his well-known book *The Competitive Advantage of Nations* (1990), identified four sources of competitive advantage:

1 *Factor conditions:* skilled labour and other high quality inputs of capital and infrastructure.
2 *Firm structures:* relationships of trust and co-operation within firms and incentives for long-term organic growth.
3 *Related industries:* geographical concentrations of related expertise and trust and co-operation within supply chains.
4 *Demand conditions:* well-informed demanding consumers in open competitive markets.

This taxonomy is quite consistent with our themes of competition and co-operation (which bear directly on 2, 3 and 4 above), fostering far-sighted companies (which bears on 2 and 3) and mobilising people's potential (which bears on 1). While government can do a great deal to influence all of Porter's elements of competitive advantage, it should recognise that it is itself a fifth source of competitive advantage or disadvantage. Multinational businesses deciding where to locate production or invest capital consider not only the four conditions listed above, but also political and macroeconomic stability, levels of taxation (and the quality of services it finances), and the probity and predictability of public administration. Any tendency to globalisation exposes not only business but also governments to increased competition.

In effect, therefore, national governments are in competition with each other in providing conditions which will encourage business to thrive. This fifth element in competitiveness prompts our remaining theme, consistency in policy, as an important component of good government. It is also the element most obviously missing in the UK, which otherwise has a high standard of public administration.

The government is moreover a major player in the economy, not least in purchasing goods and services. The way in which it fulfils that role has a bearing on Porter's idea that the quality of demand is important. Exacting customers make for strong firms. So while government must offer a welcoming environment for companies, in its direct dealings with them it should provide a stimulus rather than a feather bed.

Outline of Policy Chapters

This chapter has linked the problems identified in Chapter 1 with the four policy themes that inform the individual policy chapters which follow. These chapters are grouped into three sections, as indicated in Diagram 2.1 which provides a route map through the report.

The first section concerns companies and their management. Chapter 3 addresses how government can best improve manage-

Diagram 2.1: A Route Map to *Promoting Prosperity*

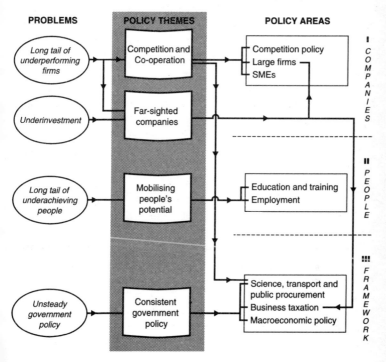

ment performance by boosting product market competition while not impeding the potential benefits of commercial co-operation. Chapter 4, on policies for far-sighted management, deals with topics in corporate governance and the relations between the financial and other business sectors. Chapter 5 focuses on smaller firms. The second section concerns people as workers. Chapter 6 deals with education and training and Chapter 7 addresses employment issues. The third section concerns other aspects of the national economic framework. Chapter 8 deals with aspects of both hard and soft infrastructure and public procurement, Chapter 9 considers the corporate tax system and Chapter 10 looks at macroeconomic management.

PART ONE

COMPANIES

3

COMPETITIVE PRODUCT MARKETS

Competitive product markets must be central to any effort to improve the competitiveness of British companies. Stimulating competition requires the reform of competition policy itself and efforts to raise the quality of consumer demand. Two aspects of UK competition law are priorities for reform. First, the overall design of competition policy should be shifted more towards the prohibition approach with legal penalties for specified anti-competitive practices. Second, some of the institutions of competition policy require an overhaul to make policy more effective and less prone to political interference.

For any developed economy, effective competition in the domestic product market is the lifeblood of competitiveness. Effective competition comes from a combination of high-quality demand, made possible by well-informed, discerning consumers, and from a set of regulations and authorities which prevent anti-competitive behaviour such as market rigging and other abuses of market power.

It is clearly the government's responsibility to ensure effective market competition, primarily through competition policy but also through policies designed to encourage highly discerning customers. Current arrangements are too confusing, too weak and too often plagued by political interference to be fully effective. Tightening competition law is not inconsistent with the government encouraging a degree of co-operation among firms where appropriate, as we argue elsewhere, but this is not as straightforward as promoting competition.

Why Government
Must Champion Competition

In proclaiming the virtues of competition, we are certainly not breaking new ground. Two centuries ago, Adam Smith described monopoly as 'a great enemy to good management'; subsequently economists and politicians alike have argued that competition is the enemy of business complacency. By putting downward pressure on costs and reducing slack, competition provides incentives for efficient business organisation and innovation. Faced with competition, management is forced to seek advantage in the marketplace, either by introducing a more efficient means of producing the same product or by producing a wholly new product or service. In other words, competition forces firms to try to win market share through innovation in products, processes or organisation.

What does this praise for vigorous competition mean for public policy? Despite the clear evidence that competition is good for both individual companies and national economic performance as a whole, companies often do their utmost to stifle it. Government intervention is therefore required both for natural monopolies – such as some utilities – and to prevent or act against anti-competitive practices in other industries. The principal form of intervention is formal competition policy, involving statute law and various regulatory authorities, but another element consists of measures taken by the government to stimulate high-quality demand.

The primary responsibility of government in this area is to ensure that markets are and remain highly competitive. In the past it was believed that companies required some degree of monopoly power in order to make adequate investments in R&D and therefore produce innovations which were rightly seen as central to competitive advantage. This belief underpinned government policies designed to produce 'national champions' in certain industries (Tomlinson, 1994; Silberston, 1981). There is no evidence that these policies were effective. Of course, large and successful British companies should be valued, provided that

58

they have achieved their status in the cut and thrust of competition, and government should always 'support success'. What the government definitely should not do, however, is try to construct these champions artificially through forced mergers or guaranteed markets, as happened in the past.

All the main political parties in Britain have now embraced competition as an important element of their policies for promoting British competitiveness so, to a large extent, we are pushing against an open door. For example, the third Competitiveness White Paper states that open markets 'enhance both business efficiency and consumer choice and offer the surest route to the promotion of UK competitiveness' (Cabinet Office, 1996a: para 9.30). The White Paper coincided with a flurry of activity in the competition policy field by the Conservative government, with a consultation document on reforming current arrangements in March 1996 foreshadowing a draft Competition Bill in August. Even the CBI, which as the representative of mainly large businesses might be expected to have reservations about tough competition policy, has argued that 'effective competition policy works to the ultimate benefit of both business and consumers and is essential in underpinning the UK's international competitiveness' (CBI, 1996b: 5).

Given this apparent consensus among academics, policymakers and business representatives about the value of strong competition, and some signs of government action in this area, it might be wondered what this Commission can add. In fact, although this is a policy area where everyone seems to agree on the general goal of promoting competition, there is intense disagreement about the most appropriate strategy for doing so, and about how far we should travel down the competition road. In this sense, competition policy is rather like education and training: everyone agrees that it matters for economic performance and that current arrangements are inadequate, but all argue strenuously about the tenor and extent of reform required. In calling for extensive reform to produce a significantly tougher competition régime, we place ourselves at the radical end of the spectrum, with the government and the CBI at the opposite end.

Rough Guide
to Competition Policy

All developed countries have some form of competition policy, involving legislation and statutory competition authorities. In general, regulations are intended to deal with three potentially unfair means by which firms might acquire market power: through collusion with competitors, through merger with competitors and through practices designed to force or keep competitors out of a market, such as unfair and predatory pricing. Policy may also be designed to ensure that companies with some degree of market power, even though they have achieved dominance by fair means, are unable to abuse their position to the detriment of consumers.

Companies based in Britain are subject to both UK and EU competition law, although the latter in practice tends only to affect large multinational companies. The various statutes and competition authorities present companies with a complex mosaic of rules, procedures and penalties covering the main forms of anti-competitive behaviour.[1] This complexity is compounded for UK-based companies by significant differences between UK and EU regulations. EU law is essentially *prohibitive* in that certain practices are deemed unlawful and severe penalties are available to punish transgressors. UK law, by contrast, is primarily *reactive* in that the competition authorities can only stop an anti-competitive practice once it has been discovered and have minimal powers to punish transgressors.

In the United Kingdom there are four Acts of Parliament[2] applied by four different authorities[3] to deal with three different types of anti-competitive behaviour. EU law deals with similar behaviour through two main Articles of the Treaty of Rome and through the European Commission and the European Court of Justice. Additionally, at the national level there is separate legislation and a regulator for particular privatised industries such as water, gas and telecommunications. The three main forms of anti-competitive behaviour tackled by the legislation are those mentioned above: *collusive agreements* between firms which restrict competition, *abuse of market power* by individual firms

60

or groups of firms, and *mergers and takeovers* which unduly restrict competition.

Collusive agreements

One of the main functions of the Director-General of Fair Trading (DGFT) and his staff (the Office of Fair Trading, OFT) in the United Kingdom is to seek out and deal with any collusive agreement between firms which unduly restricts competition damaging the 'public interest'. The most obvious agreements of this type are cartels and other agreements to raise prices, reduce output, segment a market or share out tenders for contracts in a locality or industry. Such agreements have two undesirable consequences. First, consumers pay higher prices because output is lower, leading to poorer economic performance. Second, the firms that are party to the agreement have little incentive to improve their efficiency or innovate, as neither activity will give them advantage in the market.

There is discretion in the legislation for the competition authorities to find that, although an agreement is restrictive, it does not damage the public interest. This is an implicit recognition of the value of co-operation between firms, which we believe needs to become more explicit in the reform of legislation. The regulations are summarised in Table 3.1.

EU policy on collusion is governed by Article 85 of the Treaty of Rome, which prohibits agreements between firms, or practices that may prevent, restrict or distort competition and thereby affect cross-border activity or trade (see Appendix B on p. 85). The body charged with administering the system is Directorate General IV (DG IV) of the European Commission. In recognition of the potential value of co-operative agreements, there are explicit provisions for specific exemption of agreements or practices 'which contribute to improving the production or distribution of goods or to promoting technical or economic progress, while allowing consumers a fair share of the resulting benefit'. The exemptions can either be specific to a particular agreement or cover a category of agreements (block exemptions). The latter include exclusive distribution agreements (such as car dealer-

Table 3.1: Regulations on Restrictive Agreements

---

1 The Restrictive Trade Practices Act 1976 requires all firms involved in these agreements to register them with the DGFT, who also has limited powers to seek out unregistered agreements if he or she has reason to believe that an agreement exists.

2 The DGFT then has a statutory duty to refer all agreements to the Restrictive Practices Court (RPC) which is composed of a high court judge and two others.

3 In reviewing the agreement, the judges have to be satisfied that the restriction(s) meet one or more of eight 'public interest' criteria defined in Section 10 of the Act (see Appendix A on p. 83).

4 If the agreement passes this test, there is then the so-called 'tail-piece', which is a general clause stipulating that the agreement must not be unreasonable when one considers the balance of interests and potential outcomes.

If the Court determines that the agreement does indeed act against the public interest, then the agreement will be struck down and the arrangement has to be abandoned. But the Court and the DGFT have no power to fine companies.

6 In order to prevent the referral of trivial agreements to the Court, there is a provision in the legislation for the DGFT to ask the Secretary of State to discharge him of responsibility to refer a particular agreement. This is known as a Section 21(2) order. There can also be plea-bargaining by the parties to the agreement, who may modify it in order to secure the approval of the DGFT.

---

ships), exclusive purchasing agreements and franchising arrangements.

In order to qualify for an exemption, the parties involved must notify the Commission of an agreement. Informal guidance on the agreement's likely status is offered by the Commission in the form of 'comfort letters', though these are not legally binding.

There is also scope for the parties to modify an agreement in consultation with the Commission, but these informal settlements do not bind the European Court of Justice, which ultimately decides whether an agreement is allowable.

Abuse of market power

When a company or group of companies dominates a market, there is a danger that this position of dominance may be abused to the direct detriment of consumers (through excessive pricing or price discrimination) or to potential competitors wishing to enter the market (through predatory pricing or vertical restraints on the activity of suppliers or retailers). In practice, it is difficult to determine whether or not a particular activity constitutes an abuse of a dominant position. For example, aggressive pricing by a dominant firm may be a legitimate response to competition in order to maintain market share, or it may be 'predatory' (designed to finish off weaker competitors). The key difference between the two is in the sustainability of lower prices and the intent of the party involved. Intent is not easily determined. In both cases, the consumer will benefit from lower prices in the short run. Whether competitors are able to respond and survive, however, determines whether in the long run consumers will continue to benefit from lower prices, or suffer reduced choice, higher prices or both. The newspaper price war in the 1990s is a case in point. Will benefits for consumers today, in terms of lower prices, ultimately result in reduced competition with one or more newspapers going out of business?

Legislation in the UK provides a twin-track route for investigation and action against anti-competitive practices adopted in order to preserve a monopoly (the Fair Trading Act 1973) and similar practices by a single firm which may not exercise market power (the Competition Act 1980). The process is described in Table 3.2. The investigations of the Monopolies and Mergers Commission (MMC) into monopolies have attracted almost as much attention as its investigations of proposed mergers; Table 3.3 summarises MMC decisions since the late 1980s. Among the most prominent have been those concerning compact discs, beer

Table 3.2: Regulations on Abuse of a Dominant Position

1 The DGFT investigates a particular market or practice after receiving a complaint or acquiring evidence of abuse.

2 If the DGFT believes that there is a monopoly and a case of abuse to answer, his or her findings are passed directly to the Secretary of State, under the Fair Trading Act, who can either accept undertakings to remedy the situation by the firm(s) concerned or refer the matter to the Monopolies and Mergers Commission (MMC) for further investigation.

3 After hearing the evidence and investigating the market, the MMC first considers whether or not a monopoly exists and then, providing that it does, whether or not the practice is against the public interest on the basis of five criteria in the Fair Trading Act (see Appendix A) and sends a report on this to the Secretary of State.

4 If the MMC report produces 'no adverse finding' (i.e. the practice is not against the public interest), the matter ends there.

5 If the MMC report produces 'an adverse finding' (the practice is against the public interest), the Secretary of State has three options. He can ask the DGFT to obtain undertakings from the firm concerned, he can make an order to rectify the situation, or he can choose to take no action.

6 Under the Competition Act, the DGFT can either unilaterally accept undertakings to remedy the situation from the firm concerned or recommend to the Secretary of State that the matter be referred to the Monopolies and Mergers Commission. The process then proceeds similarly to stages 3–5 above.

7 There is no right of redress under either of these Acts for parties affected by such practices, such as competitors (or previous competitors driven out of the market) or consumers.

Table 3.3: MMC Monopoly Decisions Since 1990

Year	Against the public interest	Cleared
1990	Carbonated soft drinks New cars New housing warranties Razors and razor-blades	Soluble coffee Car parts Indirect electrostatic photocopiers
1991	Matches and disposable lighters Promotion of TV companies' products	Cross-Solent ferry services
1992	Contact lens solutions Wholesale newspaper supply Private medical services Animal Waste Mid and West Kent bus services Southdown Motor Services Limited	Fine fragrances
1993	Supply of films to cinemas	Exhaust gas equipment Condoms Historical on-line databases Mortgage valuations Impulse ice-cream sales Recorded music
1994	North-east England bus services Performing rights in musical works Video games	

Source: Office of Fair Trading, *Annual Report of the Director-General of Fair Trading*, various years.

and ice-cream retailing. There have been numerous complaints about the inconsistency of MMC decisions, both from the companies being investigated and the consumers and competitors said to be suffering because of particular practices.

At the EU level, Article 86 of the Treaty of Rome deals with monopolies (see Appendix B). It prohibits the abuse of a dominant position in a market and details four examples, including predatory pricing, discriminatory pricing, actions against the interest of consumers and restrictive contracting. No exemptions from Article 86 are permitted. Once it begins an investigation, the European Commission has wide powers to solicit information from the parties concerned and to impose fines if the required information is not supplied or is inaccurate. The Commission examines both the alleged abusive practice and whether the firm or firms involved are in a dominant position in the market concerned.

The Commission has wide enforcement powers and can impose severe penalties for infringement of Articles 85 and 86. Large fines, although possible, are something of a rarity and most cases are settled through negotiation. Firms that have been found against by the Commission can appeal to the European Court of First Instance and subsequently to the European Court of Justice.

Mergers and takeovers

Mergers and takeovers can represent attempts by firms to achieve a dominant position in a market. The UK regulations covering mergers and acquisitions have four main parts outlined under the Fair Trading Act (1973), as shown in Table 3.4. Whatever the criticisms of merger policy, it does have one advantage over the other two areas of competition regulation: it is based on the principle of prohibition. Mergers with certain characteristics are not allowed until approved or passed by the competition authorities.

The MMC is obliged by law to judge the merger by five 'public interest' criteria as defined in Section 84 of the Fair Trading Act, taking into account 'all matters which appear to them in the particular circumstances to be relevant'. The criteria include consideration of the impact of the merger on the balance of industry and employment, and the promotion of new techniques and products,

Table 3.4: Competition Regulations Concerning Mergers

---

1 Mergers can be referred to the MMC either if they create or enhance a 25 per cent market share or if the combined assets of the merging parties exceed a certain sum (currently £70m).

2 The DGFT advises the Secretary of State on whether to refer a merger to the MMC, with the decision ultimately lying with the Minister. In addition, the DGFT typically takes advice from an inter-departmental Whitehall committee, the Mergers Panel, about prospective referrals.

3 If the merger is referred, the MMC examines whether it may be expected to operate 'against the public interest', using the same Fair Trading Act criteria as in monopoly cases.

4 If the MMC does not find that it operates against the public interest, the merger cannot be prevented by the Secretary of State. But if the MMC finds against the merger the Secretary of State has three options. He can follow the MMC's recommendations to the letter, which might mean blocking the merger altogether or enforced divestment of certain operations post-merger, or he can vary the conditions imposed on the bid by the MMC, or he can allow the merger without conditions.

---

as well as competition and the interests of consumers (see Appendix A). In fact, very few qualifying mergers actually make it to the MMC investigation stage. For example, of 231 qualifying cases in 1994, only 8 (3.5 per cent) were referred to the MMC by the Secretary of State on the recommendation of the DGFT. This proportion is also declining: the corresponding figure for 1990 was 10 per cent. In most years, the great majority (over 80 per cent) of proposed mergers are horizontal (between similar firms in the same industry) rather than vertical or diversified.

The European Commission has exclusive jurisdiction over any mergers with an EU dimension (the firms concerned have significant cross-border trade) where the aggregate worldwide turnover of all the undertakings concerned is more than 5 billion ECU, and the aggregate EU-wide turnover of each of at least two of the undertakings concerned is more than 250 million ECU, unless each of the companies achieves more than two-thirds of its turnover in a single member state. The criteria for assessment are strongly competition-based. Mergers which create or enhance a dominant position and significantly impede competition are prohibited. Technical and economic efficiency considerations will be taken into account only so long as they are to the advantage of consumers and do not pose an obstacle to competition.

What Is Wrong with UK Competition Policy?

Our working group on competition policy consulted a number of UK companies affected by competition policy as well as various experts. Our conclusion from these consultations is that there are three main problems with current UK law in this field: it is *too confusing*, it is *too weak* and it is *too often plagued by political interference*.

Too confusing

Even the brief description of competition policy given above is quite complex, and no attempt has been made to highlight the nuances or detail the sub-clauses. There are three main sources of confusion: the broadness of the regulations themselves, which allow for a number of potential loop-holes and stages before a practice is declared anti-competitive; the degree of discretion enjoyed by the competition authorities; and the unclear mix of domestic and EU law.[4]

The complex nature of the legislation gives the impression of inconsistency in policy application, which in turn leads to uncertainty for businesses as to how a particular market strategy or practice will be regarded by the authorities (Aaronson, 1992). As *The Economist* put it in April 1995, 'the unpredictability of competition inquiries is compounded by fair-trading laws which are complicated or confusing'.

Firms react to this uncertainty in one of two ways: they are either excessively cautious, not risking new tactics in case these should somehow violate competition rules, or they ignore the regulatory implications of their activities and proceed regardless. The latter reaction is more common in the United Kingdom thanks to the second – and more important – problem with UK policy, namely its weakness (Aaronson, 1992). It is this mix of complexity and weakness which most strongly characterises UK competition policy.

Too weak

UK competition policy does not do what it is supposed to do, namely prevent or remedy anti-competitive behaviour. A combination of factors contributes to the weakness of current arrangements. These include the reactive rather than prohibitive nature of the legislation, the lack of effective penalties against undesirable behaviour (including redress for damaged parties), inadequate powers of investigation for the DGFT, a tendency to leniency, and the broad ambit of the public interest criteria which allows too many anti-competitive practices through the net.

A single example of competition policy at work amply illustrates the problem. In the 1970s and early 1980s, there came to light a series of collusive agreements in the ready-mixed concrete industry. Local contractors had been meeting to share out the work in an area. The arrangement was that each time a contract came up, all but one of the group would bid high; the low bid would pass to each member of the group in turn. Given the geographical restrictions on the customer – ready-mixed concrete deteriorates after travelling much more than twenty miles – these seemingly independent contractors were able to rig the market. It was not until the mid-1980s, however, when the OFT brought action for contempt of court on the grounds that the struck-down agreements were still in operation, that the companies concerned were actually fined for their behaviour (National Consumer Council, 1995).

Too political

Under current arrangements, the Secretary of State's role in the application of competition policy causes yet more uncertainty for companies and regulators. Both the predilections of individual ministers and party political considerations can influence individual competition policy decisions; the two most recent Secretaries of State (Michael Heseltine and Ian Lang) have demonstrated very different interpretations of the national interest. This leads to a significant undermining of the role of the DGFT and the MMC, and further encourages companies to gamble on a favourable outcome from any review of their activities.

Lessons from EU competition policy

Critics of UK competition policy often make unfavourable comparisons with European competition policy arrangements, which are said to be simpler, tougher and more independent of political control. EU policy also has its critics, however, who have focused in particular on the backlog of cases waiting for approval from DG IV, the causes of which are insufficient resources and the submission of too many trivial cases which clog up the process (Aaronson, 1996). The resulting huge delays in decision-making are often cited as the principal reason not to go down the prohibition route in the United Kingdom (CBI, 1995a). They have also led to suggestions that some of the European Commission's powers should, in line with the principle of subsidiarity, be delegated to national competition authorities. At the moment, it is hard to see how this would work in practice in the UK, given that our institutions are so different from those of the EC. Nevertheless, European competition policy (at least that concerned with issues other than mergers) is almost certainly superior to UK policy in terms of its clarity, its lack of complexity and its substantial penalties for infringement of the rules. In all three of these areas, we have much to learn from the EU approach to anti-competitive practices.

Five Principles for Effective Policy

There are so many dimensions to competition policy and so many apparent problems that it is easy for any discussion of policy to degenerate into a long list of the pros and cons of particular reforms. This certainly comes across in much of the evidence on competition policy submitted to the Commission. In order to avoid this, policy-makers need first to determine and adhere to certain basic principles of competition policy. It is then possible to determine which of the many proposed reforms actually have merit and in what order they should be enacted.

There are five principles which are fundamental to competition policy, and which must be followed if that policy is to be reformed: it must ensure effective choice for consumers; it must take account of the market; it must seek to minimise the cost of compliance for companies; it must recognise the national interest; and it must aim for a level playing field worldwide.

Effective choice for consumers

First and foremost, competition policy should be about promoting competition in the marketplace in order to guarantee effective choice for consumers. It should be pointed out that 'effective' does not necessarily mean that more competitors are always better (or, indeed, fewer competing companies are always worse) for consumers. In some markets, two producers who fight for market share may be more effective than ten producers, where one is able to dominate the others. This principal objective leads us to argue that a policy based on prevention is most desirable. All rules-based systems work more effectively if they are able to prevent undesirable behaviour rather than punish it after it has taken place. In competition policy, this is particularly the case when an undesirable practice has long-term implications for competition in a particular industry or locality. Punishment after the fact of, for example, predatory pricing by a dominant market player will help neither a company that went out of business because of the dominant firm's activities, nor the consumers faced with reduced market options. Effective prevention depends on a number of different aspects of policy, including clarity, the magnitude of potential penalties involved, the investigatory powers of the competition authorities, and the overall attitude of public agencies towards competition.

Awareness of the market

Product and service markets range in scope from very local to regional, national, European and global. It is vital that the competition authorities are clearly able to identify and assess the market in which a particular company or group of companies is trading at an early stage of any investigation. For example, concern may be expressed that the UK has only one or two producers of motor vehicles. This may be perfectly acceptable, however, provided that these producers operate in an international market and there is sufficient opportunity for overseas producers to enter the UK market. Understanding markets will become even more important as globalisation affects more and more products and services.

Minimise the costs of compliance

Competition policy should aim to minimise the costs, both for companies and for the public purse, of preventing undesirable behaviour and promoting desirable behaviour. Clear rules and guidelines are the most effective means of doing this. Compliance costs for firms and the competition authorities themselves will be reduced by a preventive rather than a reactive policy framework.

Recognise the national interest

Although we were concerned about how widely the 'national interest' might be defined – which has implications for our first and third principles, above – we recognise that in certain unusual circumstances the promotion of effective choice may have to come second to the national interest. This might apply, for instance, to certain key strategic industries.

A level playing field worldwide

Tougher competition policy in the United Kingdom will promote prosperity through improved business performance, but unless other countries are prepared to act similarly some UK firms will be at a disadvantage. These firms could end up caught in a double bind: forced to accept greater competition at home while at the same time hamstrung by rules protecting domestic producers in other countries. There must be co-ordination between the various national and international competition agencies, particularly as many markets are broadening from domestic to international level. Cave (1996) points out that there is already some evidence of companies indulging in 'régime shopping' between domestic and international competition policy. For the UK, greater co-ordination with EU competition policy is of course of particular importance, but there are also global competition rules and issues which will need attention.

We believe that a government committed to tougher competition policy should proceed with these principles as their guide to reform. Five reforms in particular stand out as requiring immediate implementation. The first three involve a shift towards a prohibition approach to competition with new investigatory powers for the competition authorities and stiffer penalties for anti-competitive behaviour. The last two involve revision of the roles and responsibilities of the Secretary of State, the OFT and the MMC. There is also a case for changes in the public interest criteria to give clearer signals to both companies and the competition authorities.

Changing the Approach

A marked shift towards a prohibition approach in competition policy, based on prevention rather than reaction, would represent a bold policy change and demonstrate a clear commitment to the promotion of competition. Although much has been promised in this field by recent governments, there has been a notable lack of legislation. As Lord Borrie, the former DGFT, has stated, 'government policy towards the promotion of competition and the restraint of cartels and monopoly power has been marked by lack of will, dither and uncertainty'.[5] A Department of Trade and Industry (DTI) White Paper on restrictive agreements (DTI, 1989) simply gathered dust until the DTI brought out a consultation paper in March 1996 which covered very similar ground (DTI, 1996a). Although the government has produced a draft Competition Bill for consultation, this refers yet again to restrictive agreements and recommends only limited strengthening of monopoly rules. It is high time that the 1989 proposals were implemented, and also widened to cover abuses of market power as well as restrictive agreements, with the addition of appropriate investigative powers and penalties to ensure that the reforms have teeth.

A shift towards prohibition requires three main changes in current arrangements: a change in the general tenor of the legislation; an increase in investigatory powers for the competition authorities, particularly the DGFT; and a toughening of the penalties available for the authorities to discourage particular activities or arrangements.

Towards prohibition

Prohibition should be enacted in British legislation in a manner similar to Articles 85 and 86 of the Treaty of Rome (see Appendix B). All agreements which restrict the activities of one or more parties should be assumed to be anti-competitive and therefore invalid, although with some block exemptions and scope for appeal against decisions in individual cases. The block exemptions should be similar to those contained in Article 85. There should be an assets test, with only agreements involving firms with assets above a certain level submitted for scrutiny; this would ensure that trivial agreements do not clog the works, thereby streamlining the scrutiny and approval process. Additionally, there should be scope for the OFT to provide the equivalent of a 'comfort letter' in advance of a Restrictive Practices Court hearing.

The proposals described above deal primarily with restrictive agreements. A future government should go even further, however, by outlawing abuse of market power by dominant firms (in other words, something similar to Article 86). In its 1992 Green Paper *Abuse of Market Power* (DTI, 1992), the government asked for opinions on three different routes for reform of the rules in this area. These have become known as Options 1, 2 and 3:

Option 1: strengthen existing legislation on anti-competitive and exploitative behaviour;

Option 2: introduce a prohibition on anti-competitive and exploitative behaviour by enterprises with significant market power;

Option 3: introduce prohibition alongside the existing monopoly provisions.

The main results of the consultation exercise, shown in Table 3.5, were that a majority (63 per cent) of the 143 submissions indicating a preference supported Option 2 or Option 3 (DTI, 1993). Responses from SMEs and consumer groups tended to favour a distinct shift towards a prohibition approach. Opinion was divided, however, as to which of these two options was best. Option 1 was favoured by a majority of large companies and the utilities, which obviously feel they have the most to lose from a prohibition approach, and their opinions were given excessive weight. The government concluded that since there was no con-

Table 3.5: Results of Consultation on the Green Paper, *Abuse of Market Power*

Option	Large firms	SMEs	Consumers	Regulators	Utilities	Lawyers	Others	Total
1/No change	13	3	–	1	8	9	8	42
2	1	10	–	2	2	14	6	35
3	1	16	4	6	1	3	6	37
Other	1	–	–	–	–	1	1	3
No preference	2	5	–	1	6	3	9	26
Total	18	34	4	10	17	30	30	143

Source: Trade and Industry Committee (1995a), Table 4.
Notes: *Option 1:* Strengthening existing legislation on anti-competitive behaviour and exploitative behaviour. *Option 2:* Introducing a prohibition in place of existing legislation. *Option 3:* Introducing a prohibition alongside the existing monopoly provisions.

sensus on which option represented the best way forward, it should choose the least radical option of strengthening the existing system.

The shift to prohibition will not be easy. There are bound to be teething problems in determining the boundaries of the exemptions, and in changing the mindset of competition authorities and companies. More than offsetting these difficulties, however, is the deterrent effect which the prohibition approach would have on anti-competitive behaviour. This represents the biggest single advantage of such an approach over the present system.

A prohibition approach must be accompanied by tougher penalties for anti-competitive practices. The most common criticism of current competition regulations is that, despite the range of remedies in current law, there are no fines for anti-competitive behaviour. As a result, there is little incentive not to engage in anti-competitive behaviour. Collusion and abuse of market power are perfectly rational under the current system because, even if detected, the firm is merely instructed to discontinue the practice. At present, the main constraints on firms are EC legislation and the possibility of contempt of court proceedings if an undertaking to the Restrictive Practices Court is broken.

The absence of penalties in the United Kingdom is contrasted with the power of the European Commission, which can fine perpetrators up to 10 per cent of their EU turnover. Large fines make headlines and, even though rarely levied, they still serve as a deterrent. US anti-trust legislation permits even more severe penalties: violations of the main regulations embodied in the Sherman Act can be prosecuted as felonies. The US Department of Justice typically brings criminal prosecutions in cases where it believes that the defendants knew their actions were illegal. Convicted defendants are subject to large fines, jail sentences or both (White, 1993).

There is a case for going even further. As well as giving the authorities power to levy fines on offenders, third parties (including competitors and consumers) could be given enhanced rights to seek redress for damages caused by anti-competitive behaviour. For example, firms forced out of business by predatory pricing could sue the offending company. Williams (1993:108) argues that 'British competition policy is seriously weakened until safeguards against predation in the form of proper compensation for victims are introduced.' Such a change would, however, carry the danger that prohibitive potential costs from actions by consumers and by companies going out of business would restrict innovative market behaviour by companies.

> **Recommendation:** The government should adopt a prohibition approach to restrictive agreements and the abuse of market power with stiffer penalties for anti-competitive behaviour, including fines up to, say, a maximum of 10 per cent of turnover in the market concerned.

Increased powers

Increased powers of investigation for the competition authorities are required to accompany a shift towards a prohibition approach. Under the Restrictive Trade Practices Act, the DGFT can issue a notice asking for details about a suspected unregistered agreement only if he or she already has grounds for believing that such an agreement exists. In general, the powers of the OFT and MMC are very limited compared with those of the European Commission's investigators and the US anti-trust authorities. Both the last two have the power to enter premises and demand business records and oral explanations on the spot, and they can levy fines for withholding information. John Bridgeman, the current DGFT, has gone on record demanding powers similar to those of his overseas colleagues, stating that: 'extra power to demand information and supporting documents would be invaluable . . . our effectiveness in following up any suspected or alleged collusion is severely diminished by our inadequate investigatory powers'.[6] The present government has promised increases in the DGFT's powers for a long time, but action has been singularly lacking.

> **Recommendation:** There should be a substantial increase in the powers of the Director-General of Fair Trading and his staff to investigate suspected anti-competitive behaviour.

Reforming the Competition Authorities

Much of the political debate about competition policy has centred on the need for reform of the competition authorities. There have been proposals for unification of the OFT and MMC, for new names for these organisations (the CBI has suggested 'Competition Authority' and the 'Competition Commission'), for greater use of the courts, for a much reduced role for the Secretary of State and for the professionalisation of MMC commissioners. Unfortunately, some of these reforms have become political totems, which has lowered the quality of discussion. We believe that of these proposed reforms, the two most important are the reduction of the influence of the Secretary of State and the realignment of the responsibilities of the OFT and MMC.

Reducing the influence of the Secretary of State

Aaronson (1996:11), among others, makes a strong case for limiting the role of the Secretary of State to policy formation and guidance rather than direct decision-making about individual competition policy cases: 'if case-by-case decisions are made by Ministers without the public advice of an independent body, there will be a suspicion that special interest groups (particularly the dominant firm involved) have influenced the decision'. He draws a useful analogy with tax policy, where parliament enacts laws but, because interpretation of particular cases is often complex, it is left to the Inland Revenue or Customs and Excise to assess the tax due from an individual company. There is an appeal mechanism, but it does not involve a minister since this would undermine confidence in the fairness of the system. Aaronson argues that there is no obvious reason why political influence in competition policy should stretch any further than it does in tax policy. The government's response to this common criticism of current arrangements is that the tripartite structure 'provides an important safeguard by ensuring that where there are adverse findings, the merits of the case may be examined by more than one body' (Trade and Industry Committee, 1995a:ix).

Although there is general agreement among many commentators on the need for change in the Secretary of State's role in competition policy, there is a divergence of opinion on what the new role should be. The National Consumer Council and the Labour Party argue that the Minister should only appoint the heads of the two regulatory agencies (or single unified agency). Others, such as Aaronson, argue that a unified competition authority should be required to take account of ministerial guidance on competition policy, with the courts as a check that it was doing so. Some members of the Commission Working Group were worried about the extension of the role of the courts that Aaronson's proposal would imply. Another suggested option was to make ministerial decisions more transparent, through a requirement to publish a report in those cases where the Minister did not fully accept the recommendations of the competition authorities.

A more radical option would be to remove the Secretary of State from playing any role in individual competition policy cases, but this is hardly realistic politically. There is also an argument that regulatory accountability means that an elected individual should be responsible for certain key decisions. Greater transparency seems the most desirable option so that the Secretary of State's decisions will be less open to lobbying from special interest groups.

> **Recommendation:** The Secretary of State's role in competition policy should be made transparent through the publication of a report with reasons for his decisions.

Realignment of OFT and MMC responsibilities

The three-tiered structure of competition bodies (OFT, MMC, Secretary of State) is said by some critics both to waste resources and encourage inconsistency and leniency (Aaronson, 1996; National Consumer Council, 1995; Trade and Industry Committee, 1995a). In abuse of dominant position and merger cases, three sets of staff have to brief themselves on the details of a case. This means duplication of effort that wastes public resources. The multiplicity of regulators also leads to inconsistency and even leniency against anti-competitive behaviour because the parties have three opportunities to evade significant action. If any one of the three agencies is unconvinced that a particular merger or action conflicts with the public interest, then nothing happens. One common proposal for dealing with these problems is to merge the OFT and MMC into a single competition authority with separate departments charged with investigating, prosecuting and ruling on anti-competitive behaviour.

The main justification of the current division of the prosecution and judicial arms of competition policy into separate bodies is that the MMC is a truly impartial judge, since it never instigates or chooses a case. It therefore has no axe to grind and no prior view of any case which is due to come before it. One of the participants at the Commission Working Group argued that the experience of DG IV is instructive in this area. This European competition body is said to be particularly distrusted by business, and there is particular concern that, having initiated an investigation, DG IV may be reluctant to conclude that it was wrong. The participant went even further, arguing that 'the loss of the perceived independence of the MMC would be the single most damaging thing that could happen to the UK's system of competition policy'.

There is a real question as to whether the integrity of the judicial arm of competition policy could be kept intact in a unified authority. Our view is that the OFT and MMC should be kept as separate agencies but their responsibilities should be altered. The OFT should have a more explicit investigatory and prosecutory role, while the MMC should have an explicitly adjudicatory role, in order to reduce investigatory duplication and increase consistency. This would require greater resources for the OFT to investigate suspicious commercial agreements, activities and markets, and fewer (if any) investigatory resources for the MMC. It would then be up to a company investigated and accused by the OFT of anti-competitive behaviour to argue its case against the OFT at the MMC.

Recommendation: The responsibilities of the OFT and MMC should be realigned to make the OFT the principal agent of investigation and prosecution with the MMC concentrating on adjudication.

Boosting High-Quality Demand

It is well understood that governments have to establish certain rules governing company behaviour in the product market as elsewhere, which is why most of our recommendations in this area concern competition policy. We believe, however, that the government should do all it can to raise the quality of demand, which requires well-informed, discerning consumers. The government can probably do little directly to make domestic consumers become more discerning (though as Chapter 8 argues, it can aim to do this in its own procurement activities), but it can certainly do more to ensure that consumers are better informed. The government and its agencies collect certain types of information about companies and their products which, if more freely available, would help consumer choice, including for instance the health and safety record of restaurants and hotels and the performance of manufactured goods against recognised quality standards.

Although there must inevitably be concerns about breaching certain commercial confidentialities, there is surely a case for putting more of this information into the public domain, for example through the Internet. Because there are bound to be limits to the type of information the government should disclose about companies, we do not make a detailed recommendation on this issue. But the potential benefits of having better informed consumers lead us to recommend that the next government should at least review the boundaries of current commercial confidentiality legislation, and become more predisposed to disclosure of government information rather than being disposed to secrecy.

Recommendation: The government should be predisposed to public disclosure of the information it has about companies where that would enable consumers to make more informed choices.

Conclusion

Given our comments in Chapter 1 that the gains from market lib-eralisation have largely run their course, it may seem surprising that we advocate such deep reforms to competition policy in this chapter. In fact, having reviewed policy over the last decade or so, we find this is one area where the government has promised much and delivered little. Good intentions have not translated into effective action. 'National champions' are an important fea-ture of national economic success, but they should emerge through the cut and thrust of market competition rather than the back-door route of forced mergers and state subsidies. The deter-mined pursuit of *competition and co-operation* must be an inte-gral part of the government's programme to shorten the long tail of poor performing British firms, and tougher competition policy must be a crucial element in that programme. We believe that the five recommendations outlined in this chapter will demonstrate clear intent and improve business competitiveness.

A prohibition approach on restrictive agreements and abuse of market power should be adopted immediately and there should also be stiffer penalties for anti-competitive behaviour in the form of fines up to, say, a maximum of 10 per cent of turnover in the market concerned, as with EU policy. This will require a sub-stantial increase in the powers of the DGFT and his staff to inves-tigate suspected anti-competitive behaviour. Reform of the competition authorities should involve greater transparency in decisions by the Secretary of State so that his or her decisions will be less open to lobbying from special interest groups. In addition, the responsibilities of the OFT and MMC should be realigned to make the OFT the principal agent of investigation and prosecu-tion and the MMC more clearly adjudicatory in character. Finally, the government should review commercial confidential-ity legislation and change its predisposition to the disclosure of information about companies with a view to enabling consumers to make more informed choices.

APPENDIX A

The public interest criteria as they appear in the Fair Trading Act, 1973, section 84

In determining for any purposes to which this section applies whether any particular matter operates, or may be expected to operate, against the public interest, the Commission shall take into account all matters which appear to them in the particular circumstances to be relevant and, among other things, shall have regard to the desirability:

a) of maintaining and promoting effective competition between persons supplying goods and services in the United Kingdom;

b) of promoting the interests of consumers, purchasers and other users of goods and services in the United Kingdom in respect of the prices charged for them and in respect of their quality and the variety of goods and services supplied;

c) of promoting, through competition, the reduction of costs and the development and use of new techniques and new products, and of facilitating the entry of new competitors into existing markets;

d) of maintaining and promoting the balanced distribution of industry and employment in the United Kingdom; and

e) of maintaining and promoting competitive activity in markets outside the United Kingdom on the part of producers of goods, and of suppliers of goods and services, in the United Kingdom.

The public interest criteria as they appear in the Restrictive Trade Practices Act 1976, Section 10

a) that the restriction or information provision is reasonably necessary, having regard to the character of the goods to which it applies, to protect the public against injury (whether to persons or to premises) in connection with the consumption, installation or use of those goods.

b) that the removal of the restriction or information provision would deny to the public as purchasers, consumers or users of any goods other specific and substantial benefits or advantages enjoyed or likely to be enjoyed by them as such, whether by virtue of the restriction or information provision itself or of any arrangements or operations resulting therefrom.

c) that the restriction or information provision is reasonably necessary to counteract measures taken by any one person not party to the agreement with a view to preventing or restricting competition in or in relation to the trade or business in which the persons party thereto are engaged.

d) that the restriction or information provision is reasonably necessary to enable the persons party to the agreement to negotiate fair terms for the supply of goods to, or the acquisition of goods from, any one person not party thereto who controls a preponderant part of the trade or business of acquiring or supplying such goods, or for the supply of goods to any person not party to the agreement and not carrying on such a trade or business who, either alone or in combination with any other such person, controls a preponderant part of the market for such goods.

e) that, having regard to the conditions actually obtaining or reasonably foreseen at the time of the application, the removal or the restriction or information provision would be likely to have a serious and persistent adverse effect on the general level of unemployment in an area, or in areas taken together, in which a substantial proportion of the trade or industry to which the agreement relates is situated.

f) that, having regard to the conditions actually obtaining or reasonably foreseen at the time of the application, the removal of the restriction or information provision would be likely to cause a reduction in the volume or earnings of the export business which is substantial either in relation to the whole export business of the United Kingdom or in relation to the whole business (including export business) of the said trade or industry.

g) that the restriction or information provision is reasonably required for purposes connected with the maintenance of any other restriction accepted or information provision made by the parties, whether under the same agreement or under any other agreement between them, being a restriction or information provision which is found by the Court not to be contrary to the public interest upon grounds other than those specified in this paragraph, or has been so found in previous proceedings before the Court.

h) that the restriction or information provision does not directly or indirectly restrict or discourage competition to any material degree in any relevant trade or industry and is not likely to do so.

APPENDIX B

Articles 85 and 86 of the Treaty of Rome

Article 85

1 The following shall be prohibited as incompatible with the common market; all agreements between undertakings, decisions by associations of undertakings and concerned practices which may affect trade between Member States and which have as their object or effect the prevention, restriction or distortion of competition within the common market, and in particular those which:

a) directly or indirectly fix purchase or selling prices or any trading conditions;
b) limit or control production, markets, technical development, or investment;
c) share markets or sources of supply;
d) apply dissimilar conditions to equivalent transactions with other trading parties, thereby placing them at a competitive disadvantage;
e) make the conclusion of contracts subject to acceptance by the other parties of supplementary obligations which, by

their nature or according to commercial usage, have no connection with the subject of such contracts.

2 Any agreements or decisions prohibited pursuant to this Article shall be automatically void.

3 The provisions of paragraph 1 may, however, be declared inapplicable in the case of:

– any agreement or category of agreements between undertakings;

– any decision or category of decisions by associations of undertakings;

– any concerted practice or category of concerted practices;

which contributes to improving the production or distribution of goods or to promoting technical or economic progress, while allowing consumers a fair share of the resulting benefit, and which does not:

a) impose on the undertakings concerned restrictions which are not indispensable to the attainment of these objectives;
b) afford such undertakings the possibility of eliminating competition in respect of a substantial part of the products in question.

Article 86

Any abuse by one or more undertakings of dominant position within the common market or in a substantial part of it shall be prohibited as incompatible with the common market in so far as it may affect trade between Member States. Such abuse may, in particular, consist in:

a) directly or indirectly imposing unfair purchase or selling prices or other unfair trading conditions;

b) limiting production, markets or technical development to the prejudice of consumers;

c) applying dissimilar conditions to equivalent transactions with other trading parties, thereby placing them at a competitive disadvantage;

d) making the conclusion of contracts subject to acceptance by the other parties of supplementary obligations which, by their nature or according to commercial usage, have no connection with the subject of such contracts.

NOTES

1 These are described in more detail in Hay (1993) and National Consumer Council (1995).

2 The Fair Trading Act 1973, the Restrictive Trade Practices Act 1976, the Resale Practices Act 1976, and the Competition Act 1980.

3 The Director-General of Fair Trading, the Monopolies and Mergers Commission, the Restrictive Practices Court and the Secretary of State for Trade and Industry.

4 These and other points are elaborated on in DTI (1989), Hay (1993), National Consumer Council (1995); and Trade and Industry Committee (1995a).

5 In evidence to the Trade and Industry Committee's inquiry into monopolies (1995a: para. 69).

6 Speech to the European Policy Forum in London, 30 January 1996.

4

FAR-SIGHTED MANAGEMENT

We want to promote efficient companies which adopt best practice and take a far-sighted view of their business. In this chapter we identify external and internal obstacles to the building of such companies in the United Kingdom. This leads us to focus on relations with the financial institutions representing company shareholders and the culture and governance structure of companies. The aim is to maintain a market in corporate control in the interests of efficiency and to take steps to alter corporate culture and improve relations between management, shareholders and other stakeholders in the interests of far-sightedness.

The central theme of this chapter is that the state must do what it can to foster efficient and far-sighted companies. An efficient company is characterised by responsiveness to customers and employees, and a determination to adopt and operate best practice in management. A far-sighted company aims to be in business indefinitely and seeks to maximise its returns over a long period of time. A long-termist approach to investment in research, training, plant and capital equipment generally follows. Efficiency is mainly driven by product market competition (see Chapter 3). Managerial accountability structures and the market in corporate control are also, however, supposed to promote efficiency and it is these that form the focus of this chapter.

In developing customer loyalty, the managers of far-sighted companies will also seek to develop productive relationships both within the firm and between the firm and key outside associates, such as suppliers or financiers. In long-term relationships lies a substantial part of a firm's ability to generate value added.

A far-sighted firm must be and remain highly competitive. That means not so much the ability to screw the last halfpenny out of any deal as the ability to engage the enthusiasm and commitment of employees and business associates, to induce them to make the investments of skills and capital that will be jointly beneficial. The importance of co-operation, against a background of competitive markets, should be clear.

In Hirschman's famous distinction, developing productive relationships means stressing 'voice' rather than 'exit'. If there are practices and procedures whereby shareholders, employees or suppliers meet with management to consider how jointly to improve performance (voice), those groups will be less predisposed to selling, leaving the firm or ending the commercial relationship when dissatisfied (exit). That such practices or procedures are a strength which promotes better company performance is amply documented (for example, Blair, 1995; Kay, 1993; Kenworthy, 1995; Sako, 1996). Mari Sako's study of the motor-car components industry for the Commission showed clearly that those companies which had 'voice' relationships with employees or suppliers outperformed – in hard, cash terms of higher productivity and greater profitability – those which did not.

In theory at least, more people are now getting this message. The Employment Department, for example, has stated that 'effective employee involvement is not just a matter of good employee practice. It is, above all, a prerequisite for business growth in a modern economy' (Employment Department, 1994). Moreover, the RSA's *Tomorrow's Company* report claimed that 'a majority of UK company leaders now appear convinced that an *inclusive* approach to business relationships provides a route to sustainable success' (RSA, 1995:1). Lip-service is one thing, but practice is another. There is much evidence that in both their investment decisions and in their approach to building relationships too many British companies are short-termist. The key issue, therefore, is what prevents companies behaving in the way most informed people now agree they should?

In the search for external obstacles to far-sightedness, we consider the City – a prime target for commentators agonising over

British short-termism. In looking for internal obstacles, we enter the area of corporate governance, which has been much discussed in recent years. We do not wish to revisit all those discussions since we are looking at governance from a particular point of view. We are concerned with the contribution that it can make to business competitiveness through facilitating efficient and far-sighted companies. We concentrate less on questions of how governance structures should protect the legal rights of those involved with the business or prevent breaches of business ethics, important though those issues are both in their own right and in relation to a firm's reputation. Having reached conclusions on these issues, we set out some policy proposals.

UK Company Myopia

Chapter 1 documented the long tail of underperformance among British companies, and how their investment in research and physical capital is less than that of competitors in other countries. Short-termism is partly to blame for these problems and this is confirmed by two types of evidence: on the nature of investment decision-making and on the length and nature of relationships between management and others involved in the company.

Investment criteria

Perhaps the clearest indicator of short-termism is the existence of a policy of undertaking investments only if they are expected to pay off quickly. There is strong evidence that some UK firms use pay-back criteria which tend to limit investment to projects that are believed to guarantee high and/or rapid returns. These criteria can be measured in terms of internal rates of return (IRRs, also known as hurdle or target rates of return) and/or pay-back periods. Any project which is expected to yield lower returns than the company's IRR, or which is expected to yield such returns only in the long term, will not receive funds to proceed. In theory, the IRR is set with reference to a measure of the cost of financial capital plus some risk premium to take account of the margins of error in calculating expected returns. Risk will depend on such things as the volatility of demand, costs and technical factors. The pay-back period (the period of time in which the investment is expected to recoup the capital invested plus some return) reflects management's and investors' discount rate (the extent to which they prefer rewards sooner rather than later).

Numerous studies have shown that UK companies have, on average, very high IRRs (Bank of England, 1995; Miles, 1993; Rough, 1996) and pay-back periods which are very short (Hutton, 1995; Miles, 1996). Pay-back periods in particular are found to be much shorter than in other countries where surveys have been conducted, and are sufficient in themselves to explain the UK's relatively low investment rate. While these studies examine or ask questions about investment, it must be supposed that many managers will regard training or research expenditures in a similar light; they will be reluctant to undertake these expenditures unless they are thought to have a rapid pay-off.

Given open capital markets and a highly developed financial sector, why do so many UK companies treat the cost of capital as being so high? One argument is that the decline in inflation is quite recent and managers still do not trust that it will last; they are therefore building an inflation premium into expected returns. Some managers told us that they were not yet sufficiently convinced of interest-rate stability to bring down their IRRs. Yet this cannot be the whole or even the main part of the story. The difference in yield between index-linked and standard government bonds shows the financial sector is currently discounting inflation of around 4 per cent over the next ten years or so. Even adding a substantial inflation risk premium does not go far to explaining hurdle rates approaching 20 per cent.

These high hurdle rates have apparently persisted even during the current recovery, when profitability has much improved (Figure 4.1). A corollary has been a dividend pay-out ratio which has grown significantly since the mid-1970s and is now substantially higher in the UK than in all our major competitors (Table 4.1 and Figure 4.2). Firms have not wanted to invest their earnings and have instead returned an increasing proportion of them to shareholders.

Figure 4.1: Profitability in UK Companies, 1970–95

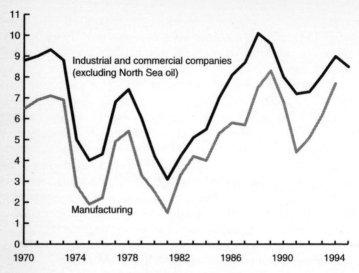

Source: ONS – First release ONS(96) 95 – 5 July 1996.

Notes: Includes North Sea oil companies up to 1975. Manufacturing only available to 1994. Data are net rate of return on capital employed.

In theory, dividends should reflect the balance between residual earnings available for distribution and the internal requirements for investment. In practice, they tend to be set so as to avoid going below the previous year's level, almost irrespective of current performance (Mayer and Alexander, 1991; Mayer, 1994). Managers, then, do not regard dividends as in any way an optional payment; they plan instead to maintain and increase them. Given that retained earnings fund the great bulk of investment in the UK – over 90 per cent between 1970 and 1994, according to Jenkinson and Corbett (1996) – a view that dividends must be kept high and rising is an important component of a high estimated cost of capital. This reflection leads to another puzzle. If equity capital is for some reason very expensive, why should firms not borrow to invest or, indeed, to finance other productive expenditures such as training or research? Interest

Table 4.1: Dividend Yields in the G7, 1992–93

Country	1992	1993
UK	3.9	3.9
Canada	2.5	2.6
France	2.9	2.9
Germany	1.7	2.1
Italy	1.6	2.2
Japan	0.8	0.8
USA	2.7	2.8

Source: Bond *et al.* (1995), Table 1.

Note: Dividend yields measure dividend payments in relation to equity values rather than current profits and are closely related to the payout ratio. Bond *et al.* state that 'internationally comparable data on dividend payout ratios are not so easily available but some recent estimates [from the DTI] confirm the same ranking with the payout ratio in the UK being higher than any other major economy in 1992'.

rates now are low in relation to hurdle rates and borrowing receives a more favourable tax treatment than raising equity, since interest payments are tax deductible. Yet the study by Jenkinson and Corbett shows that British firms borrow less than firms in most other countries, including the United States, France and Japan (in transatlantic jargon, they are 'under-leveraged').

These facts make it seem unlikely that a simple 'shortage of capital' has any role to play in explaining short-termism or underinvestment. None the less, if we are looking for external constraints to far-sightedness, City–industry relations clearly merit further scrutiny.

Productive relationships

The evidence on the extent to which British management forms long-term, productive relationships with employees and other groups involved in the company is less straightforward than the evidence on investment criteria. None the less, it supports the

Figure 4.2: Dividend Payout Ratio by UK Companies, 1970–94

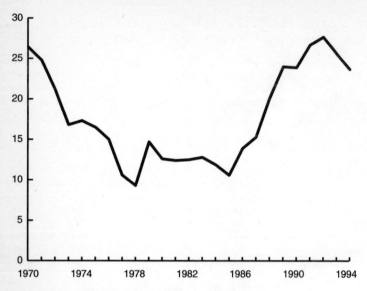

Source: Economic Trends Annual Supplement, 1996.

Note: The graph shows total payments of cash dividends on ordinary and prefer-ence shares by UK industrial and commercial companies, as a percentage of total gross trading profit net of stock appreciation.

view that too few British companies are far-sighted. For example, British employees tend on average to stay with the same employer for a shorter period than employees in most other OECD countries apart from the United States, where turnover is much higher than the rest of the developed world (Table 4.2). In addition, while it is well known that union representation has dropped enormously in the UK since 1980, there has been rela-tively little take-up of 'human resource management' voice mechanisms, such as quality circles and consultative committees, specifically designed to promote employee performance (Mill-ward, 1994; TUC, 1994).

Measuring the length and nature of relationships with suppli-ers is not easy, but evidence of UK stand-offishness in this area is nevertheless striking. Despite the example of Japanese best-practice supplier relations demonstrated by Nissan, Toyota and Honda in their subsidiaries in the United Kingdom and the spur this has given to some British producers to adopt similar arrangements, many UK companies still see little value in spending time developing supplier relationships. A recent study of medium-sized UK companies concluded that '73 per cent of middle market companies disagree that they should operate in partnership with their larger customers, preferring instead to maintain an adversarial commercial relationship' (Coopers and Lybrand, 1994:78). International comparisons of the length and nature of relationships both within firms and between firms confirms that the United Kingdom is among the two or three countries with real deficiencies in this area (Kenworthy, 1995). This general finding is reiterated in a detailed study of automotive manufacturers in nine developed countries (Andersen Consulting, 1994). There are, however, some encouraging signs of change, including the setting up of an industry forum in the automotive sector involving both large car companies and their suppliers (see Chapter 5 for more details).

Table 4.2: Enterprise Tenure in Selected OECD Countries, 1991

	UK	USA	Canada	France	Germany	Japan	Switzerland	Average (13 countries)
Average tenure (years)								
All	**7.9**	6.7	7.8	10.1	10.4	10.9	8.8	8.7
Men	**9.2**	7.5	8.9	10.6	12.1	12.5	10.4	9.8
Women	**6.3**	5.9	6.5	9.6	8.0	7.3	6.6	7.1

Source: OECD (1993), Table 4.1.

Notes: Enterprise tenure measures how long an individual has been employed by their current employer. Details of tenure are omitted for six of the thirteen countries included in the average (Australia, Austria, Finland, Netherlands, Norway and Spain).

The conclusion which emerges from the above review of the evidence is that too few British companies are truly far-sighted in their approach to investment decisions and in their relationships with the key individuals, groups and other companies which are involved in making the company a success or failure. We need to ascertain why this is so before examining what, if anything, the government should or can do about it.

The City's Role

There have been some entertaining, if misleadingly lurid, depictions of the City's role in company short-termism. A common stereotype is that of the CEO continuously watching a computer screen to monitor the firm's share price. Behind this mythical figure is the allegation that too many British companies are trying to maximise short-run shareholder value at the expense of other groups in the firm and of long-run performance.

Institutional investors

The United Kingdom is said to suffer from the problem of short-termism both because of the greater importance of equity as a form of finance compared with most other countries and because of the peculiar form of shareholding in British companies (Hutton, 1995; Albert, 1993). A much larger proportion of British shares is held by institutional funds than in any other country; pension and insurance fund holdings have doubled to 60 per cent of all shares in the last thirty years (75 per cent if foreign funds are included; see Table 4.3). The performance of the funds themselves is measured quarterly. Therefore, it is argued, they need industrial and commercial companies in which they invest to return good short-term results. Their commitment to any single company may be negligible, particularly if they are 'performance' funds, not obliged to follow the stock market index. That means that fund managers' response to a company which fails by their criteria is to sell. In that sense the funds are 'absentee owners' who acknowledge no responsibility for the governance or performance of a company. As long as they have rights

Table 4.3: Structure of Share Ownership in Four Countries [a]

| | UK | | Germany | USA | Japan |
Ownership category	**1963**	**1994**	1991	1991	1991
Pension funds	**6.4**	**27.8**	–	24.8	0.9
Insurance companies	**10.0**	**21.9**	10.6	5.2	17.3
Investment companies and other financial companies	**12.6**	**10.1**	–	9.5	3.6
Overseas investors	**7.0**	**16.3**	17.7	6.7	4.2
Total fund managers	**36.0**	**76.1**	28.3	46.2	26.0
Individuals	**54.0**	**20.3**	16.8	53.5	23.1
Others [b]	**10.0**	**3.6**	54.9	0.3	50.9
Total	**100.0**	**100.0**	100.0	100.0	100.0

Sources: Gaved (1996), Table 8.1 and Kester (1992), Table 4.

Notes: a Data are percentage of ownership by value of shares.

b 'Others' include corporate cross-holdings, bank holdings and government stakes. These are only significant in Germany (39.2 per cent corporate holdings, 8.9 per cent banks) and Japan (25.2 per cent corporate holdings, 25.2 per cent banks).

of 'exit', they do not care about 'voice'. Moreover, they are said to see little value in management giving voice to other groups within the firm, such as employees, suppliers or customers.

Many institutional investors have, for tax reasons, a particular thirst for dividend income over capital gains. Chapter 9 deals with the tax distortions responsible for that. It seems misplaced, however, to blame fund managers for companies' reluctance to borrow, which is the reason for the predominance of equity finance. Nor can other financial institutions such as banks be blamed for low borrowing, at least by large companies. Even if British banks have behaved more like a cartel than a competitive sector in the past, the opening of London to foreign banks has led to the loans market becoming very competitive. Demand, not supply, is lacking in that market.

In any event, fund managers universally repudiate the suggestion that their own short assessment period forces them to take a short-term view of companies. Ultimate beneficiaries (the pension funds which put their money with the professional fund managers) understand, say the managers, that bets on companies take time to pay off. Success as a fund manager consists in taking a long-term view of a company and making a contrarian bet by buying more or fewer of its shares than its weight in the market index warrants. Such a position will typically be held for years. At any time enough of the 'bets' should be paying off to satisfy the fund manager, and he or she will not be tempted to 'close' other bets simply because the companies in question have long-term strategies. In corroboration of this, fund managers point to the high share prices of biotechnology companies that have yet to make a profit at all (Lindey, 1996).

Several of the fund managers whom we consulted also had their own story about the rigidity of dividends. In plain terms, they argued that dividends were a virility symbol for managements keen to maintain status. Indeed, one fund manager stated he sometimes suggested to companies that they should consider reducing their dividend in order to get them over particular trading difficulties or to fund new investment projects, but that managers almost unanimously argued that they could never cut the dividend. Corporate management believes that the market will penalise companies which cut their dividends, which are as much about signalling management's confidence in the future performance of a company as they are about distributing the earnings from past performance (Allen, 1992).

Takeovers

Why do managers show such concern about market reactions and their share price? One reason is that managers themselves often hold shares, or options to buy shares, on the grounds that this helps them to identify with the interests of shareholders. Another reason is that many managers are concerned about the threat of hostile takeover, which is easier if their share price is low. The volume of takeovers in the UK topped £25 billion in 1995, of which about one-quarter were hostile (Mayer, 1996). The threat of takeover may be at the back of the minds of many boards of directors when they make strategic decisions.

Mergers and acquisitions are an important part of business strategy and hostile takeovers are an ultimate discipline on management. The statistical and other evidence, however, is that these tools have come to be relied upon excessively in the United Kingdom. The majority of takeovers do not result in increased returns for the shareholders of the bidding company, though they generally benefit shareholders of the company being bought (Mayer, 1996). It is unclear that the merged company is generally more productive than its component parts.[1] Indeed, there is currently a fashion for de-merging, 'downsizing' and 'focus'.

The main criticism levelled at the 'takeover culture', however, is not that many takeovers are misguided but that this culture affects management behaviour in many firms in regrettable ways. Certainly, it inhibits managers from ignoring shareholders' interests, as it is supposed to do. But, if managers believe shareholders are short-termist (whether they are or not), a concern with the share price may also inhibit managers from taking long-term measures in their company's interest. The takeover culture could thereby inhibit not only long-term investments, if these threaten short-term earnings, but other developments important to creating far-sighted companies, in particular long-term relationships with workers or suppliers. The incentives for such 'stakeholders' to enter 'implicit contracts' with existing management are weakened if management itself is perceived as precarious. Employees or suppliers may agree with management to behave in a certain way, for example, to promote company recovery. This will often involve the former making 'investments' in the company, such as a pay cut or an increase in effort by employees or acceptance of delayed payments by suppliers (Blair, 1995). Their investments in the company's future may be rendered valueless, however, if the management disappears after a hostile takeover; the new management may insist on renegotiating the contract. It is better, therefore, to insist on cash on the nail. The prevalence of the takeover mechanism arguably biases British business relationships towards explicit contracts and low-trust relationships rather than implicit contracts with high-trust relationships.

An important question is why the UK has such a high level of takeover activity. Two particular sets of City actors are blamed for encouraging it: investment bankers, who can earn large fees for devising and implementing deals; and institutional investors, who, as shareholders in target firms, tend to be ready to sell to a hostile bidder and, as shareholders in acquiring firms, fail to prevent takeovers.

Once again, institutional investors mainly plead not guilty. The tendency for industrial managers to seek growth by acquisition rather than by investment was said by many fund managers to be nothing to do with them. Many company directors found wheeling and dealing much more fun than laboriously assessing capital investments and minding the store. (Diversification by water companies who neglected their leaking pipes was cited as one example.) Mergers and acquisitions are often a more rapid route to a larger company, bigger remuneration and mention in the Lex column of the *Financial Times*. Indeed, as Gerry Robinson and Rocco Forte found out in their battle for Forte,[2] corporate managers involved in hostile bids can become something like soap opera stars, especially if they are proposing to take over or defend a well-known company.

Lack of trust

The source of the problem is neither clear nor simple. Many fund managers are ready to take a longer view and to arrive at understandings with managements; others, running performance funds, believe their responsibilities to their own clients dictate an arms' length relationship with firms and a readiness to buy and sell whenever an immediate advantage can be obtained. The overall impression is that managers cannot count on the degree of commitment they would like from the City, but also the financial institutions are not so averse to long-term strategies and dividend fluctuations as many managers suppose. Put another way, with a good story or a good record you can keep your share price up even as you follow a long-term strategy; yet if your share price does fall, your shareholders may well sell you to a hostile bidder without compunction. On the other hand, deal-making proclivities are far from unique to the City and the observations of some fund managers, about the eagerness of some company managers to play the takeover game, have justification.

Other groups and commissions have looked at the relationships between financial institutions and commercial and industrial companies and their findings are generally consistent with our own. The Myners Report, a City-industry working group which reported on the ideal company-investor relationship, also stressed the importance of long-term values and a working partnership. It believed that 'open and informed dialogue between investors and corporate management can overcome this lack of confidence, and leads to mutual trust rather than antagonism and suspicion' (Myners Report, 1995).

Those words touch the heart of the problem. We have found a considerable lack of mutual confidence among the groups concerned. Whether or not short-termism exists, plenty of business players firmly believe that it does; moreover, each is inclined to blame each other for being its cause. One clear lesson which emerges is that it is vitally important to improve the communication and information flow between companies and investors. Some funds are already moving towards a more active stance in monitoring and discussing company performance so that they can better distinguish incompetence from long-termism as an explanation for low dividend flows. The nature of some other funds, however, makes it difficult for them to follow suit. Improved reporting is necessary and new channels of undistorted communication may be needed. We make specific proposals below.

Corporate Governance

As shown above, the financial sector cannot be blamed entirely for short-termism. The culture and attitudes of managers in some industrial and commercial firms are quite congenial to a short-term, deal-making approach. In other words, there appear to be internal obstacles in some companies which prevent them becoming far-sighted. These are matters of business culture and judgement, and as such are not easily tackled by public policy. Certainly bureaucrats and politicians are not in a position to second-guess managers about how to run any particular business. Moreover, attempts to secure compliance with any single, necessarily abstract, model of how a business should be run would almost surely be both ineffective and expensive. The objective must be to nudge attitudes and business practice towards far-sightedness. Ideally, the way companies are assessed, the interpretation that directors have of their duties and corporate governance structures should all reflect such a shift.

The issues of corporate culture, how companies view their functions and, in particular, how directors view their duties take us into deep water. A readiness to work in partnership with other stakeholders to build a company's strength over the long term may conflict with a narrow view of shareholder interests if it detracts from immediate profits or weakens the share price. There are two possible justifications, however, for taking a far-sighted view. First, it can be argued that such a view is in the shareholders' own interests; second, it can be argued that the company is not simply the property of its shareholders but is an organic entity concerned with the livelihoods of many different stakeholders. These justifications embody two alternative philosophies of what companies are for, which have been labelled the 'shareholder' and 'stakeholder' models. Adherents of the different philosophies see the structures of corporate governance as being designed to address two quite different problems.

The *shareholder model* was exemplified in the deliberations of the Cadbury Committee, set up in 1991 in the wake of high-profile corporate fraud cases. The Committee defined corporate governance as: 'The system by which companies are directed and controlled. Boards are responsible for the governance of their companies. The shareholders' role in governance is to appoint the directors and the auditors and to satisfy themselves that an appropriate governance structure is in place' (Cadbury Committee, 1992:15).

This reflects the orthodox view in the United Kingdom that a company is simply the property of its shareholders. As Colin Mayer points out, this traditional view leads to governance being essentially concerned with solving a 'principal–agent problem' (Mayer, 1996). Since the interests of management (the agent in this case) and shareholders (the principal) do not necessarily coincide, governance mechanisms exist to bring management's behaviour in line with that which the owners – that is the shareholders – wish to see.[3]

In contrast, the *stakeholder model* depicts the company as an organic entity whose interests are not identical with those of the shareholders. The management of a company requires the reconciliation of different interests and the development of mutually beneficial relationships between all groups involved in the successful functioning of a firm, including at least some employees, management, shareholders, customers, creditors and suppliers. The organisation is envisaged not as something owned by shareholders and controlled by managers more or less in their own interests, but as an entity of which managers are the trustees, balancing the interests of all the groups crucial to its long-term success. Corporate governance is thus the system whereby managers are ultimately held accountable to all stakeholders for their stewardship.

It is often said that companies in the United Kingdom and the United States are generally governed according to the shareholder model, while in countries such as Japan, Germany and Switzerland the stakeholder model is dominant. This generalisation then leads to a polarised debate about the relative merits of the Anglo-American shareholder model and German-Japanese models in terms of their effects on profitability and productivity (e.g. Fukuyama, 1995; Thurow, 1993). In fact, each country's system is a product of its history and institutions, and the wholesale importation of models or even elements of models will lead to unpredictable outcomes and is unlikely to work. We do not see the task as to pick the best system and import it, but rather to study how different systems solve the common problems of business governance and finance and then to consider how to improve the UK's own system so that it better solves the problems we face.

Each way of viewing the company has its strengths and weaknesses. Clearly the stakeholder view is conducive to fostering long-term relationships, but it carries its own dangers. The diffusion of responsibility to a number of different stakeholders can insulate management from any accountability, making it torpid and inefficient. Moreover, stakeholder companies may react more slowly to rapidly changing circumstances given the need to bring the different groups within the company along. Even those who sympathise with the stakeholder idea of the company acknowledge the difficulties in deciding who the stakeholders actually are; that is who are the people whose 'investment' in a company in cash or commitment is essential to its success? The answer must be contingent on the anatomy of individual companies and industries. For example, in some companies certain suppliers will be stakeholders because of the need for high-trust, co-operative relationships, but other suppliers to the same company may not be considered stakeholders.

The shareholder model has the mirror-image weaknesses and strengths. The company can be decisively run and can be fast on its feet when reacting to changing market circumstances, and the existence of a single dominant group of owners means that, in principle, management can have clearer objectives and accountability. This model can, however, lead management to become obsessively concerned with maximising earnings per share over a relatively short time horizon. In the end the company ceases to be seen as a business concern and becomes simply a capital market vehicle. Managers become preoccupied with the share price and with buying and selling bits of the business, merging and de-merging, in an effort to extract a quart of shareholder value from the pint pot of capital invested. Organic growth and its wellsprings in corporate capabilities and committed relationships are neglected. However, while shareholder pressure, real or imagined, can induce such behaviour, it is not really in the long-term interests of shareholders themselves.

It is possible for a company to be well run by managers following either model. Yet we believe the dominant pressures on managers in the UK have changed decisively during the past two or three decades, introducing new biases in management. From the end of the Second World War to the late 1970s, businesses generally confronted tight labour markets with unemployment never above 4 and often below 2 per cent; shareholders were generally individuals who did not trade their portfolios actively, and in any case capital controls prevented them from investing abroad. The dominant pressure on firms was from the labour market. 'Short-termism' in such a context consisted of overmanning to avoid expensive industrial conflict and to maintain a reserve of labour for any expansion; the shareholders could be expected to put up with it. In that world, to emphasise stakeholder interests would be to accentuate a bias that already existed.

Today, however, the situation has changed radically. Unemployment has more than doubled; more significant still, one adult male in five has no job. The labour market is considerably more flexible than it was. Overmanning is no longer endemic. In contrast, shares are now held by institutions, ready to buy and sell; investments compete globally in the absence of exchange controls. Yielding to short-termism now more often means paying out high dividends and neglecting the development of the business and a skilled and committed workforce.

In this world, it is no longer dangerous to emphasise that in a good company the interests of the various stakeholders should be considered by management. People making a contribution to the company, be it of capital, labour or specific expertise, are working together for common profit. Maximising long-term profit, which accrues to shareholders, will generally require co-operation with employees, suppliers and others. Similarly, a company run well in the long-term interests of all stakeholders will pay primary attention to its markets and the satisfaction of its customers, and will also generally do well by its shareholders. It may therefore be difficult, when looking at the performance of a well-run company, to know whether its managers favour the shareholder or stakeholder philosophy.

We have defined the difference between the two competing corporate philosophies in terms of the objectives of the company. Others have regarded the issue more as a question of how firms determine their business strategy, whether the determination is made by managers alone or through a more 'political' process involving stakeholders. Thus firms can be ranked according to the objectives they profess, ranging from undiluted maximisation of shareholder value to balancing increasingly broad stakeholder interests; they can also be ranked according to the extent of management licence, ranging from managers being one voice in a joint decision-making process with shareholders or stakeholders, through to managers being substantially autonomous with periodic review of their success or failure.

On the latter issue, we are firm believers in managerial responsibility. A good management team will consult stakeholders because they are an important source of information and feedback about the business. It will also take account of their interests in order to elicit their co-operation and enthusiasm. Someone in the firm has to take decisions, however, and in making that decision they must balance different interests and take responsibility for doing so. That is the right and duty of the manager.

Cultivating Corporate Cultures Which Value Long-Term Relationships

The second half of this chapter considers potential policy interventions to tackle both the external and internal obstacles which prevent more British companies becoming far-sighted. In policy terms, we believe that the government should focus on two objectives: cultivating a corporate culture which recognises the value of developing long-term, productive relationships; and improved information flows and mutual understanding between players in the financial sector and company management.

Directors' duties

Directors' duties, as defined in Section 309 of the Companies Act, are both fairly permissive and subject to little if any enforcement. The Act states that 'the matters to which the directors of a company are to have regard in the performance of their functions include the interests of the company's employees in general, as well as the interests of its members'. In theory, therefore, depending on what is understood by the interests of the company's 'members', the current definition of directors' duties permits them to take a far-sighted approach. In practice, however, UK business culture has viewed the 'members' as the company's shareholders and this has been reinforced by case law and the Takeover Code (Deakin and Slinger, 1996). Moreover, the members' interests are often assumed to be summarised rather narrowly in the share price. In other countries the notion of maximisation of shareholder value above all else is absent. For example, the German fiduciary duty is also to promote the interests of the company as a whole, but that has been described as 'its own survival and the continued fulfilment of its functional responsibilities towards shareholders, employees, suppliers, customers, state and society' (Melville-Ross, 1996).

For most British managers that would go too far. In order to help change company culture, rather than imposing new legal obligations on directors, we favour the rephrasing of directors' duties in order more clearly to permit a broader approach. Certainly it is important not to constrain directors to do anything against the long-term interests of shareholders; rather, they should be free from an excessively narrow interpretation of their fiduciary responsibilities which could actually work against the company's interests. An example of such a formulation is given below. It draws heavily on, though is not identical to, one enacted in the US State of Pennsylvania (Orts, 1992):

> In discharging the duties of their respective positions, the board of directors, committees of the board, individual directors and individual officers should, in considering the best interests of the company according to their business judgement, consider the effects of any action upon employees, suppliers and customers of the corporation, and communities in which offices or other establishments of the corporation are located.

Recommendation: The government should clarify directors' duties as currently stated in the Companies Act to enable directors to take a broader view of their responsibilities.

Enabling stakeholders to become shareholders

The practice of issuing non-voting stock or the issuing of new stock to insiders such as employees or suppliers is quite legal but has often been discouraged by a combination of stock exchange rules and condemnation from institutional shareholders, notably in the Institutional Shareholders' Committee's code of practice. This discouragement stems from the fact that such measures have been seen as a means of forestalling hostile takeovers.

It is well known that in continental Europe corporate take-overs are more difficult than in the United Kingdom. US corporate law and practice is also a good deal more tolerant of anti-takeover defences than is ours. Devices such as shark repellents, whereby directors are elected for three-year overlapping terms, or poison pills, whereby existing shareholders acquire new rights when a bid is made, are customary (Deakin and Slinger, 1996). Several states have also enacted anti-takeover statutes, which are optional in that companies can either opt in or out of their provisions. For example a state may impose a high tax on any short-term profits by raiders acquiring shares in connection with a bid.

We do not wish to shackle the market in corporate control and there are good reasons for maintaining the proscription on devices which are called into effect exclusively to forestall a hostile bid. But current pressures against issuing certain types of shares, simply because they may have the effect of forestalling takeovers, go too far. There is no reason why companies should not issue different kinds of shares, including non-voting shares. There is a market, after all, and no one is compelled to buy these shares. This argument has been recognised at EU level, where there are plans to standardise rules in different countries towards a maximum of 50 per cent of a company's equity being non-voting. Such a rule would be particularly useful for the directors of a smaller firm wishing to raise capital without losing control of their company, and this point is discussed in that context in Chapter 5.

An important case is the provision of shareholding rights for employees. There are already some incentives for individual shareholding by employees, but there should be increased pro-motion of Employee Share Ownership Plans (ESOPs). There is no reason either for discrimination against employees holding shares collectively, through a core holding of shares held by a trust. That would afford individual voting rights for employees and would provide the potential for a representative structure for employees based on trusteeship. There are very few such schemes in existence, and even fewer were set up primarily to increase employee involvement (Pendleton *et al.*, 1995), but ESOP trusts could be useful in some businesses. To enable such schemes to have permanence, two changes in law are necessary. First, laws governing trusts must be simplified so that the same trust can hold and distribute shares. Second, the current requirement on companies to eliminate any collective holding of shares within twenty years must be removed (Schüller and Erdal, 1996).

> **Recommendation:** Trust law should be simplified to allow blocks of shares to be assigned to employees collectively and held for them indefinitely, and current practices limiting the issuance of non-voting shares should be liberalised.

Takeovers

Merger and acquisition may be inhibited at the margin if new freedoms to set up ESOP trusts and issue non-voting stock are exercised, but the effect would surely be very small and takeovers will remain an important element of the UK system. Takeovers should continue to play their role of ultimate deterrent to sleepy management, but without unnecessarily restricting the development of long-term relationships. Limited additional protection for employees after a takeover would encourage their co-operation without deterring mergers based on sound strategies or the existence of important synergies. To that end, some legislative changes would be advantageous. In the State of Pennsylvania, there is a provision for severance pay for workers dismissed within a certain period of a takeover. UK law provides a more general right to redundancy compensation, but this applies only to workers who have been with a company for at least two years; the right should be extended to apply to all workers immediately after a takeover. This would achieve two, albeit limited, objectives. First, those few takeovers motivated purely by the potential for asset stripping rather than productive synergies would be marginally discouraged because of the extra cost involved. Second, the one group who tend to lose out as a result of a takeover, the employees of the acquired company who lose their jobs, would receive a small share of the benefits from the takeover.

Pennsylvanian law also provides that a new owner cannot cancel collective agreements with trade unions for a five-year period following a takeover. UK law has no provision to entrench collectively agreed terms and conditions following takeover; indeed, collective agreements are generally not legally binding. The UK Transfer of Undertakings Regulations of 1981 do not apply to a change of ownership by share transfer. We believe that new owners should inherit the civil liability of former owners for personal contracts.

In the past, merger and acquisition were sometimes preferred to organic growth because accounting conventions gave companies more latitude to write off good will in the balance sheet of an acquired company than they had in dealing with depreciation of physical investments. This enabled creative accountancy to show rising earnings per share in the years following acquisition. Such a stratagem should have fooled no one in an efficient capital market, but there is some evidence that such manoeuvres were important motivators in some takeovers. Changes in practice now under way should eliminate this bias against organic growth in future. Subject to these changes going ahead, we are reluctant to see further administrative intervention in the market for companies, other than the usual anti-monopoly regulations.

Recommendation: There should be no new administrative restraints on takeovers, but contracts between management and individual employees should be binding, and redundancy rights should be extended for a period after an acquisition.

Employee involvement

In order to underpin our belief in the benefits of consultation with employees and also our reluctance to impose specific governance forms on companies, we recommend an extension of statutory employee rights to information and consultation. The current mandatory duties to consultation and information refer only to recognised trade unions within workplaces and cover the following areas: collective redundancy, transfer of undertakings and health and safety. This should be extended in two ways. First, workers not represented by trade unions should be included. All workers whether full- or part-time should have individual rights to consultation on collective redundancy, transfer of undertakings and health and safety, with employees and management being left free to determine the form consultation should take. Second, rights should be extended to include timely provision of information on management proposals involving significant changes in employment numbers, working conditions, corporate strategy, financial matters and restructuring; that is, information that would be provided anyway through company reports.

> **Recommendation:** There should be an extension of individual employee rights to information and consultation.

Improving Information Flows about Corporate Performance

Since long-term business success depends on the involvement of shareholders, employees and other groups, and on investment in capacity, R&D and training, the range of information on which companies are required to report should be extended to include these less tangible investments and factors. Providing this information will facilitate more effective bench-marking against other firms and allow the state of a company's relations with key stakeholders, and hence its longer-run prospects, to be better monitored.

Enhanced information flows will do two things. First, they will help to reduce misunderstandings between institutional investors and management about corporate performance and strategies. Second, by improving awareness of firms' long-term investments and relations with business partners and stakeholders, they will have a more generally educational function. We believe that when the information is available, investors will take it into account when making their assessments of the long-term prospects of a firm. Also the mere fact of having to publish such information will increase the attention that managers pay to the things being disclosed. Over time, reporting requirements are powerful influences on perceptions and attitudes.

What should companies report on?

Companies already report adequately on payments to shareholders and investors but we would like to see four main innovations in company reporting. Companies should report on:

- their corporate objectives, future plans and prospects;
- the development of the skills and capabilities of their employees;
- relationships with their customers; and
- their other trading relationships, including those with suppliers.

While companies should be obliged to make disclosures under the four headings above, it is quite impracticable to set out exactly what information should be disclosed. The specific nature of the information reported will surely differ across sectors and businesses. Beneath a very general requirement to disclose information under the above four headings, businesses should be free to consult and determine what it is most useful to disclose. Industry-level consultation could determine best practice for different businesses, and appropriate standards should be developed in a 'bottom-up' way.

Specific elements under each heading could include the following. On *corporate objectives, future plans and prospects*, companies could provide a corporate mission statement, information about corporate intentions and long-term shareholder value estimates using forecasts of the impact of planned investments and R&D activities. On *the development of skills and capabilities of employees*, companies could provide data on changes in labour productivity, turnover and on training. For example, on training, companies could be required to record and report the proportion of the workforce (employees and management) which had access to employer-funded training in the previous period, company expenditure on training, and the evaluation of skill needs within the firm. Other possibilities are developments in the production process such as quality circles and consultation procedures like works councils. On *relationships with customers*, companies could report results from customer-satisfaction surveys and report on initiatives to improve customer awareness of the company's products or services. On *trading relationships including those with suppliers*, companies could report information on arrangements for consultation and dissemination of best practice through the supply chain and the performance of supplier companies in meeting deadlines.

A number of British companies, including Unipart and the NatWest Group, have already chosen to go beyond the narrow confines of the statutory rules governing company reporting, and even beyond the Cadbury and Greenbury codes, to publish such information. The recently published Body Shop Social Audit, which comprehensively assessed the company's relationships with employees, shareholders, suppliers, customers and non-governmental organisations, provides one model of enhanced reporting (Body Shop, 1995). Balanced Reporting Scorecards are another initiative which have been used by firms such as Apple Computers to assess performance, not only on gross margins and equity return but also on core competencies, distribution systems, supplier performance and customer satisfaction. The Scorecard data have been used to develop business strategy and have been incorporated into senior executives' compensation plans (Kaplan and Norton, 1993).

An argument against enhanced reporting requirements is the cost it imposes on companies. Any increased requirements on business, whether of reporting or anything else, are a cost burden and can be bad for competitiveness. Yet, since most good companies will already have such monitoring in place, new costs would in fact be borne by those companies with the most to gain. Moreover, requirements to produce and provide additional information could improve the operation of the capital market, facilitate co-operation between stakeholders and provide all players with a much better basis on which to make long-term decisions. There is, of course, the risk that the information would be ignored or that the companies would find ways to report favourably on adverse situations. These difficulties occur, however, with any sort of reporting and have not led anyone to propose the abolition of annual accounts, for example.

> **Recommendation:** There should be extended reporting requirements under the Companies Act and companies should be encouraged, through the development of 'best practice' codes, to state their objectives more fully and to report on non-financial performance measures.

Encouraging institutional investors to become more involved company owners

A number of recent assessments of City–industry relations have urged institutional investors to be more involved in the companies in which they invest. Examples include the best practice guidelines for pension funds issued by the NAPF (National Association of Pension Funds) and the description of a 'model institutional investor' set out in the recommendations of the Myners Report, both of which stress the fiduciary duties of the institutions and emphasise the beneficial impact of increasing their monitoring role as owners (NAPF, 1995).

Indeed, there is at the moment something of a sea change towards increased involvement by institutional investors. For example, one of the largest UK fund managers has recently appointed a corporate watchdog to monitor the performance of firms in the fund and hold discussions with some of those not doing well. Several fund managers also told us that they were involved in more informal dialogue with companies than in the past. This has been prompted in part by the Cadbury Code, which provides points of pressure on which to question firms about their policies (Holland, 1995). Gaved (1996) found that investor involvement often takes the form of a lead investor doing the cajoling on behalf of others.

We doubt, however, if this movement on its own will go far enough. It is expensive to monitor companies adequately and most institutional fund managers do not pretend to do more than fairly cursory research on many companies. The research available from stockbrokers or investment banks is slanted since these institutions have much more interest in encouraging deals and trading than in improving corporate management. Some pooling of resources is worth considering to improve monitoring and to boost the impact of interventions by individual investors. One way forward may be seen in the example of the United States, where problems of diffuse ownership have led to the development of joint investor bodies.

The US Council of Institutional Investors, founded in 1985, addresses investment issues which 'affect the size or security of plan assets'. The Council has almost 100 pension fund members and is recognised in the United States as a significant voice for institutional shareholder interests, providing services such as research, legal advice, data collection, publications and some personnel and administration support. In addition to these basic kinds of support structures, the Council also provides 'activism programs aimed at facilitating solution of problems in underperforming portfolio firms'. To this end, it regularly issues a focus list of poorly performing firms so that its members can, at their discretion, attempt to influence performance in the listed firms. Examples of firms under scrutiny in 1995 were Salomon, Toys 'Я' Us and Upjohn. A recent study found that firms experiencing poor share-price performance before appearing on the focus list showed an average 11.6 per cent increase in share price above the Standard and Poor 500 index in the year immediately after appearing on the list (Opler and Sokobin, 1995). These authors concluded on the basis of this finding that 'co-ordinated institutional activism creates shareholder wealth'.

We support the formation of an equivalent UK Council of Institutional Investors (CII). A few of the US Council's functions are already carried out in the United Kingdom by the NAPF and the ABI (Association of British Insurers), and they would need to be involved in the formation of the CII, which would concentrate on the research and publication functions which they do not carry out. The government should make subscription to the CII a requirement for funds operating in the United Kingdom. A CII, with compulsory membership for all pension, insurance and other savings funds, would strengthen the hand of investors without reducing diversity of opinion; individual investors and funds would still go on seeking to form their own views of firms and the market and act accordingly.

A perennial soft spot in the UK system of corporate governance is the position of non-executive directors (NEDs). Despite considerable recent improvements in the system, triggered by the Cadbury and Greenbury reports, NEDs still have multiple functions, which can lead to conflicts of interest, and doubts remain about their standing and independence from other directors in exercising a monitoring function. Individual fund managers are reluctant to attempt to appoint NEDs, as they have no wish to divide the management team and often do not even have a list of candidates for such a role. The CII would never have the power of appointment, which would remain with companies themselves. One could imagine the CII, however, encouraging underperforming firms to appoint an NED from a list of people enjoying the confidence of institutional investors. In time, alongside other bodies, the CII could become one significant source for the selection and training of potential NEDs.

> **Recommendation:** A Council of Institutional Investors should be set up to monitor and research underperforming companies. It should publish a list of those in which it lacks confidence. The government should make subscription to this body mandatory for any investment fund wanting to trade in the UK.

There is also a case for establishing a new bench-marking institution for companies outside the quoted sector. At the moment, there are private bench-marking services but these are based on the fairly limited data reported in company accounts. Since many medium-sized firms seem to be unaware of their own deficiencies (Coopers and Lybrand, 1994), a future government should perhaps consider establishing the equivalent of the National Audit Office (NAO) in the private sector. This organisation could, like the NAO, choose an issue on which it intends to monitor firm performance (probably in specific regions and/or sectors) and publish bench-mark tables by sector and region. The issues could range widely to include, for example, defect rates, productivity, innovation, process management and customer relations. These company league tables would, like school league tables, at least open up the eyes of underperforming management to their deficiencies. The National Bench-marking Office, as this body might be called, would be able to access much more information on company practices and performance. There are practical difficulties with this proposal and we have no wish to increase the bureaucratic burden on business, so we make no firm recommendation. The idea warrants serious consideration, however, and its potential should be assessed by a joint business–government working party.

Conclusion

Our recommendations in this area are modest. We wish to avoid upheaval in company law and practice while making incremental changes that encourage more far-sighted companies. To this end, our intermediate objectives are to improve the information flow and relationships between management and institutional shareholders in order to mitigate 'short-termism', and to encourage a broader view of directors' responsibilities and remove impediments to the development of long-term relationships by businesses – in other words, fostering stakeholding.

The government should amend the legal definition of directors' duties to enable directors to take a broader view of their responsibilities. This should be reinforced by extending reporting requirements on non-financial performance measures for the guidance of investors, NEDs, employees and others. Closer relations and exchange of information with institutional shareholders should be encouraged through the establishment of a Council of Institutional Investors, which would also reinforce the position of NEDs within underperforming companies. There should be no new administrative restraints on takeovers, but current practices limiting types of shares issued, or their issuance to employees, should cease and the market should be allowed to price such shares and companies as it will. Trust law should be simplified to allow blocks of shares to be assigned to employees collectively and held for them indefinitely. Agreements between management and individual employees should be binding for a period on successor managements after an acquisition and there should be extension of redundancy rights. We believe these measures represent a series of prudent, practical steps through conflicting considerations towards the encouragement of more far-sighted companies.

NOTES

1 Academic opinion is not quite unanimous, however, and Higson and Elliott (1994) and Marsh (1993) assert that the outcomes of hostile takeovers are generally more positive than those of agreed mergers.

2 See the *Financial Times* (24 January 1996) for a typical piece highlighting the personalities in a bid. Burrough and Helyar's (1990) bestseller on the leveraged buy-out of RJR Nabisco at the end of the 1980s is probably the best-known account of how individual corporate managers can become so swept up in winning the battle for a company that they lose sight of the prize.

3 In one key respect, these governance structures clearly fail to deal with conflicts of interest. The dual role of NEDs – both advisers to the board of management and custodians of the shareholder interest in matters like directors' remuneration – gives rise to tensions which are not well balanced. But these issues have no direct bearing on competitiveness and we do not consider them further.

5

WORLD-CLASS SMEs

*Small and medium-sized enterprises (SMEs) are responsible for
more than half of the output and employment in the UK private
sector. Government policy already targets SMEs for substantial
assistance, but the various schemes currently operating require
rationalisation. They are too geared to providing standardised
support services and not enough to stimulating SMEs to work
out their own requirements and to help themselves through the
creation of networks or co-operative associations. Finance is an
important area where co-operation in mutual guarantee schemes
should be encouraged.*

Large firms may generate the newspaper headlines, but SMEs
account for 99 per cent of all UK firms and roughly 60 per cent
of output (Trade and Industry Committee, 1995b). In the past
few years, virtually all job growth has occurred in smaller firms.
The UK government has directed a number of initiatives at SMEs
in recent years; indeed, we now have a plethora of policies which
are badly in need of rationalisation.

The enormous number and heterogeneity of small firms make
blanket prescriptions for them inappropriate. Our guiding principle is to help them tackle their problems by promoting self-
help. We support 'bottom-up' identification of needs rather than
exclusive reliance on 'top-down' provision of services. The latter
tends to be standardised in its approach, and cannot deal with
the specific needs of different sectors and localities. Many EU
countries as well as Canada and the United States are now introducing policies to encourage the formation of self-help networks,

in which companies benefit by learning from and co-operating with each other (Pyke, 1992; Humphries, 1995).

In the first part of this chapter we briefly review the importance of SMEs; then we consider the role of networks and how to promote them; finally, we make a proposal for the rationalisation of current support policies for SMEs. In the second part of the chapter we concentrate on finance for investment, often cited as the single biggest problem for SMEs. We reject some common myths about their finance, but identify two particular difficulties: access to finance for new high-tech firms, and an excessive tendency to use short-term debt. Here, too, co-operation between firms can overcome some of the problems of risk and increase their attractiveness to investors.

SMEs in the UK

It is usual to distinguish three different categories of SMEs: micro firms with up to 10 employees, small firms with 11–99 employees and medium-sized firms with 100–499 employees. Over 95 per cent of SMEs are micro firms; this group includes many self-employed sole traders such as construction workers, barristers and computer contractors. Although there is a range of estimates of the number of SMEs in the economy (Storey, 1995), the latest official figure is 3.5 million, up from less than 2.5 million in 1979 (Figure 5.1). Most of this growth is accounted for by 'second-job' self-employment, and around one million businesses are self-employed owners with no employees (DTI, 1996b). Only about 3,000 UK firms (less than 1 per cent of all firms) are *not* SMEs.

The massive increase in SME numbers over the last decade and a half has occurred for a variety of reasons, notably the spread of contracting out by both large private companies and public sector organisations, changes in technology reducing the need for large-scale production facilities in many industries, changes in government policy which have actively promoted SMEs, and significant increases in unemployment and part-time working which have encouraged many people to start up on their own.

Figure 5.1 shows the stock of firms in the economy. Currently, there are on average about 400,000 business closures and a sim-

Figure 5.1: Number of Enterprises in the UK, 1979–94 (*millions*)

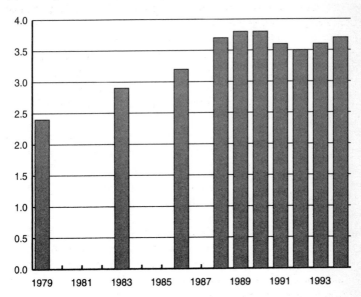

Source: DTI (1996b), Table 1.

ilar number of start-ups (virtually all of which are SMEs) each year. This means that more than one-tenth of the 3.5 million businesses which are in operation at the start of each year will have closed down by the end of it, to be replaced by a similar number of new firms. This degree of turnover is significantly higher than in other EU countries, particularly Germany (Midland Bank, 1994), though not all closures are failures; mergers and acquisitions account for some, retirement of the owner-manager for others. Public policy needs to tackle the reasons for the failures as well as promote start-ups.

About 60 per cent of UK private sector output is generated by the SME sector, split roughly between micro firms (10 per cent), small firms (20 per cent), and medium-sized firms (30 per cent) (Trade and Industry Committee, 1995b). The SMEs' share of employment is greater than their share of output. Table 5.1

Table 5.1: Employment by Firm Size in the UK, 1979–91
(*% of total*)

Size of firm	1979	1986	1991
Micro (1–10)	20	28	28
Small (11–99)	20	20	22
Medium (100–499)	18	17	17
Large (500 +)	43	36	33

Source: Storey (1995), Table 2.5.
Note: These figures do not necessarily add up to 100 due to rounding.

shows the trend since 1979. There has been a marked shift in employment away from large firms to SMEs, in particular to micro firms. This is a continuation of the trend in employment in the UK since the early 1960s; during the first two-thirds of the century, employment in SMEs decreased. Despite this increase, the share of UK employment in SMEs is still lower than the EU average (Figure 5.2). Firms with 1–49 employees account for only one-third of employment in the United Kingdom compared with nearly one-half of employment in the EU as a whole. Italy, Greece, Denmark, Spain and Ireland in particular have a much higher proportion of employment in SMEs than does the UK. This has much to do with very different levels of employment in small hotel, restaurant and catering enterprises (DTI, 1996b).

The increasing importance of small firms to the economy has resulted in their being subject to greater attention from academics and policy-makers. Although the evidence is that the number of micro firms is growing fastest and such firms are particularly prevalent in the poorer countries of the OECD and in low-productivity sectors, many commentators and academics see smaller firms as having particular advantages in responding to globalisation. For example, they may be better able to create innovative niche products or respond to changing markets (Porter, 1990; Hirst and Thompson, 1996). There is also evidence that faster-growing SMEs in the United Kingdom in the 1990s are also more likely to have innovated and to be involved in exporting than slower-growing SMEs (Cosh *et al.*, 1996a).

Figure 5.2: UK and EU Employment by Firm Size (% *of total*)

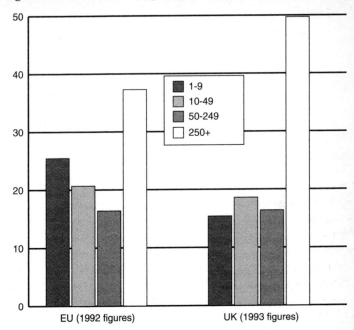

Source: DTI (1996b), Table 11.

Nevertheless, there are problems associated with being small, especially being very small. These include a limited customer base, sometimes consisting of only one or two large firms, which can mean that small firms are vulnerable to unfair trading practices and late payment; difficulties in accessing information on product markets, particularly export markets; lack of a breadth of expertise across management areas such as finance, marketing, IT and training; and high costs of regulatory compliance. On the last point, Bannock and Peacock (1989) have shown that the cost of VAT compliance can be as much as 2.5 per cent of turnover for small firms compared with only 0.07 per cent for firms with more than £2 million turnover. In order to tackle these problems, governments in every country have policies directed specifically at helping SMEs to get started, grow, become more efficient, innovate, gain access to new product markets and make use of new information technologies.

Promoting Networks:
A New Approach to Industrial Policy

Value of networks

Inter-firm collaboration has been present for some time in sectors such as advertising, fashion or television. Firms with complementary skills come together in semi-permanent partnerships in order to produce products for markets where a high degree of customisation is often necessary. Other industries, such as pharmaceuticals, appear to be moving in the same direction though in a slightly different way; here partnerships are developing between the large multinationals and small flexible research companies which feed innovations and developments through to the large firm (Fairtlough, 1996). Porter (1990) goes so far as to claim that the key to growth for small firms is to gain strength by co-operation and collaboration, and through clusters and formal and informal networks to mould their environment and their markets for maximum benefit. There is accumulating evidence for his claim (Birley *et al*., 1991; Pyke, 1992). In the United Kingdom in the 1990s, faster-growing and innovative SMEs are more likely to be involved in partnership and collaborative arrangements than slower-growing and non-innovative SMEs (Kitson and Wilkinson, 1996).

For SMEs these inter-firm linkages are one method of overcoming the problems of small size. By sharing resources they can achieve economies of scale in areas such as marketing. They can also create joint alliances with complementary skills and form local production chains, or clusters. The latter may be defined as geographical areas in which small firms (often family enterprises) specialise in different phases of the production of one single product in a market characterised by both co-operation and competition. Clustering is a feature of the conspicuous economic success of northern Italy. In the town of Carpi, for example, there are nearly 750 firms producing finished clothing products with 1,900 local and independent sub-contractors (Pezzini, 1996). Clusters are characterised by quick responses to change and the production of tailored goods through flexible specialisation. In his analysis of such Italian clusters, Brusco (1992) pointed out the sharp delineation between the vigorous competition taking place between similar firms, and the strong co-operation between firms at different stages in the production process.

It is often difficult to tell why particular clusters emerge. They seem to be less common in Britain, although there are certainly examples such as the high-tech SMEs in the Cambridge area. Keeble (1996: 1) found that 60 per cent of Cambridge high-tech SMEs 'maintain close links with other local firms, primarily in terms of suppliers, services and research collaboration'. In general, however, a culture of collaboration is not widespread among UK SMEs.

Types of co-operation

Lichtenstein (1993) defines three types of co-operation:

- joint solutions to common problems (joining forces and resources);
- development and exploitation of mutually complementary strengths (utilising combined skills, competencies and facilities); and
- developing the quality of sub-contracting links (both upwards and downwards).

In practical terms, several different types of network or association can be identified:

- *Supplier networks*, which help to reduce information problems between large firms and their suppliers, and which have been spreading as outsourcing increases in manufacturing.
- *Social networks*, such as Chambers of Commerce or trade associations, which provide opportunities to exchange information, provide joint services, set standards and network in more general terms.
- *Specific functional networks*, such as Business Angels for finance, or technology transfer centres.

- *Clusters or industrial districts*, as described above.
- *Consortia*, small groups of complementary firms which join forces either for a particular project or for a series of projects in order to produce a final product.
- *Informal networks*, which may involve firms with a variety of partners ranging from universities, service providers to complementary firms or even ex-employees.

Diagram 5.1 shows how these different kinds of networks can be simply categorised depending on the content of the relationship – resources, skills and capabilities, or support and information –

Diagram 5.1: Types of Network

Type of co-operation	Resources	Skills and Capabilities	Support and Information
 POOLED	Shared equipment and facilities Co-operatives	Industry service centres	Industrial parks Business parks Incubators
 SEQUENTIAL	Resource trading networks Bartering networks Subcontracting networks	Joint production networks Strategic alliances Suppliers' networks	Trade associations Chambers of Commerce Roundtables Business forums
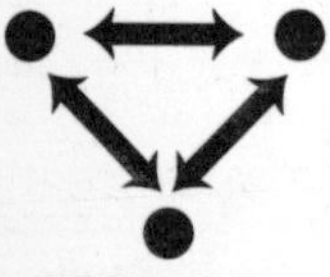 RECIPROCAL		Consortia Learning networks	Support groups CEO networks

Source: Derived from Lichtenstein (1993).

and on the type of co-operation. 'Pooled' refers to the sharing of common needs between similar firms; 'sequential' indicates co-operation between companies or organisations which produce inputs for each other (for example in the supply chain); and 'reciprocal' refers to collaboration between firms with complementary assets.

The UK government is aware of the importance of networks. The DTI told us that there is a pilot project of network brokers in Business Links to help small firms co-operate. Seedcorn finance was provided for a sectoral joint initiative within the automotive industry to establish best practice and encourage bench-marking among the supply chain, and informal Supply Chain Network Groups are being formed in a variety of industries. Nevertheless, these initiatives are *ad hoc* and are not as systematic or advanced as some of the programmes of our competitors, particularly those in Denmark, Italy, and the United States.

Rationalising Business Support Services

Smaller firms face particular problems in resourcing many business activities taken for granted by larger firms and have to rely on outside expertise and inputs. The question for SMEs is where to get this assistance, whether it be information about export markets, new technology, finance or marketing. Recognising these difficulties, all industrial countries have developed organisations, both private and public, which are designed to advise SMEs. In the United Kingdom these organisations have proliferated over the last two decades and now include Regional Technology Centres, TECs, Business Links, Chambers of Commerce, trade associations, innovation centres and university-business links. Yet SMEs still regularly complain that they do not know who to approach for information and do not know about different government schemes designed to help them.

The government recognises that Britain's system of business support for SMEs requires an overhaul. The DTI commented in March 1996 that 'businesses have difficulty in discovering exactly what is on offer and often find that the various government schemes are not tailored precisely enough to their needs'(Cabinet Office, 1996c:3), despite there being over 200 such initiatives. One small business response to a DTI survey is typical: 'the government is running a lot of potentially useful schemes that most small businesses have never heard of'(Cabinet Office, 1996c:3). Such comments prompted the DTI to question the whole system of business support in Britain in early 1996, and to invite recommendations for reform.

The government's principal response so far to this problem has been to promote its latest support body, Business Links, as the means of amalgamating business advice and support in a single local institution. Its vision of Business Links is that these will provide a true one-stop shop for SMEs, formed by partnerships between local support bodies such as TECs, local authorities, Chambers of Commerce and Enterprise Agencies. There are now over 250 Business Links operating across Britain, though many are very new. They are charged with providing a range of core and additional services, where relevant to a local area. Initial funding for each Link comes from the DTI, but they are intended to be self-financing within three years of establishment, generating income from TECs, clients and private sponsorship.

Business Links have had very little time to develop, but there is a general consensus among commentators that they have serious flaws. In a report on business support structures for the British Chambers of Commerce, Bob Bennett of LSE found that 'at a local level, instead of a proper partnership with local agents such as Chambers, the government is developing its own agents [Business Links] to compete with the private sector . . . this entails a lack of development of trust with the business community'(Bennett, 1995:ii). Similarly, an Institute of Directors' membership survey in 1996 found that general awareness of Business Links was low and only 5 per cent of respondent firms had made use of them. Respondents expressed concern about the quality of the Business Link staff and the independence of the advice offered. Some members concluded that 'some of these problems might have been avoided if Business Links had remained a sign-posting organisation as opposed to a competing service provider'(IoD, 1996a:2).

The nature of the problem is thrown into sharp relief when we look at one critical issue for SMEs – technology transfer. The relatively poor innovation record of British industry is one factor behind the long tail of underperforming firms. Closely related to this is the poor diffusion of new technology, particularly among SMEs (Miliband, 1990; CEST, 1995). Yet there is a range of different public and private bodies at work trying to promote technology transfer, including research and technology organisations, regional technology centres and technical database providers. Most SMEs are simply not aware of these bodies: 69 per cent of small firms responding to a recent Chambers of Commerce survey wanted to be made more aware of technology opportunities (BCC, 1996). Clearly, Business Links need to be more effective in informing SMEs about such organisations.

In light of these and other reports we conclude that the current Business Link approach is flawed, because:

- Business Links are providing marketable services as well as information for SMEs, they are competing with private providers and are thus unlikely to offer impartial advice.
- Much of their advice involves duplication of the work of existing public bodies and can result in 'turf wars' between competing providers.
- Services provided by Business Links are standardised and 'top-down' rather than being responsive to local needs.

Business Links should not provide marketable advice, since this will discourage them from providing unbiased non-marketable information and advice. We wish to see Business Links acting as signposts for small firms, steering them towards the best providers of a particular service rather than providing it themselves through 'one-stop shops'. Although it was never envisaged that Business Links should compete with the private sector, many Business Link chief executives have seen the organisations as business opportunities and have thus reduced their potential to encourage the rationalisation of existing service provision. The pressure on Business Links to be self-financing within three years, and hence to become profit centres, is proving counter-productive and should be removed.

The guiding principle for business support should be self-help by SMEs, involving articulation of their own needs and greater input into the decisions about providing services at a local level. Government should act as a catalyst to promote networks of support provision through Business Links.

An example of such co-ordination in action can be found in the north-east. Here local universities collaborate under a framework called Higher Education Support for Industry, which includes a network of facilitators who direct enquiries from SMEs to the appropriate academic expert or department. Linked to this, the local Regional Technology Centre has built up databases of technology support agencies and is developing joint marketing of support services in collaboration with the Business Link (Charles, 1996). Funding for this initiative has come from the European Regional Development Fund.

The benefits of networks of this type are illustrated by Coopers and Lybrand (1995) which showed that almost half of hypergrowth SMEs (defined as those which have at least doubled both turnover and employment in three years) use technology transfer networks to gain access to new technology, compared with only 28 per cent of slower-growing firms. Networking among existing institutions, directed particularly at breaking down cultural differences between SMEs and universities, seems to be particularly valuable in this process (CEST, 1995); by working together and creating a forum for interaction with businesses, universities can engage directly with companies in order to create partnerships. Charles (1996) summarised the way in which such networks should be developed:

> There is a need to get the person with the right expertise connected with the SME relatively quickly. This requires databases of existing expertise, a means of passing on enquiries, protocols for inter-agency cooperation and an environment of collaboration rather than competition.

The ultimate aim is therefore to promote the increased networking of SMEs with public and private service providers, with the government acting as a catalyst to promote information flows and interaction between relevant groups. Rather than providing marketable services to firms, Business Links should co-ordinate local public agencies and maintain databases of private sector expertise relevant to SMEs, promoting networking between these organisations. It should be an impartial provider of advice, and should not be side-tracked by trying to compete with other groups, either public or private.

Recommendation: Business Links should become predominantly sign-posting bodies to public- and private-sector service providers. They should no longer be required to become self-financing.

Encouraging Networks

Supplier networks

A supply chain is one of the easier areas to promote beneficial collaboration. A supply chain is made up of a large number of small- and medium-size firms, only some of which will have direct contact with the large-firm customer. The general tendency in the United Kingdom is towards arms' length interaction between suppliers rather than close co-operation. For example, in the Middle Market Survey (Coopers and Lybrand, 1994), 73 per cent of medium-size firms had maintained adversarial relationships with their large-firm customers.

Productivity gains can often be realised through the firms in the supply chain adopting best practice by increased collaboration and bench-marking with other companies. Ideally, the initiative should come from within industries or sectors, but the government could support and encourage them through means such as seedcorn finance. One such initiative has come from the Society of Motor Manufacturers and Traders, which set up an Industry Forum 'to drive for and support the achievement of sustainable world-leading competitiveness in the UK-based vehicle and components industry'. This sectoral forum, or network, is charged with ensuring that all companies in the supply chain are 'aligned in terms of the measures that meet and beat customer expectations, i.e. quality, cost and delivery' and 'that real practical improvement is implemented within suppliers by putting in engineers who have "hands on experience" of factory improvement programmes to work alongside the local workforce'.[1] Firms pay a fee for this expertise, which is also subsidised by money from the automotive unit of the DTI. The Forum aims to be self-financing within four years. Another element of the Forum's work relates to the introduction of a standardised measurement system, which enables firms to assess their own performance and that of their customers and suppliers. This provides an incentive for collaboration between firms in order to remove defects and adopt best practice.

This example has a number of desirable features. It is voluntary and internal, developed and refined out of the needs of a particular sector rather than imposed by legislation. It is therefore more likely to generate enough improvement in performance to be self-financing. Also, by developing expertise in bench-marking and collaboration, the Forum can provide useful feedback to the public sector, advising on policies directed at smaller firms and promoting the networking of the various agencies and bodies which provide business support services.

Although the results of this initiative and the measurements involved have been made available by the government to other sectors, it is still an isolated example. The extension of this kind of government–business partnership to other sectoral organisations could be facilitated if there were a well-publicised budget in the DTI available for seedcorn finance of supply-chain networks in any sector. The initiative and application for support would come from the sector itself, backed up by a costed plan of action. There would undoubtedly be some deadweight losses entailed in a public scheme of this kind, but they would, like the financial scale of the scheme itself, be small.

Peer-group networks

Most SMEs are not within tight supply chains. There is therefore a need to transfer the principles of bench-marking and networking to self-help groups and organisations catering for a wider range of firms. Inter-firm networking is already a successful practice in some countries. In Denmark, for example, small-firm networking has been developing over a period of some time, and after an analysis of 500 firms covering 100 networks, the Danish National Agency for Industry and Trade concluded that it was 'completely convinced that business networks are job and export creating'.[2] The United Kingdom has begun to adopt some of these practices through the development of pilot Network Centres, set up by TECs and Business Links, with network facilitators trained by Business Net Ltd, an offshoot of the Danish Technology Institute.

Business Net sees networking as 'bringing businesses together in a joint venture or alliance to achieve a competitive advantage which is not possible individually'. It gives examples of the kinds of projects it supports with the help of network brokers:

- Jointly purchasing raw materials at a better price and quality than the individual firm could command.
- Developing and successfully marketing new products that deploy significant strengths within individual firms.
- Establishing agents and distributors in new markets.
- Investing in important production equipment for shared use.
- Pooling individual products into complete product ranges attractive to significant purchasers.
- Utilising complementary production equipment and labour forces.
- Sharing access to markets or distribution opportunities based on the complementarity of product ranges.

The role of the network broker or facilitator is to 'ensure transparency of information, the successful resolution of conflicts between firms, and continuity in running the network'(Pyke, 1992).

The Business Net initiative is to be applauded, but there are more ways to encourage networks. The broker does not have to be an independent expert; the role could equally be played by different individuals or institutions depending on the nature of the collaboration. International examples use trade associations, banks, accountants, innovation centres and universities (especially for research and development) to promote networks. There are some examples in the United Kingdom: Barclays Bank in

Yorkshire has brought together small-firm entrepreneurs in woollen textiles, and St John's Innovation Centre in Cambridge has sought to promote technology linkages and networks among firms (Keeble, 1996). The West Midlands Clothing Resource Centre was established to service 500 small firms, providing computer-aided design facilities, management support and other initiatives designed to 'upgrade the industry as a whole from a low-wage, low-investment and low-productivity sector to one where higher levels of investment and productivity could support improved wages and working conditions'(Marshall, 1990).

There are lessons to be learned too from the 'service system' instigated by ERVET (the Agency for Economic Development for the Region of Emilia-Romagna), which acted as a catalyst to promote service centres for a variety of industries. Although initiated by government funding, over time the centres have become self-financing, thus releasing public funds for other projects. A further example can be found in Carpi, where the knitwear service agency CITER[3] has developed a computer system which links thousands of small firms to information about export markets. The important feature of these examples is that the centres are developed at the instigation of the firms themselves and respond to particular sectoral needs rather than having their activities predetermined from outside.

We believe that more work needs to be done to investigate the best forms of co-operation within the UK, but see a more network-oriented policy as providing a cost-effective way to promote self-help and respond to particular needs.

Recommendation: The government should initiate an information campaign about the value of SME networks and investigate the most appropriate means for encouraging their formation, perhaps involving financial bursaries for successful proposals.

Access to Finance

At periodic intervals since the 1930s, when the Macmillan Committee reported on finance for firms in Britain, at least half a dozen separate committees of 'the great and the good' have identified a 'finance gap' for SMEs.[4] A gap is generally seen as the failure of some SMEs with commercially viable propositions to obtain investment capital from financial institutions. After reviewing the latest evidence and consulting widely on SME finance, we conclude that the market for SME finance actually works quite well. We reject some of the widely held views concerning a general market failure in this area. There are, however, two important areas where improvements should be made: the inadequate provision of finance for *new high-tech SMEs,*[5] and short-termism in the *type of finance* used by many SMEs.

A recent OECD survey of the financing of innovation in developed countries concluded that 'investing in innovation in existing small businesses and through enterprise creation is becoming more crucial in determining relative national economic performance'(Guinet, 1995:16). Ensuring an adequate supply of finance to such firms is therefore important. Cutting down on the use of short-term forms of finance, specifically bank overdrafts and late payment, would also help to reduce a domino effect of SME failure in recession when efficient firms may be dragged down with the rest.

Potential problems in both areas stem in technical terms from 'asymmetric information'. Both lenders and borrowers (or prospective borrowers) have insufficient information to make efficient decisions about who should receive finance or what type of finance to demand. Solving these problems requires once again a balance between competition and co-operation in the market.

Scotching some myths

A summary of the different allegations about the provision of finance for SMEs can be found in Table 5.2, together with a judgement on their accuracy. Certain criticisms can be rejected mainly because of significant changes in the last decade or so. First, there is no general finance gap for SMEs: the Cambridge Survey of 2,000 small firms in the late 1980s and early 1990s (Cosh, 1996) revealed that between 80 and 90 per cent of finance required by these firms was successfully obtained (see Figure 5.3),

Table 5.2: Charge Sheet on Finance for SMEs

Charges	Verdict/Evidence
1 Investment capital is generally scarce for SMEs.	**False.** Most SMEs report few difficulties obtaining finance.
2 Investment capital is relatively expensive for SMEs.	**False.** Bank margins are no higher in the UK than Germany.
3 It is difficult for high-tech firms to obtain finance.	**Partly true.** Theoretical and empirical evidence of difficulties in early stages especially regarding venture capital.
4 Finance for start-ups is scarce.	**Probably False.** Especially in the 1980s. It is hard to measure the number of failed potential start-ups, but there is some evidence that venture capitalists are now more reluctant than in the past to invest in start-ups.
5 SMEs rely too much on short-term finance.	**True, but less so than in the past.** Late payment is still a problem, with a domino-effect of failures in recession. Both a demand and supply-side problem.
6 Banks are inflexible in their approach to SME customers.	**Partly true.** Collateral is still a significant feature in bank loans. Allegation that banks foreclose too quickly on firms in trouble is not proven.
7 Venture capitalists reluctant to provide 'patient' capital for SMEs.	**Partly true.** But there is some evidence that SMEs are also reluctant to sell equity.
8 SME owner-managers lack financial management skills.	**Probably true.** There is some evidence that this affects firm performance.

and this fits with other evidence (Aston Business School, 1991; Rosewell, 1996). Second, finance is no more expensive for SMEs in the UK than elsewhere. For example, bank lending margins in

Figure 5.3: SME Access To Finance

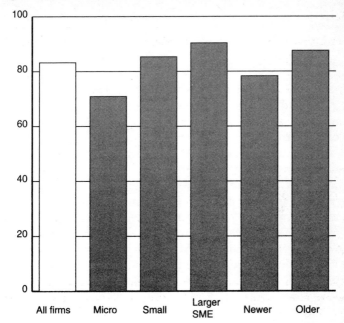

Source: Cosh (1996), Figure 3.

Note: Data are percentage of firms (sample = 2,028 SMEs in 1993) which obtained the funds they sought from various sources.

the UK and Germany (which is widely credited with having a particularly pro-business banking system) are very similar for firms of a similar size (Midland Bank, 1994; Bank of England, 1995). Third, start-ups do not have excessive difficulties obtaining finance and, in any case, it should not be too easy to raise finance. Easy money means that too many unsustainable businesses get started; for proof of that, one has only to look at the bad debts carried by the main four clearers in the early 1990s because of their enthusiasm to lend money to all-comers during the Lawson boom. Given the persistently high levels of business start-ups in the United Kingdom compared with our competitors, it is hard to believe that there is a general problem of finance for start-ups. Finally, there is evidence of an increasing variety of finance available from banks for SMEs with a substantial growth in term lending at the expense of overdrafts in the 1990s (Bank of England, 1996).

Finance for new high-tech firms

Many young new technology-based or innovative firms (hereafter referred to as new high-tech) may face problems finding finance because the scientific and technological knowledge involved creates an extra degree of uncertainty for finance providers. David Storey of Warwick University describes this phenomenon as the 'hairdresser v. the PhD' problem. Consider a typical bank manager faced with two requests for investment capital: one comes from an individual in an industry which the manager knows well (such as hairdressing), and the other comes from an area about which the manager knows little (such as virtual reality or telemedicine). The bank manager knows all the right questions to ask the hairdresser regarding the location of the premises, the expertise and experience of the owner and the degree of local competition. With a high-tech proposal, the manager hardly knows where to start. Thus, quite sensibly, the manager will offer finance to the hairdresser but not the high-tech firm, even though the former is just as likely to fail and will probably see much lower long-term returns than the latter (Storey, 1996). That this happens in practice is supported by case-study evidence that new high-tech small firms find it more difficult to obtain bank finance than their larger or less innovative counterparts (Advisory Council on Science and Technology, 1990; Oakey, 1984). High-tech firms in general do not, however, appear to be particularly disadvantaged (Moore, 1994).

It is generally thought that high-tech small firms are exactly the market gap which venture capital is designed to fill. Classic venture capital is seen as equity investment in new, often high-tech ventures which banks are reluctant to support. The venture capitalist is supposed to take a longer-term perspective, willing to forgo any returns in the first few years of an investment in the expectation of reaping very high returns once the product in question gets to market. The new high-tech entrepreneur and the venture capitalist seem to provide exactly what the other is looking for: expertise and enterprise on the one hand, the funding required to seize new opportunities and generate profit on the other (Latter and Garnsey, 1995).

This stylised view of what venture capital does, however, is becoming ever more divorced from reality. As the UK venture-capital industry has expanded rapidly in the last fifteen years, there has been a steep decline in the proportion of venture-capital investment in young, high-tech firms. The proportion of UK venture capital invested in such firms dropped from 26.4 per cent in 1985 to under 10 per cent in 1992 (see Table 5.3). In contrast, in the United States the proportion of funds going into such ventures has remained relatively high and steady at around 70 to 80 per cent. Gordon Murray, a leading expert in this area, comments:

> Young, high-tech-based firms produce innovative products and services, sell internationally and benefit the economy. But in the UK this potential is being stifled by difficulties in attracting financial support from professional investors, particularly for start-up and early-stage ventures.[6]

There are at least four explanations as to why venture capitalists are seemingly reluctant to invest in young high-tech firms:

- *Objectives are not aligned.* Despite the common view given above, there is in fact evidence that the objectives of entrepreneurs and venture capitalists are not aligned. For example, entrepreneurs do not want to issue equity since they believe that their intellectual expertise merits a relatively greater ownership stake – and degree of control – than the financial contributions of the venture capitalist. This problem is reinforced by the fact that UK equity markets have traditionally discouraged the issuance of dual-class shares, as noted in Chapter 4. We believe that our recommendation to eliminate such restrictions will help to reduce this problem of incompatible objectives.

- *Lack of expertise within venture capital funds.* There is evidence that venture capitalists, just like bankers, perceive that 'new high-tech' means 'high risk', partly because they may lack the necessary expertise to understand the products in question. In consequence, venture capitalists routinely impose higher rate-of-return demands when assessing a new high-tech proposition (Murray and Lott, 1995).

- *Earnings prospects when floated.* Both the above explanations could just as easily apply to the US venture-capital market as to the UK. Clearly, there must be more specific explanations for the reluctance of UK venture-capital firms to invest more in this area. One explanation concerns the prospects for high returns when the high-tech firm is floated (which is the ultimate objective of most venture capitalists and many entrepreneurs). Beecroft (1994) points out that the price/earnings

Table 5.3: Technology Investments in the UK, Europe and the USA by Venture Capital Firms, 1985–92

Year:	1985	1986
UK:		
Total no. UK companies financed	517	600
Technology – % no. total investments	30.9	26.5
Total value investments (£ million)	278	384
Technology – % value total investments	26.4	17.8
EUROPE:		
Total no. investments	n.a.	n.a.
Technology – % no. total investments	n.a.	n.a.
Total value investments (ECU million)	n.a.	n.a.
Technology – % value total investments	n.a.	n.a.
USA:		
Total value investments ($ million)	2670	3242
Technology – % value total investments	77.0	70.9

Source: Murray (1994), Table 1.

ratios for high-tech firms are higher in the United States than the UK and, in addition, newly floated high-tech firms attain their high price/earnings ratio more quickly in the United States. Therefore, the relative weakness of the UK equity market in smaller high-tech companies may play some part in the reluctance of venture capitalists to invest heavily in such companies. The fledgling Alternative Investment Market (AIM) has a long way to go before it can catch up with the USA's NASDAQ in terms of expertise and understanding of high-tech companies.[7]

- *Structure of the venture-capital industry.* Finally, it is argued that the proportion of captive funds directly funded and controlled by banks, pension funds or other institutions may prejudice venture capital investment against high-tech firms

1987	1988	1989	1990	1991	1992*
1174	1326	1302	1221	1196	1297
25.6	21.4	23.7	23.6	20.8	18.0
934	1298	1420	1106	989	1251
15.7	8.9	12.4	12.9	13.1	9.0
n.a.	5078	5439	5362	6907	6197
n.a.	32.0	30.4	29.0	25.5	24.4
n.a.	3452	4271	4126	4632	4701
n.a.	20.7	20.4	19.7	16.1	16.0
3977	3847	3395	1922	1358	2543
63.5	60.5	67.4	72.8	80.0	76.0

Note: *BVCA statistics included for the first time in 1992 debt provision by venture capital firms. UK 1992 statistics are therefore not directly comparable with earlier years.

(Beecroft, 1994). Captive funds, especially bank subsidiaries such as Midland Bank's Regional Enterprise Funds and NatWest's Pioneer Fund, raise funds on the short-term money markets or from their parent companies. They insist on current income to pay their funding costs and therefore tend to invest in later-stage companies, where they can obtain a running yield on their investments in the form of dividends. Interestingly, recent research suggests that pioneering innovation, which is most risky, though with the greatest potential pay off, is more likely to be funded in the UK than 'follower' innovation (Cosh *et al.*, 1996b). The relative reluctance to fund the latter could contribute to the maintenance of a tail of underperforming firms by slowing down the diffusion of best practice.

Even if these arguments explain why so little venture capital finds its way to young high-tech firms, they do not explain why there has also been a steep decline in the proportion of funds going into this area. There seems to be some absolute limit to venture-capital investment in young high-tech firms in the United Kingdom and the massive expansion of the venture-capital industry has accordingly led to a dramatic drop in the proportion of such investment going to new technology-based and innovative firms. Put simply, even though there is much more venture-capital money around, high-tech firms are getting no more funding than before.

Closing the finance gap for new high-tech SMEs

The problems of finance for new high-tech SMEs revolve around risk and uncertainty. Both these factors are of course essential features of all capital markets, but if uncertainty is too great there are likely to be problems in providing sufficient finance at reasonable cost and in an appropriate format. Public policy should therefore be directed at helping to reduce risk and uncertainty in this area, especially by encouraging the spread of best practice to the long tail of underperforming firms.

Given that many entrepreneurs are reluctant to give up equity to venture capitalists, and that equity supply from venture capital is limited, it is necessary to encourage banks to provide more finance in this area. Our main recommendation for reducing uncertainty for the banks is that the government should actively encourage the setting up of *mutual guarantee schemes* (MGSs). Mutual guarantee schemes are used extensively in Europe (see Table 5.4) and are specifically designed to reduce asymmetric information problems associated with finance for SMEs (see Table 5.5).

Central to these schemes is the involvement of the real experts in an industry – the firms already operating in it – in a co-operative structure with banks and other trade-related associations to pool information about the credibility of a particular project (Deakins and Philpott, 1994). There is, therefore, a strong element of networking in an MGS since it specifically involves SMEs helping themselves and each other to gain access to finance more easily by reducing uncertainty and pooling risks.

Local loan guarantee consortia are well established in Italy (Hughes, 1994). In Modena for instance, one consortium founded in 1974 had 3,500 artisan members by the late 1980s. By 1989 this consortium had guaranteed 10 billion lire in loans and had only 70 million lire in unrecovered debts. The loans are mutually guaranteed by the scheme members, who have an incentive to monitor other members to try to prevent default, and a strong moral pressure not to default themselves.

These MGSs appear to be using networks of co-operation among the business community to reduce information problems in the assessment of investment proposals by finance providers. A rather different example of the power of business groupings is provided by the case of the UK finance director of a multinational motor vehicle manufacturer, who told us that his company had negotiated with the banks on behalf of its dealers and had secured much better terms than the dealers had been able to obtain when acting alone. The one concern with MGSs is that they have the potential to operate as closed shops, with established firms preventing new entrants from gaining access to reasonably priced finance. Hence policies to promote MGSs should also be designed to maintain competition while increasing co-operation. The involvement of banks and Chambers of Commerce should help in this regard.

Hughes (1994) argues that because there are significant start-up costs for firms initiating an MGS, 'there is likely to be an undersupply of such schemes unless the state underwrites or subsidizes their creation'. In partnership with local Chambers of Commerce, trade associations, TECs and other network facilitators, the government will need to provide some seedcorn finance for MGSs. This will not involve significant expenditure since MGSs are likely to form relatively slowly, but the potential effects in deepening the finance market are great. Seedcorn finance could be withdrawn, through a request for repayment, if the network were guilty of restrictive practices.

Recommendation: Information flows between banks and new, especially high-tech, borrowers should be improved, with mutual guarantee schemes employed to reduce uncertainty. These should receive some seedcorn money, which should be conditional on the mutual guarantee scheme not operating to restrict competition.

Table 5.4: Mutual Guarantee Schemes in the EU

Country	Number of MGSs	Average amount of finance agreed ECU (000s)
Belgium	18	19
Denmark	12	n.a.
France	286	11
Germany	28	87
Italy	642	n.a.
Luxembourg	2	16
Spain	23	35

Source: Hughes (1994), Table 11.6.

Improved information flows between venture-capital providers and potential or current high-tech firms could also be achieved through the establishment of an Investment Opportunity Network (ION), through which prospective lenders and borrowers could be matched. This network could be built on the success of the five Informal Investment Demonstration Projects set up by the DTI in 1992 (Mason and Harrison, 1995). In these projects, TECs were provided with matching finance to establish a register of local informal investors (or Business Angels), and then marry these with local firms seeking small amounts of investment capital. There are also some private-sector initiatives in this area, but they are very specialised and limited. This approach to improving information flows should be deepened and broadened so that it includes other forms of equity investors apart from business angels, and so that it spreads across the country.

The main medium for the ION would ideally be the Internet. We envisage 'links' between the home page of the ION and the

Geographical coverage of MGSs	*Industries*
Organised locally often parallel with Local Credit Associations	All industries
Mostly regional, otherwise national	Selected industries
Usually local or regional	Selected industries
Organised regionally	All industries
Mostly regional in their operations	Selected industries
National	Selected industries
Mostly regional but two national MGSs	All industries for regional MGSs. Two for nationally operating MGSs: road transport, construction

Table 5.5: How a Mutual Guarantee Scheme Works

1 Individual firms wishing to borrow money for a particular project present details of that project to an elected or representative assessment board of the MGS. A fee is paid to cover administrative costs and the guarantee.

2 Provided that the board is satisfied with the business credentials of the applicant and the prospects of the proposal, it will provide a guarantee to underwrite any bank loan to pay for it.

3 The applicant can then go to a bank with the proposal backed by a guarantee.

4 In the event that the firm defaults on the loan, the MGS will pay the loan back to the bank and will itself seek recovery from the defaulter.

5 MGSs typically also negotiate with the banks more favourable interest rates for their members to reflect the guarantee. Therefore although the loan applicant has to pay a fee to the MGS, because default rates are relatively low total financing costs are reduced.

---

alternative commercial networks, which would then probably perform even better than at present. The financial kick-start for the use of the Internet would have to come from the ION itself. Although this is some way down the road, the ultimate aim should be an easily accessible, up-to-date network of investors with information on industries of interest by region, size of investment required, and so on. There should also be sub-networks for particular industries, individual regions and different types of investors. Because of the valuable information contained on the ION and its sensitivity, subscribers, whether companies or individuals, would need to pay a fee in order to conduct a search. This would help to ensure that only those individuals and companies genuinely interested in finding finance would use the service. Investors, especially business angels, could remain anonymous in the first instance if they wished, with the details of potential investment opportunities being passed to them so that they could decide privately whether to contact the company or individual requiring finance.

> **Recommendation:** Action should be taken to improve the market in equity capital, including the establishment of an Investment Opportunity Network and the relaxation of restrictions on the issuance of non-voting equity.

We do not recommend any new tax incentive schemes to promote equity investment, partly because of doubts about the effectiveness of such schemes in the light of the well-documented abuses of the Business Expansion Scheme in the 1980s and early 1990s (Hughes, 1994). In the interests of policy stability, once tax-based schemes are established they should be left relatively unaltered for at least five years so that investors and companies seeking investment can have some faith in their longevity. On this basis, we would expect the government to review the experience of the Enterprise Investment Scheme in 1998 and Venture Capital Trusts in 2000.

Short-termism and SME finance

Despite some movement away from overdrafts as the primary form of finance for SMEs, too many small firms are still reliant on short-term debt. This is symptomatic of other short-termism problems. Figure 5.4 shows CBI data from the early 1990s on the debt structure of SMEs in five EU countries, including the UK. The United Kingdom is clearly distinguished by the fact that more than half of all debt is in the form of overdrafts compared with around 10 per cent in Germany and 30 per cent in Italy, France and Spain. Since that time there has been a shift towards longer-term loans by British banks and their business customers. For example, David Lavarack, the head of Small Business Services for Barclays Bank, reports how Barclays has changed its approach in recent years: 'Since the mid 1980s Barclays has adopted a policy of lending long-term to its small business

Figure 5.4: Debt Structure
of SMEs in the EU

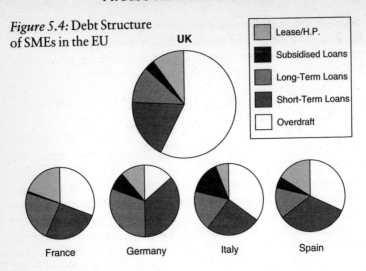

UK

Lease/H.P.

Subsidised Loans

Long-Term Loans

Short-Term Loans

Overdraft

France   Germany   Italy   Spain

Source: CBI (1993), Table 1.

Notes: Short-term loan defined as less than five years. The year of the data is not reported (probably 1992 or 1993).

customers ... This longer-term approach to finance helps to encourage businesses to develop a long-term culture generally.' (Lavarack, 1996:56)

Despite this, the latest Competitiveness White Paper remarked that 'there is evidence that UK SMEs are still more reliant on short-term finance than their European counterparts'(Cabinet Office, 1996a: para. 10.8). The most significant problem with shorter-term forms of debt is that in recession these tend to get called in rather quickly, thereby exacerbating the financial problems caused by the drop in demand.

The way forward

In attempting to wean SMEs and their banks even further off short-term debt, we would do well to emulate some aspects of the German system, such as better information flows and co-operation between banks and business. However, government cannot encompass that and should not attempt to achieve it with onerous new regulations. For medium-sized and larger firms, banks are now generally prepared to negotiate individual loan contracts tailored to the needs of the company; for example, to hedge particular risks to match repayments to cash-flow projections. Small companies do not have the standing to negotiate in that way and may take overdrafts because they offer flexibility in drawing on credit. Ideally, the banks should offer fixed-term loans to small businesses with certain standard flexibility features such as discretionary draw-down and some automatic rollover rights. We believe that private initiative will move in that direction, and we doubt if a public subsidy of the cost of such flexibility features is necessary. But the government should keep the situation under review.

The short-termism problem is partly due to SME demand. A British Chambers of Commerce survey of small firms in 1991 found that 49 per cent of them had never considered long-term finance, even though most clearly recognised that it was available to them (Middleton *et al.*, 1994). This suggests that some degree of financial training for SME owner-managers would be useful. To this end, we would like to see more developments along the lines of the Small Business Initiative (SBI), a National Westminster Bank sponsored project in Norfolk which aims to enable SME owner-managers to access good quality financial management training at times convenient for them. In the beginning, the SBI entailed entrepreneurs being provided with cheaper bank finance (at lower rates or with no bank charges) for a year after completing a free financial management training course. In successive tranches, the SBI has been modified so that participants have paid a greater proportion of the fees for the course and have received less generous rewards for completion. The SBI has been a great success; it now encompasses all four main banks and has operated in other parts of England as well as Northern Ireland. Moreover, there is substantial evidence that bank-business understanding and relationships improved markedly for those firms involved in the initiative, even with firms receiving preferable rates or lower charges.

The success of the SBI leads us to recommend that the DTI persist with its proposal to establish a *Financial Management*

Certificate (FMC) designed for SME owner-managers, the possession of which would provide an extra incentive for banks and other investors to supply finance to such firms. Flexibility in the delivery of learning materials and teaching for the FMC is crucial to its success. We would expect to see it at the forefront of the courses on offer in any open learning agency, but individual entrepreneurs should be able to access material and courses in local colleges and universities. In the early stages of its existence, before the FMC becomes a recognised badge of financial competence for SME owner-managers, the government may probably have to subsidise access to courses. However, the experience of the Small Business Initiative is that people will be prepared to pay reasonable fees for the training once the FMC gains currency among business and lenders alike.

Recommendation: The government should help to establish a Financial Management Certificate specifically designed for SME owner-managers.

Late payment

In addition to bank finance, an important source of working capital to SMEs is their late payment of suppliers. Hughes (1994) reports that, especially for service-sector SMEs, the level of trade debt can be as much as 35 or 40 per cent of total liabilities compared with around 20 per cent for larger firms. One of the most direct sources of business failure is the domino effect of trade debtors failing, leading to serious cash-flow problems for otherwise healthy businesses. There are many victims here, but few real culprits, since the great majority of small firms rely too heavily on trade debt for their working capital. We do not believe that a statutory right to interest holds the key to this problem. Small firms will be reluctant to enforce such a right against powerful large-business customers, whereas the latter will probably be only too willing to do so against their own small customers. In addition, late payment practices in other European countries do not suggest that a statutory right to interest actually succeeds in reducing late payment (Bank of England, 1996).

Late payment has become an ingrained business practice in Britain, and there are no easy solutions and therefore we offer no single firm recommendation. There are some relatively minor measures which could be taken, however, and we offer three in particular:

- The government itself must set good standards and ensure that other public bodies such as local authorities and quangos pay promptly.

- New reporting requirements on company payment policy (recommended by the current government) should be strengthened by an auditor's statement concerning actual payment practice, which must be published in the annual report.

- There should be a business information campaign on the collective peril of late payment and the potential benefits of factoring as one way to prevent failure due to cash-flow crises.

Conclusion

We have tackled the particular problems of SMEs by focusing on self-help initiatives, involving networks of firms and by very specific issues relating to finance. In particular, Business Links should become sign-posting bodies linked to networks of public- and private-sector service providers. The requirement to be self-financing should be removed. The government should initiate an information campaign about the value of networks of SMEs and investigate the most appropriate methods for encouraging their formation, perhaps involving financial bursaries for successful proposals. Information flows between banks and new high-tech borrowers need to be improved, with mutual guarantee schemes employed to reduce uncertainty. These would require some seed-corn money and would have to be made conditional on the MGS not operating to restrict competition. Action must be taken to improve the market in equity capital, including the establishment of an Investment Opportunity Network. The government should be active in establishing a Financial Management Certificate specifically designed for SME owner–managers. There are no easy answers to the late payment problem. We believe that cultural change will only happen slowly through good public payment standards, new reporting requirements on firms and a public information campaign.

NOTES

1 This information was provided to us by Graham Broome, Chief Executive of the Society of Motor Manufacturers and Traders Forum.

2 Business Net Ltd provided us with a great deal of information on the Danish initiatives and their role in training network brokers and setting up network projects in the UK together with Business Links.

3 CITER stands for Centro Informazione Tessile dell'Emilia-Romagna.

4 These include the Industrial and Commercial Finance Corporation in 1945, the Radcliffe Committee in 1959, the Bolton Committee in 1971, the Wilson Committee in 1980, and the Trade and Industry Select Committee in 1994. Most recently, the Bank of England in three annual reports on finance for small firms (1994, 1995 and 1996), has pointed out continuing market failures. In addition, there are various groups representing small firms, including the IoD, the Federation of Small Firms and the Forum of Private Businesses, which regularly produce reports critical of the banks and other finance providers.

5 Strictly, when we use the term 'new high-tech', we are referring to young innovative and new technology-based firms (NTBF).

6 Quoted in *Observer* (16 June 1996).

7 This was confirmed by several comments from high-tech entrepreneurs and financial analysts in 'Fast Movers Want to Go to America', *Independent on Sunday* (30 June 1996).

PART TWO

PEOPLE

6

IMPROVING SKILLS

Knowledgeable, motivated people are a key element in national competitiveness. Britain's education system is underperforming in important respects. There is a long tail of underachievers and levels of numeracy, literacy and adaptability are too low. School effectiveness must be raised and the underachievers caught early by increasing resources for nursery and primary education. The tendency for children to specialise too early, with the result that graduates have competencies which are too narrow, must be progressively eliminated. Traineeships should be universal for those leaving the school system at the age of sixteen. Adults must have access to quality learning opportunities, particularly in the area of general skills, so they can retrain more easily. The current funding bias against sub-degree level and part-time learning should be ended. Education is the government's business, but there are many types of training which are best left to the private sector to provide. The government can contribute, especially for smaller firms, by helping to develop new modes of training using new technology.

Skills and knowledge have always been crucial to wealth creation. As a consequence of globalisation and the information revolution, the qualities of a nation's workforce are becoming ever more important. This chapter outlines strategies to mobilise people's potential, so boosting Britain's skills base.

Education and training have been subject to more upheaval in two decades than most other policy areas.[1] Yet almost every assessment of the UK skills base, both by government and independent experts, suggests major reforms are still required.[2] In addition, virtually everyone has an opinion – often a different opinion – about what should change. Just commenting on reform proposals in reports from the CBI, IoD, TUC, Sir Ron Dearing and various select committees, let alone government investigations into education and training, would make a substantial report.

Our focus here is relatively narrow: the role of education in business success rather than in citizenship or life generally. Moreover, we are not specialists in education policy. Therefore, we avoid giving detailed views on such things as the minutiae of the National Curriculum, the requirements of specific GNVQs and NVQs, or the respective merits of full-class versus group-based learning. Instead, after a brief discussion of the importance of education and the role of government, we detail three broad ways in which we believe continuing failures in Britain's education and training system are undermining business success and suggest some ways in which they can be corrected.

Skills, Prosperity and Economic Performance

Most commentators accept as given that education and training are a significant determinant of economic performance and that the government has a major role to play in terms of funding, provision and regulation. Robert Reich's influential *Work of Nations* epitomised this view. If a country is starting from a situation of general literacy and numeracy, however, economists are not unanimous that further education is necessarily its best way to improve economic performance, especially when the education is financed and directed by the state. Therefore it is worth asking whether or not improvements in education and training in the United Kingdom will do much to increase prosperity and also what role government should play in orchestrating or financing those improvements.

Importance of education

There is a great deal of research into the impact of education and training on the performance of individuals, companies, industries and countries (Ashton and Green, 1996; Barro and Sala-i-Martin, 1995; Booth and Snower, 1996; Prais, 1993). Although there are alternative interpretations of the empirical evidence (Robinson, 1995b), we draw four main conclusions from our review:

- There is a positive correlation between educational attainment and national prosperity. The evidence confirms that education causes prosperity (as well as vice versa). For instance, a feature of the success of the Asian Tigers, such as South Korea and Singapore, has been their huge investment in education and training. The UK government's third White Paper on Competitiveness, in commenting on the rise of Asian competitors, states that much of their growth is explained by 'increased employment, notably of workers whose skills have been enhanced by improved education systems' (Cabinet Office, 1996:14). Similarly, in discussing the remarkably swift economic rise of Singapore, the *Skills Audit* states that 'the strategy for skills has been seen as a crucial element supporting economic development and overall must be judged as highly successful' (DfEE, 1996:79).

- Competitive levels of education and training are important for national success but are not a panacea. Among countries with similar levels of GDP per head there is wide dispersion of educational attainment. For example, the proportion of the population of Italy without secondary education is more than double that of Sweden or the United Kingdom yet Italy has a similar standard of living.

- Comparisons of the same industry across countries regularly reveal that higher skills (measured in terms of both academic and vocational qualifications) are associated with higher productivity.[3] The only exception to this pattern appears to be the United States, where factory productivity is consistently higher than it is in Europe despite the much lower levels of skills typical in American workforces. According to Mason and Finegold (1995), however, a small minority of shopfloor workers in the United States are graduates who provide a core of production management skills among other relatively low-skilled workers, and employers and the education system are much more geared towards continuing education for adults than they are in the United Kingdom. One expert in the area, David Soskice, has argued that the United Kingdom should aim to follow the US model (Soskice, 1993).

- There are generally positive 'returns' to the individual from education and training, especially higher education and employer-backed training. Better-qualified people command higher salaries and have much better employment opportunities than the less well qualified. Moreover, this pay-off has been increasing markedly since the early 1980s, as illustrated in Figure 6.1. In the early 1980s the Department of Education and Science estimated the rate of return on higher education at between 20 to 30 per cent, with social sciences and engineering degrees resulting in higher pay-offs than the arts and natural sciences (DES, 1988). A more recent study for the Department suggests that the pay premium for a degree has remained high despite the increase in student numbers. Lissenburgh and Bryson (1996) estimate a higher education premium of 14 per cent for men and 24 per cent for women, but report that now engineering and natural sciences lead to higher returns than arts and social sciences.

There has been considerable investigation of the effect of different types of employee training on subsequent employment and earnings. Generally, full-time, off-the-job training seems to provide particularly large benefits for the individual concerned. Payne (1990) reports that average pay was 28 to 34 per cent higher for participants in such training and that the probability of finding work in the same vocational area increased by 25 percentage points. A more recent study by economists at the Institute for Fiscal Studies also suggests that the largest pay-offs come from employer-provided, off-the-job training geared towards a particular vocational qualification, although the conclusions are tentative since the study did not control for the duration or level of courses (Blundell *et al.*, 1996).

Figure 6.1: Median Male Earnings by Highest Qualification in Great Britain, 1979–93 (*as percentage of median earnings for all males*)

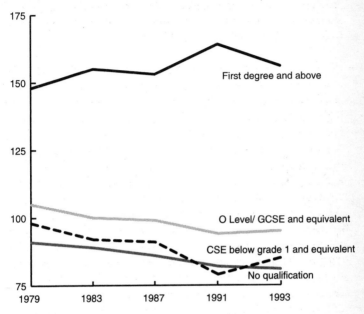

Source: DfEE (1996), Figure 3.1.

Government's role

These results raise an important issue. Since there are measurable gains for the individual in educational achievement and for firms in having a better-trained workforce, do these not provide sufficient incentive for private investment in both education and training?[4] Why does the government need to intervene further or increase public resources for education and training? In fact, there are good reasons to believe that individuals and employers, left to their own devices, would invest too little in skills, even if individuals could more easily borrow to finance educational investment. Such investment may be risky for the individual, even though the average return to society is not. The necessary borrowing may look particularly prohibitive for those with few assets or a low family income. Employers may also be under-standably reluctant to pay for their employees to learn general skills which are just as likely to yield rewards for other employers, society or the individual as for the sponsoring employer.

The government should be particularly involved in education and training where the market for skill acquisition works least well – to remedy market failure. The market is most likely to fail where social returns are highest. And that is in learning basic or generic rather than specialist skills. Moreover, 'the social rates of return tend to decrease with higher steps of educational attainment, where private returns are high' (Leuven and Tuijnman, 1996:10). In the early stages of learning, there are also likely to be 'asymmetric information' problems in that children and some less-educated parents are likely to underestimate the value of education. These considerations provide a powerful argument for the most important realms of government action being in education of children plus general education for adults. In the areas of specialist adult education and training there is a greater danger that the government will end up paying for skill formation which would have happened without its intervention – technically known as a deadweight problem. With these findings and implications in mind we turn to a review of the situation in the United Kingdom.

Poor Skills and Business Underperformance

Having reviewed copious written evidence, heard the views of numerous business people and consulted many academic experts, we believe that despite notable recent improvements in Britain's skill base, there are three broad failings in the country's education and training system which can be directly related to business underperformance.

- *A long tail of underachievement:* Very few of our competitors can better us in the quality of our graduates and we are beginning to match them in terms of quantity. But far too many young people still leave school with few or no qualifications. Moreover, very few of them get the opportunity in later life

160

to make up for their earlier underachievement. British business performance would benefit hugely from a levelling-up in the educational performance of the current and future workforce.

- *Children specialise too early:* We have come across too many examples of the damaging consequences of early specialisation among most British children; it seriously undermines business performance. This specialisation means that many young people leave school after their A Levels with only a rudimentary grasp of mathematics, English or both, and only a distant memory of learning a foreign language. The possibility of dropping maths or science at the age of sixteen compounds a weakness in these subjects, already evident among younger children.

- *Lifelong learning is a reality for too few adults:* Good employers recognise the benefits of both training their own workers in specific skills and enabling them to broaden their horizons through adult education. Although there have been marked improvements in the number of employees receiving work-related training and participating in adult education, their numbers are still too low and access is still very limited for low-skilled adults.

Long tail of underachievement

Britain's education and training system produces polarisation. We are probably educating and training a larger proportion of the current and future workforce to a higher level than ever before. Improvements in education and training have undoubtedly occurred in recent years. Less than half of young people stayed on in full-time education at sixteen in 1983–4. Now around three-quarters do. Similarly, a third of eighteen-year-olds now enter higher education compared with only 14 per cent in 1987. Exam grades and the proportion of passes seem to be on an upward trajectory (Figure 6.2). More employees than ever before are receiving training at work (Machin and Wilkinson, 1995). Skill shortages, though still reported by many employers,

Figure 6.2: GCSE and GCE O Level Attainments in England, (1983/4–94/5)

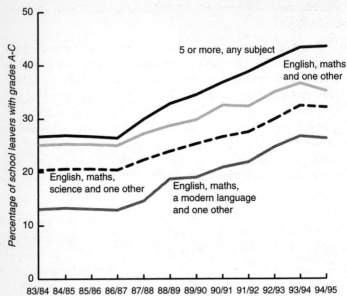

Source: DfEE (1996), Figure 5.5.

are significantly below the levels reported when unemployment was at a similar level in the late 1980s.

Yet there remains an uncomfortably large group of children, young people and adults who lack the basic skills required for them to be employable or even to function properly as citizens. The government's priority must be to decrease this polarisation. There is a pertinent analogy here with British business performance in that we have roughly the same proportion of leading companies as our major competitors but too many lagging companies compared with them. Similarly, the cream of our education system probably matches that elsewhere (though we have a weakness in maths, where there is less cream than in other subjects). But too many people are completely failing to gain marketable skills from their education and there are far too many failing schools. As the CBI recently remarked, 'although the best

162

in the UK is world-class, the tail of education and training under-performance is striking' (CBI, 1996a:13).

Three pieces of evidence confirm the long tail of underachievement in Britain:

- *Performance against the National Targets for Education and Training:* One of the most important initiatives in recent years has been the setting of specific targets for the nation in education and training outcomes. The targets began in 1991 as a CBI initiative, but the body responsible for assessing progress towards the targets (NACETT – the National Advisory Council on Education and Training Targets) has since been widened to include TUC representation. The targets have attracted strong government support and have been used as bench-marks in all three Competitiveness White Papers. They specify a proportion of the workforce which should attain certain qualifications by the year 2000 and are summarised in Table 6.1, which also shows progress towards the targets. There is a clear dividing line between the very good progress towards the higher skills targets, in particular the proportion of young people entering higher education and the proportion of the workforce with at least a first degree, and the poorer performance against targets for lower-level skills. Indeed, an original target for enrolments on NVQs has been abandoned, presumably because of the low take-up by employers and employees. There has been no target whatsoever for the attainment of basic skills of literacy and numeracy for that 25 per cent of young people expected to fall short of NVQ level two.

- *National performance against our competitors:* The government's recent *Skills Audit* is a welcome attempt to bench-mark Britain's achievements in skills against some of our competitors. The report compares both qualifications obtained and multinational companies' opinions on important skills in the United Kingdom, the United States, France, Germany and Singapore. While we rank at or near the top of this short league table in higher-level skills, the United Kingdom is close to the bottom in lower-level skills (see Table 6.2). The only other

163

Table 6.1: Performance Against the National Targets for Education and Training

Skill level	Actual (%) 1995	Target (%) 2000
Life-long learning		
Workforce at NVQ level 3	40	60
Workforce at NVQ level 4	23	30
Foundation learning		
Young people at NVQ level 2	63	85
Young people at NVQ level 3	41	60
Higher education		
Cohort entering higher education	31	33
Employee training		
Organisations with >200 employees recognised as Investors in People	10	70
Organisations with >50 employees recognised as Investors in People	6	35

Sources: Robinson (1995a), Table 1; Cabinet Office (1996a), Chapter 4.

major developed country with a similarly polarised education is the United States, which has an even higher proportion of its young people participating in higher education and similar deficiencies in such basic skills as literacy and numeracy among much of the rest of the population.

• *Performance in internationally co-ordinated skills tests:* The performance of our children in internationally co-ordinated maths tests has consistently shown a wider distribution of performance than that in most other developed countries. Figures from the most recent study are shown in Table 6.3. Not only is the average performance of English school-children below that of all other countries in the study apart from the United States (reinforcing our point about the general weakness in maths),

Table 6.2: UK's Ranking Among Five Major Competitors at Different Skill Levels

Skill level	Rank (1st to 5th)
% of population with a first degree	2nd (behind the United States)
% of 25–28-year-olds with degree	2nd= (behind France)
% of population with A-level or equivalent	2nd= (behind Germany)
% of population with O-level or equivalent	5th
% of 19–21-year-olds with O-level or equivalent	4th (ahead of the United States)
Literacy of adults	5th
Numeracy of adults	4th= (with the United States)

Source: DfEE (1996).

Note: The *Skills Audit* involves an assessment of five countries: the United Kingdom, United States, France, Germany and Singapore.

Table 6.3: Scores in International Mathematics Tests of 13-year-olds, 1990

	England	France	Italy	Switzerland	United States
Average	59.5	64.2	64.0	70.8	55.3
Highest decile	89.3	89.3	88.0	93.3	82.7
Lowest decile	32	37.3	36.5	50.7	29.3
Relative variability (%)[a]	95	81	81	60	97

Source: Prais (1993), Table 3.

Note: a This is the difference between the highest and lowest decile as a percentage of the average.

but the disparity between the top and the bottom of the ability distribution is also much higher in England.

Sig Prais, a leading expert in the field, consequently argues that 'there needs now to be greater concern with the schooling attainments of average and below-average school-leavers than simply with those top-attainers who are to join the ranks of university graduates' (Prais, 1993:167). We wholeheartedly endorse this comment. Tackling the long tail of underachievement in skills should be among the first priorities for a government determined to help British business succeed.

Children specialise too early

In no other advanced industrial country do students at the age of sixteen choose only three subjects. In most systems (including Scotland) a wide range of subjects, usually between six and ten, is studied at this stage. We are far from a lone voice in criticising the early specialisation of British children, with other critics including Sir Claus Moser in a famous speech as President of the British Association for the Advancement of Science in August 1990, the National Commission on Education (NCE, 1993), and Sir Ron Dearing's review of qualifications for this age group (Dearing, 1996). Our main concern is that children are therefore dropping core subjects such as mathematics and English.

The consequences of early specialisation for business performance were borne out in anecdotal evidence from a number of employers. Typically they expressed concern that their highly skilled employees have too narrow a focus, which inhibits communication within the firm. The chief executive of a major engineering company complained, for example, that his engineers, accountants, marketing and other experts were locked into their own 'chimneys' which prevented proper understanding between the groups. As illustrated in Chapter 5, one of the difficulties in the provision of both debt and equity finance for high-tech firms is that few experts on finance in the banks or venture-capital houses have even a basic knowledge of technology.

Lifelong learning for too few adults

Among the current working population, lifelong learning is a reality for too few, despite the increase in employer-provided training. Moreover, employee training and adult education are primarily the preserve of those employees or managers in relatively large firms who are already reasonably well qualified and well paid. That was among the most important findings in the Commission's first Issue Paper by Stephen Machin and David Wilkinson. For example, whereas one in four employees with a degree in the national Labour Force Survey report some training over a four-week period, only one in twenty-five employees with no qualifications does so.

How significant is lifelong learning for business success? Our observation of the speed of change in workplace technologies in both services and manufacturing and our concerns about increasing insecurity in the labour market, have made us firm believers in the need for lifelong learning. Despite the widespread acceptance of its value, as embodied for instance in the government's Investors in People initiative to stimulate employee training, progress in extending it is too slow. The responsibility for making lifelong learning a reality lies with employers and their employees as much as with government.

Reducing the Long Tail of Underachievement

In making recommendations in this area we have been influenced by the experts in the field, since the proposals draw on much more than our personal business experiences. There is a large and internationally unusual disparity of achievement among pupils in the United Kingdom. A major cause of this disparity is diverse standards in schools and we believe this is the most urgent area for action. Another of the stronger messages we received, which we came to accept, is the importance of experience in the earliest years for eventual educational achievement. We feel confident, therefore, in urging that this problem be tackled. Reform of pre-school and primary education should aim to ensure that British children receive the best possible start in life.[5] Resources should be channelled into pre-school education and primary schools with the specific objective of ensuring that by the age of eleven all children acquire adequate literacy and numeracy. A final aspect of underachievement which should be tackled is closer to the world of work. That is the inadequate education and training of young people leaving school before the age of eighteen. We make specific proposals in that area too.

More effective schools

A school where nearly all pupils achieve at least five good grades at GCSE may well be just down the road from one where fewer than one in ten does so. The pupils' abilities on entry to the school and their social background only partly explain the divergence and there is evidence that schools vary greatly in the extent to which they advance pupils' education. A consensus seems to be forming among educationalists about the factors that make for a successful school, including effective leadership from the head, a team of well-trained teachers and considerable parental participation (Sammons *et al.*, 1995). Achieving the best possible performance of all schools is the first thing to put in hand. As managers, we firmly believe that making an operation as efficient and effective as possible should come before further investment is considered and this principle applies to the reform of education. To discuss reforms to improve school effectiveness in detail would take us too far from our area of primary concern and competence. That said, the sorts of reform to teacher training and career structure and the extra resources which are required by problem schools would probably entail more government spending (Hillman, 1996a). So far as we can judge, on the basis of expert advice, this might amount to at least £1 billion extra a year.

Recommendation: The top priority in education should be to improve the quality of teaching and learning in schools. As well as reform of teacher training and assessment, this will require increased spending.

Pre-school education

Several studies have shown that high-quality pre-school education leads to immediate gains in educational and social development, which persist through adolescence and adulthood (for example: Audit Commission, 1996; Ball, 1994; Sylva, 1994; Jarousse *et al.*, 1995). British children start their education later than many of their counterparts in other countries (see Table 6.4), which probably contributes to lower levels of achievement later in life. There is also a marked disparity among regions, cities and even boroughs in access to free or subsidised nursery places. We encourage moves to extend high-quality pre-school education to accommodate the great majority of our young children. The National Commission on Education estimated that the annual cost of publicly funded places would be £860 million (NCE, 1993).

Recommendation: The government should fund high-quality nursery education for all three- and four-year-olds whose parents want it.

Table 6.4: Percentage of Children Attending Publicly Funded Early Childhood Education, 1992

Country	Three-year-olds	Four-year-olds
France	98	100
Belgium	97	99
Denmark	76	81
Sweden	63	67
Norway	49	60
Finland	44	49
Britain	**41**	**58**
Spain	28	94
Portugal	28	44

Source: Hillman (1996a), Table 6.1.

Class sizes

Studies show that a satisfactory primary school education influences a child's subsequent educational progress in secondary school and beyond (Sammons, 1994; Goldstein and Sammons, 1994) and may have a greater impact on pupils' overall progress than secondary school education (Mortimore, 1995). By the age of eleven, many children have decided whether they consider themselves to be high or low achievers, and these self-perceptions become increasingly difficult to change. Pupils should be given as much individual attention as possible in their formative years, which depends on class size. International data on class sizes reveal that the United Kingdom is poor at providing such attention. Average class sizes in maintained primary schools are increasing (the latest figure being 26.6), with more than 20 per cent of classes having over thirty and a growing number having over forty (Department for Education, 1994). The United Kingdom now has a higher ratio of pupils to teachers than all OECD countries except Ireland and Turkey, with many countries having ratios half that of the United Kingdom. Reducing all class sizes for five- to seven-year-olds to under thirty would not be particularly expensive, probably costing less than £100 million. It would contribute greatly to achieving the objective of ensuring that all British children attain at least basic literacy and numeracy standards by the time they reach eleven.

> **Recommendation:** Class sizes in all primary schools should be reduced to thirty or under.

Young adults

The beneficial effects of our first three recommendations on competitiveness, if implemented, will be felt only in ten or twenty years' time. Yet underachievement is a reality for too many school-leavers now. We propose measures to ensure that no young adult is lost to the education and training system at the age of sixteen.

Although we welcome the significant increase in staying-on rates among the sixteen to nineteen age group since 1988 (Figure

Figure 6.3: Staying-on Rates of 16/17-year-olds in England, 1986/7–94/5

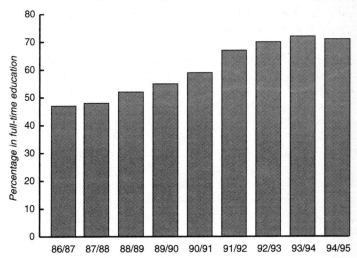

Source: Robinson (1996), Table 26.

6.3), we have two concerns. First, there are some young people staying on at school, often retaking low-level qualifications, who would be better off being trained more practically in a commercial environment. While everyone should continue education and skill acquisition after sixteen, this does not necessarily have to be at school. Some youngsters may find more motivation for academic studies when these are a formal part of a training programme whose relevance to the world of work is clearer to them. The education 'market' may be distorting the routes to further education, however, because schools and colleges are the information gate-keepers about a youngster's options. They now have a financial incentive to keep young people enrolled and may understate the advantages of apprenticeships or sandwich courses. That is one of the negative effects of the attempt to make educational institutions operate in an ersatz market, at least without adequate provision of and support for disinterested information brokers.

A yet more urgent problem is that roughly 20 per cent of the 16–19 age group are in work without any guaranteed access to training at all. We believe that both these concerns can be tackled by a single policy: the introduction of mandatory traineeships for all young workers aged under nineteen. There should be a concerted effort to ensure that everyone, both those remaining in the education system and those working, reaches at least GNVQ level 2 by the age of nineteen (equivalent to five GCSEs at Grades A–C).

Traineeships would involve the employer releasing a young employee who had not already reached the equivalent of GNVQ level 2 for the equivalent of eight hours a week for off-the-job vocational education. In addition, the youngster should have a trainer at the workplace who is responsible for practical skill development. Employers will need to be compensated for providing the on-the-job training and the day off each week (say £1,000 a year for two years) so as not to impair unduly the attractiveness of young workers. Moreover, employers are not going to take on trainees if they cost too much. The traineeship minimum wage should certainly be below any national minimum wage introduced for adults. This should ensure that employers who currently employ youngsters at higher rates of pay, but with no training requirement, would continue to employ them when there is a training requirement and it would reduce the likelihood of older workers, who carry no training obligations, being substituted for younger workers.

In advocating this replacement for Youth Training, which has become debased in the eyes of young people, we place particular emphasis on the quality of training providers, on curriculum content and on the competencies of individual trainers. The trainees should have a positive attitude towards the training they receive, otherwise it will prove fruitless. Engendering that positive attitude will not be easy, since some youngsters will have a negative attitude towards learning after their experience of school. It will require imaginative use of practical learning facilities rather than traditional textbook learning.

Our traineeship scheme is different from the government's recently announced plan to introduce National Traineeships, after consultation, from September 1997 in that our traineeships would be mandatory for employers, whereas the government's scheme as currently envisaged is voluntary (Cabinet Office, 1996a:41). Our scheme will not be costless. Layard *et al.* (1995) estimate that it will cost around £800 million per year once it is up and running.

Recommendation: Mandatory traineeships should be introduced for all young workers to ensure that they are not lost to the education and training system at the age of sixteen.

Reducing the Detrimental Effects of Early Specialisation

Sir Ron Dearing's review of sixth-form studies, completed in March 1996, was widely welcomed because its main recommendations were seen to encourage a baccalaureate-style qualification system, allowing a greater mix of vocational and academic subjects for sixteen- to nineteen-year-olds (Dearing, 1996). Some critics complained that the report did not go far enough in that A Levels remain intact. But there is a strong lobby to retain A Levels on the grounds that they are recognised by universities and employers (IoD, 1996b). We applaud moves to broaden young people's education, since sixteen is too early an age to specialise so much. But we value stability in qualifications since it takes a number of years for employers to gauge the status of new qualifications, and curriculum changes entail upheaval in schools and colleges. We have a clear idea of the ultimate objective – young people studying a broader range of subjects with everyone maintaining minimum standards of literacy and numeracy – but the upheaval required to get there should be minimised. Unification of the parallel academic and vocational streams is desirable but problematic in the medium term; therefore the priority should be to broaden the academic stream. This could be done immediately, in advance of reform of A Levels, with greater use of AS Levels. Within the present points system, the government should ensure that all universities insist on at least AS-level qualifications in English or a modern language and in maths or a science from all candidates.

> **Recommendation:** The long-term objective of phasing out A Levels should be pursued by broadening university entrance requirements.

Removing Impediments to Lifelong Learning

Adult education

The current system of funding adult education discriminates against sub-degree vocational education and part-time degrees. People who take full-time degrees have their fees paid by the state, while those who study in further education or for part-time degrees have to pay fees. Moreover, most full-time higher education students also receive maintenance grants whereas other students have to support themselves. With so distorted a system it is not surprising that we produce so few people with first-degree-level vocational qualifications. The traditional argument for discriminating between higher and further education was that since the latter predominantly consists of vocational courses, the employer reaps the benefit and therefore should pay for the course. This is clearly false since it is very hard for an individual employer to capture the whole benefit from a general (rather than firm-specific) vocational course and therefore they are not always prepared to pay for it.

Funding arrangements for adult education should be more equitable. There are a number of different options, each with different spending implications. We believe that there is a reasonable distinction between sub-degree and degree-level education but that there ought to be harmonisation within each level. We propose that all sub-degree education courses should be provided free of charge to adults meeting relevant entrance requirements. The sacrifices involved in taking these courses – reduced work or leisure time, costs of books and equipment – will ensure that people do not embark on such courses lightly. For degree-level education, there is clear evidence of a significant pay-off for the individual in higher pay and better jobs. Hence we believe that individuals should contribute to course fees. Whatever proportion of fees is paid by the individual for a particular course, it should be the same whether they are taking the course full- or part-time. We have based our costings of this proposal on 20 per cent personal contribution, but we have no strong commitment to this figure. This produces an estimated cost for the whole reform of £800 million a year. In addition, we believe that the entitlement to education should be renewable; someone should be able to enrol in further courses at a similar or lower level, say five years after completing a previously subsidised course. That would promote the widely approved aim of lifelong learning. Our proposal does not involve subsidising fees for 'recreational' adult education, postgraduate courses or tailored courses put on at the request of firms.

It is common ground among most policy-makers, employers and even some student groups that maintenance grants will sooner or later be converted entirely into loans and be repaid via the tax or national insurance system. In the long-term, this will free considerable resources, which could help to finance the reduction of fees for part-time students and those in further education.

Recommendation: Funding biases in adult education should be eliminated by making all sub-degree courses free and charging partial fees for all part- and full-time degree courses.

Employee training

Subsidising fees for vocational and part-time courses would itself be a contribution to adult learning but it would not be enough. Additional policies are needed to improve employee access to training and employer provision of it. Those policies must balance different requirements:

- To increase the volume of training.
- To target those firms not training and those employees not receiving training.
- To avoid employer and employee resentment against mandatory schemes.
- To avoid deadweight costs of incentive-based schemes.
- To encourage individuals and their employers to take charge of their own training arrangements.

Policy design will depend on how these requirements are ranked. Those favouring compulsory training levies are less worried about employer resentment and more concerned to raise the overall level of training. Similarly, although there is a case for fiscal incentives for employers who train, such as tax breaks for employers achieving a given standard rather than fiscal penalties for those who do not, such measures tend to involve high dead-weight costs. The great majority of large firms train most of their workers in the absence of training subsidies.

The current government is clearly less concerned about targeting particular employers since its principal focus, the Investors in People programme, is geared more to large firms, which tend to train anyway, than to SMEs which train less. We believe that training policies will have to concentrate much more on smaller firms than they currently do. A recent analysis of training practices, needs and difficulties among SMEs concludes, however, that a blanket policy for promoting training among such firms is inappropriate since they have very different practices and attitudes towards training (Curran *et al.*, 1996). We therefore set out an approach based on encouraging firms to learn from each other and on the use of new information technology, with the state acting as facilitator rather than director. Our policy proposals draw on the themes of networking and co-operation developed in Chapter 5.

Enabling TECs to promote employee training

Training and Enterprise Councils (TECs) are potentially the most important agents at local level for encouraging and enabling more employers to train and develop their workforce. Since their inception in 1990 TECs have attracted criticism and praise in fairly equal measure, but in the last year or so they seem to have gained greater acceptance from employers and workers. The national training accord signed between the TECs and the TUC in June 1996 was a great step forward in the establishment of TECs as permanent institutions for co-ordinating public funds for training at local level. A select committee report on TECs in February 1996 provides the most comprehensive assessment of both the role of TECs in the wider framework of training and economic development and their relationship with various government departments (Employment Committee, 1996a). Our proposal draws on some of the select committee's findings.

TEC funding needs to become more flexible. Currently, rules restrict them to spending about £65 million (just over 4 per cent) of their £1.5 billion annual budget on employee training – specifically, £55 million on Investors in People and about £10 million on Skills for Small Businesses. Most of their funding goes on youth training (about £700 million) and training for the unemployed (about £550 million).[6] While both those activities are laudable, we believe that TECs should have greater flexibility to promote training in small firms. Chris Humphries, policy director at the TEC National Council, told us that the TECs felt hamstrung by current funding arrangements and were 'desperate to do more on employee training'. Our call for greater flexibility in TEC funding echoes comments made by a number of witnesses to the select committee on TECs. One of the training providers which reported to the committee, Scope Training Limited, (Employment Committee, 1996a: appendices to the minutes of evidence, p. 19) commented that:

> In our experience the TEC budget is structured very rigidly with quite precise objectives defined for each budget heading. There is limited scope for a TEC to support or respond to training and development needs not previously acknowledged in its Business Plan. The vast majority [sic] of the TEC's budget is allowed for specific purposes before the beginning of the financial year.

Curran *et al.* (1996) also report that only one in ten SMEs has had any contact with its local TEC about training.

Recommendation: TEC funding should be made more flexible to enable them to promote employee training.

Making Investors in People more attainable

The most significant initiative to promote employee training in the 1990s has been the Investors in People award. This has become a recognisable standard in staff training and development which any firm can in principle work towards and attain. More firms each year are using IiP to examine how effectively they are using their people as a business asset. By the end of 1995 around 3,000 firms had already attained the IiP standard and a further 20,000 were registered as committed to achieving the standard. The take-up of IiP is, however, a long way from the targets set. We welcome the Secretary of State for Education and Employment's challenge to the TUC and CBI to work together to bring more organisations into IiP, but this will probably do little to bring more SMEs into the IiP fold. Appropriately, the IiP standard is not an easily won award; it takes a great deal of time and effort to achieve it. But this inevitably means that it is seen as rather unobtainable for the great majority of SMEs.

Following the approach to SME policy set out in Chapter 5, we wonder whether the IiP standard is not too restricted in being focused on individual firms. Perhaps groups of small firms should be able to achieve IiP status by clubbing together to fund and organise staff training and development. The Investors in People organisation should be charged with investigating a new joint IiP standard for groups of small firms to work towards.

Learning from large firms

The low quality of some British managers has been identified in a number of different areas, including their weakness in innovation and their lack of financial acumen, entrepreneurial flair and practical knowledge. There have been various warm words about promoting more sub-MBA management training, with little in the way of policy proposals. One option would be to extend a 'Business Angel' approach into the training arena. There are examples of large firms seconding some of their younger managers to set up and run an SME training network dealing with issues like marketing, financial management, human-resource management and supply-chain management. This is not currently done on a large scale. We believe, therefore, that it could safely be encouraged with small grants to cover the salary of training angels up to a maximum of ten days a year. Dead-

178

weight losses would be small. If such a scheme takes off, it could also provide an alternative to early retirement for redundant senior or middle managers from large companies.

> **Recommendation:** The government should encourage a business angel approach to training for SME managers.

Using new information technology

There is no doubt that technical change is now reducing the cost of certain sorts of training, particularly 'distance learning' where student and teacher are separated. Computer-based learning via interactive CD-ROMs is a reality and with the development of communications networks new possibilities are being opened up for real-time distance learning analogous to the pioneering work of the Open University using television. In future that process could be made interactive at a local level with students 'attending' virtual lectures or seminars. These developments could revolutionise training in SMEs since they permit formal learning, as well as practical experience, to be acquired at the workplace. They could also permit training to take place at times and in instalments consistent with other work and responsibilities.

We are sure that these things will happen in response to the influence of market forces. Yet all past experience tells us that the opportunities will be seized by some, with many others who could benefit even more lagging behind. Vigorous state action would accelerate the process. This is an area where scale economies are considerable. Nearly all the costs are up-front and quickly become sunk: installing networks and equipment, devising courses, writing and developing software. Once all that is done, the cost of supplying the marginal consumer is almost nil. Private enterprise has shown time and again that it can deal with such situations but it takes time, since firms are reluctant to invest on the scale necessary until a market has developed. Yet the market cannot really develop until the infrastructure, both 'soft' and 'hard', is in place. Meanwhile, consumers are charged heavily because development costs have to be met somehow and that too slows down the growth of the market.

If it is managed properly, government intervention could help business over the initial hump of market development. The government must ensure that the communications infrastructure is in place nationally; it must rapidly resolve any outstanding issues about technical standards or compatibilities so that the training network is integrated and user-friendly. It can do a great deal to publicise the possibilities and it has a vital role in providing information and accreditation of courses offered by private-sector suppliers; for those purposes we welcome the suggestion for an open learning agency – dubbed by some the University for Industry (Hillman, 1996b). Such an institution should work with TECs to reduce the cost and raise the practicality of training for SMEs.

If the open learning agency (OLA) acts as a broker, simply publicising and accrediting courses offered by companies and other institutions, it could charge for its services and be self-financing. Responding to business needs and suggestions, the OLA could also become an important commissioner of educational material for interactive learning on computers. The power of its purchasing could greatly accelerate the development of the market in software and courses. This would be more expensive in the short term but could ultimately be self-financing. Real costs would come only in providing subsidised access to the OLA. Yet that would not only help to boost training but would also accelerate the development of what could be a vital emerging industry and one where the United Kingdom could have a competitive advantage. We have not studied the options or costs in detail but our instinct is to move ahead. Detailed studies should be launched without delay.

Recommendation: The government should actively promote the use of advanced information networks in adult education and training.

Paying for Our Proposals

Our proposals do not involve massive spending commitments. Excluding the Open Learning Agency, they involve some £3.5 billion as shown in Table 6.5. How would we pay for these pro-

Table 6.5: Estimated Costs of Education Proposals

Policy proposal	Estimated cost £m per year
Better schools	1,000
Nursery provision	860
Class sizes	100
Traineeships	800
Free sub-degree education for adults	800
Total	3,560

Sources: Hillman (1996a); Layard *et al.* (1995); National Commission on Education (1993).

posals? Redistribution within the DfEE budget could achieve a lot. For instance, £2 billion a year could be saved eventually if student maintenance grants were altered to privately funded loans, leaving around £1.5 billion to be found elsewhere.

It is important to maintain perspective over these expenditures. At present there is a welcome realism in political rhetoric about the need to be careful with tax-payers' money and to economise on public spending. There are, however, priorities and everyone seems agreed that education and training top the list. Public spending on education in the United Kingdom was 5.2 per cent of GDP in 1992 figures (the last year for which we can make international comparisons) which put us fourteenth out of eighteen OECD countries in educational spending. That figure has risen to 5.4 per cent subsequently but it is still well down on the peak of 6.4 per cent reached in 1975–6. To increase spending by 1 per cent of GDP, taking the proportion back to the mid-1970s level (and incidentally to sixth out of eighteen OECD countries), does not seem outrageous. That would entail spending nearly £7 billion more annually. In such a context our proposals for a net increase of £1.5 billion a year are modest and more than consistent with the need for public economy.

Conclusion

This chapter has identified three particular failings in the British education and training system which are undermining business performance and competitiveness: the long tail of underachievement, children specialising too early, and too few adults (particularly those working in SMEs) having access to learning opportunities. We believe that one of the government's primary responsibilities is to tackle these problems and that the implementation of our reform proposals would provide long-term benefits for the UK economy.

The top priority for government action should be improving the quality of teaching and learning in Britain's schools, including reform of teacher training and assessment. All children should be given a good head-start in learning through the opportunity for free high-quality nursery education at an early age and guaranteed smaller class sizes once they reach primary school. A mandatory traineeship scheme should be introduced to ensure that young people leaving school at sixteen do not stop acquiring skills. The government should work towards a long-term goal of phasing out A Levels by ensuring that university entrance requirements are broadened. Funding biases in adult education should be eliminated by making all sub-degree courses free and charging fees for all part- and full-time degree courses. The difficulties encountered by workers in SMEs should be countered by a range of measures. These include allowing TECs greater flexibility in their use of funds; small grants being made available to encourage a Business Angel scheme for training SME managers; and the active promotion of the use of new information networks in adult training.

NOTES

1 The OECD's 1995 economic survey of the UK lists nearly 20 major changes in the institutions of education and training since 1980 and 14 current initiatives (OECD, 1995a: Tables 18 and 19). Since this report the government has announced other major initiatives such as pre-school vouchers, the Literacy and Numeracy Project and further

reform of 16–19 qualifications in the light of the Dearing Report of March 1996, to name just three.

2 For example, the 1996 Dearing Report into qualifications for 16–19-year-olds contains nearly two hundred detailed recommendations (Dearing, 1996) and the National Commission on Education produced sixteen very broad recommendations covering everything from nursery education to supporting lifelong learning (NCE, 1993). Moreover, the chapters on education and training have been among the longest in the three Competitiveness White Papers (DTI, 1994 and 1995; Cabinet Office, 1996a).

3 A great body of work demonstrating this has been accumulated since 1980 by the National Institute of Economic and Social Research (NIESR). Their main type of research involves so-called 'matched plant' studies, in which the research team investigates the performance, skill structure and organisation of two or more groups of plants producing similar goods or services in different countries to explain observed productivity gaps. The research has included such diverse industries as chemicals, biscuits, precision engineering, furniture, clothing and hotels. Germany has typically been the favoured comparator country since it is well known to enjoy a productivity advantage over the UK in many sectors. More recently, comparisons have been drawn with Dutch, French and even US plants. The accumulated empirical and case-study evidence on the impact of skills on plant-level productivity is without parallel (examples include Mason *et al.*, 1994; Steedman and Wagner, 1989; Prais *et al.*, 1989).

4 For an example of such a critique, see comments by Tarsh in the discussion section of Prais (1993).

5 We are particularly grateful to Josh Hillman, Research Fellow at the Institute for Public Policy Research, for his advice and guidance on the impact of and policies towards pre-school provision and schools.

6 All figures on TEC budgets are taken from the Employment Committee (1996a), Annex lxiii–lxvi.

7

EFFECTIVE LABOUR MARKETS

Underperformance and underachievement can ultimately lead to failure and unemployment. The consequent 'drag anchor' on the economy of long-term unemployment is a problem for everyone, including the business community. In this chapter we set out a strategy for pulling up the drag anchor by preventing the short-term unemployed from becoming the long-term unemployed and reconnecting the latter to the labour market. The current government's policy of extending in-work benefits must continue, but it necessitates a minimum wage to prevent employers transferring their labour costs to tax-payers. The minimum wage must be set at a rate that does not threaten jobs. Provisions under the Social Chapter are currently fairly innocuous, but there are potential threats to competitiveness from excessive regulation. Despite these, the need to maintain the Single Market and relations with other EU countries mean that we should opt into the Social Chapter and argue vigorously for a liberal market approach.

The United Kingdom suffers not only from a long tail of personal underachievement but also from a 'drag anchor' consisting of long-term unemployment, economic inactivity and high levels of welfare dependency. These problems combine to create not only a burden for society but also an impediment to business. Unemployment is everyone's problem. The apparent short-term advantages for business – an excess supply of labour and low wages – are illusory; in the long run every business pays, through higher taxes, reduced government investment, shortage of skilled workers and problems of social disturbance such as higher crime.

Tackling long-term unemployment is the key to lifting this drag anchor, helping to improve Britain's competitiveness. We must first examine how to prevent short-term unemployment turning into long-term unemployment, and then look for ways of reconnecting those already in long-term unemployment to the labour market. By reducing the social costs of unemployment, we can free resources which could be better employed by business.

Unemployment and Business

Although a firm's fortunes are influenced primarily by the skills and attributes of its management and workforce, general business performance is also affected by external labour-market conditions. Particularly important are the level and persistence of unemployment and the tenor of labour-market regulations. In the UK today, two important – and intertwined – problems stand out: the long-term exclusion of a significant group of the adult population from work, and a substantial increase in wage and income inequality giving rise to another significant group earning wages that do not adequately support them or their families. Both are social problems in their own right, but both also imply a fiscal burden which business cannot entirely escape. This chapter sets out a hard-headed approach for improving labour-market conditions so as to reduce the fiscal burdens on British business.

Should business really be worried about unemployment? In the case of short-term unemployment (defined as less than twelve months), perhaps there is no self-interested or economic reason why it should. High unemployment can offer opportunities for employers, particularly those employing unskilled labour, as firms then have access to a large pool of people eager to find work and a workforce anxious to avoid being out of work. There is also a negative correlation between unemployment and inflation.

The disadvantage for the economy, however, is that when there is an excess supply of labour, there is less need to provide decent terms and conditions in order to attract and retain hard-working employees. The situation also does little to encourage employers to train or value their current workforce, exacerbating the problem of low skills, and it may dull the quest for innovations to raise labour productivity. Finally, excessive levels of unemployment run the danger of seeing many of the short-term unemployed becoming long-term unemployed.

The picture for long-term unemployment (twelve months or more) is substantially different. There are no economic advantages to be gained from long-term unemployment, and there is no effect on the rate of inflation. Long-term unemployment tends to become a spiral for the individuals involved. The longer they are out of work, the harder it is for them to find work; they lose skills and, in any case, employers tend to look less favourably on them as recruitment prospects. The social and fiscal costs associated with long-term unemployment tend to go on and on.

Commentators as diverse as John Philpott of the Employment Policy Institute and Martin Wolf of the *Financial Times* have pointed out the huge cost of high levels of unemployment. Table 7.1 shows that in 1994 unemployment cost the public purse more than £22 billion, or nearly £8,500 per unemployed person. Wolf, describing the situation in the United States, points to other costs for society and business, such as high crime rates which can be readily correlated with long-term unemployment, and particularly to the social exclusion of prime-age men who would ordi-

Table 7.1: Exchequer Cost of UK Unemployment, 1994

Cost	£ million
Benefits	10,003
Administration of benefits	737
Statutory redundancy payments	222
Direct taxes	4,581
Employers' NICs	3,371
Indirect taxes	3,164
Total	22,078
Total per person unemployed: £8,429	

Source: Philpott (1996), Table 7.3.

narily be expected to participate in the labour market.[1] The exclusion problems in Britain are nothing like as great as in the United States, but preventive action is necessary now if we are to save business and social resources in the future.

We need to make sure the short-term unemployed do not become long-term unemployed, with all the costs and disadvantages this entails, and we need to find ways to reintegrate into the labour market those people already in long-term unemployment. In essence, this means expanding employment opportunities for unskilled workers. Alleviating these problems will not itself provide the key to business success. But it is hard to believe that lower unemployment – particularly long-term unemployment – and fewer workers on poverty wages could do anything other than help British business. Our recommendations for improving labour market outcomes also lead us to comment on two highly politicised issues: the minimum wage and the Social Chapter.

Achieving and Sustaining High Employment

Employment is clearly linked to GDP growth. We therefore expect that the Commission's other policy recommendations, designed to increase the UK's sustainable growth rate, will have an effect on job creation.[2] But there are three reasons for believing that higher growth alone will not be enough: the *inflation constraint*, the *long-term unemployment constraint* and *changes in demand for skills*.

Inflation constraint

If unemployment falls too far, inflation will begin to rise, which will contravene another important policy objective, that of low and stable inflation. The lower limit beyond which further declines in unemployment lead to ever-increasing inflation is known as the NAIRU (the Non-Accelerating Inflation Rate of Unemployment). The NAIRU is largely determined by structural factors such as the social security system, pay bargaining arrangements, the mismatch between supply and demand for skills and employment protection legislation. Policies designed to affect these structural factors are often known as 'supply-side measures'.

It is very difficult to determine the level of the NAIRU in advance of seeing the consequences of hitting it. Estimates range from the extremely optimistic one million by Patrick Minford (about 3.5 per cent of the current workforce, defined as the population of working age who are either in work or seeking work) up to 2.25 million (about 8 per cent), which is very close to current unemployment. Minford bases his low estimate of the NAIRU on the fact that there have been significant changes in all the structural factors outlined above since the early 1980s. Other commentators argue that the high level of long-term unemployment – itself a cause of loss of skills and motivation – and a collapse in demand for unskilled workers contribute to a stubbornly high NAIRU.

Long-term unemployment constraint

People who have been unemployed for more than one year are likely to have difficulty finding work even if economic activity is relatively buoyant. Their specific and general skills may have deteriorated or become out of date; even if they have not, they will be regarded with suspicion by many employers. This may make it very difficult to reduce unemployment to desirable levels.

Changes in demand for skills

Evidence from all over the developed world suggests there has been a collapse in the demand for unskilled labour, for two principal reasons: globalisation and rapid technical change. Increased economic growth would no doubt stimulate demand for unskilled workers, but the changing nature of work means that even a sustained period of high growth would be unlikely to absorb them all. Policies should focus in the long term on reducing the numbers of unskilled workers through education and training, but in the short term means should also be found to increase employer demand for unskilled labour.

Reducing Long-Term Unemployment

Although most developed countries have had similar experience of short-term unemployment since the early 1980s, their experiences of long-term unemployment have been quite dissimilar (see Table 7.2). This suggests that to some extent countries can choose their level of long-term unemployment, and that employment policy can play some role in its reduction.

There are several reasons why employment policy should focus on helping the long-term unemployed back into the labour market, and on preventing the short-term unemployed from

Table 7.2: Unemployment Rates in the OECD, 1983–94

Countries	1983–8			1989–94		
	Total	*Long-term*	*Short-term*	*Total*	*Long-term*	*Short-term*
France	9.8	4.4	5.4	10.4	3.9	6.5
Germany	6.8	3.1	3.7	5.4	2.2	3.2
Italy	6.9	3.8	3.1	8.2	5.3	2.9
Spain	19.6	11.3	8.4	18.9	9.7	9.1
Australia	8.4	2.4	5.9	9.0	2.7	6.2
Canada	9.9	0.9	9.0	9.8	0.9	8.9
USA	7.1	0.7	6.4	6.2	0.6	5.6
Japan	2.7	0.4	2.2	2.3	0.4	1.9
Norway	2.7	0.2	2.5	5.5	1.2	4.3
Sweden	2.6	0.3	2.3	4.4	0.4	4.0
UK	**10.9**	**5.1**	**5.8**	**8.9**	**3.4**	**5.5**
Mean	7.9	3.0	5.0	8.1	2.8	5.3
Standard Deviation (SD)	4.7	3.0	2.3	4.2	2.7	2.2
SD/Mean	0.6	1	0.5	0.5	1	0.4

Source: Jackman *et al.* (1996), Table 1.
Note: These figures do not necessarily sum due to rounding.

becoming long-term unemployed. First, as noted, the chances of an unemployed person finding a job diminish rapidly after a few months; the problem gets more intractable the longer it is left. Second, the long-term unemployed and their families are a much more serious drain on the public purse than the short-term unemployed, as they tend to develop poor health and have other social problems. Although data on whether people consider themselves happy are often scorned by economists as meaningless, there is conclusive evidence that persistent unemployment is a major cause of unhappiness (Clark and Oswald, 1994). Finally, in macroeconomic terms the long-term unemployed do little to restrain inflation, whereas employees negotiating with their employers over pay are heavily influenced by the level of and changes in short-term unemployment. Government should therefore be able to reduce long-term unemployment without the risk of stoking up inflation.

The main objective should be to prevent people entering long-term unemployment since it is so much more difficult to help those who have been unemployed for a long time. Therefore, instead of spending billions on benefits paid for doing nothing, we should use the money to get people back into work. The most cost-effective approach would be similar to that followed successfully in Sweden for three decades up to 1990, during which time the unemployment rate there averaged around 2 per cent.[3]

The essence of this approach is a fundamental change of régime, whereby after a year's unemployment anyone still unemployed is offered some form of full-time work; the option of remaining on benefit disappears. In this way those who need help get helped, while those who are able to help themselves cease to be a drain on the public purse. The OECD has in recent years argued strongly for this kind of 'active' approach, while countries as diverse as Denmark, Switzerland and Australia have moved towards it.[4] The key question is what is the best form of help?

The OECD has surveyed extensively the experience of its member countries in trying to help people back into work (Fay, 1995). It concludes that in terms of cost-effectiveness, job-search assistance generally ranks high, followed by recruitment rebates, job-creation projects and adult training (which tends to be the least effective). We would therefore propose an approach with the following features:

- After a person has been unemployed for a year, the Employment Service should have to find them work lasting at least six months, and permanent employment wherever possible.

- The work would ideally be with a regular employer, if possible in the private sector. To encourage employers to give year-long unemployed people a chance, employers would be offered a substantial financial rebate for the first six months.[5] If an employer simply sacked an eligible worker after the rebate ran out, he or she would not be eligible for another one. As the experience of the Workstart pilots has shown,[6] such an inducement would be quite attractive, especially to smaller employers, but it would probably not be enough to generate placements for all the unemployed in question. This problem would be especially severe in high unemployment blackspots, where there would have to be a parallel system of employment on job-creation projects.

- These job-creation projects would be in the non-internationally traded sector, and largely in public services. The jobs could be part-time (to maintain the incentive for these people to find a full-time job) but paid at the going rate so as not to undercut existing workers. The focus would be on additionality, providing services which would not otherwise be provided by a local authority, such as maintaining and repairing the public housing stock, providing more help in running retirement homes and amenities such as parks, swimming pools and libraries. The hope is that once individuals have reacquired both work habits and skills, they will become reintegrated into the labour market and will be able to move away from the subsidised part-time job into regular full-time work.[7]

The advantage of the job-creation approach is that the work being done is clearly additional to work that would have been done anyway. But there are legitimate concerns about how much more employable people would be after passing through such a scheme, especially in the eyes of private-sector employers.

Recruitment rebates, in contrast, are often criticised on the grounds that they simply get jobs for one lot of people at the expense of another, without any increase in total employment. Either the subsidised workers are substituted for others, or the work they do displaces that of workers in other firms who become unemployed. This criticism does not look at the full picture, however; those who are not hired because of substitution or displacement are now available to other employers. These employers now find it easier to fill their vacancies and they create more jobs. This is the standard process of labour-market adjustment, just as when a factory closes the number of jobs elsewhere rises.

The whole process proceeds much more smoothly, of course, if the monetary authorities are in tune with what is happening. When they see that there is less inflationary pressure due to the increased effective supply of labour, their monetary policy should be appropriately eased. If not, there will be more substitution and displacement, at least in the first phases of the programme. When subsidy schemes have been used in recessions, when overall demand for labour is inadequate, rates of substitution or displacement have reached 70 per cent (for every ten subsidised workers who are employed, seven non-subsidised workers lose their jobs). In the long run, substitution and displacement should not be a major offset to the effectiveness of the programme, provided it is well administered and the level of demand in the economy is adequate.

Over the long term the programme should roughly pay for itself through savings in benefits, but in the first five years the net cost could average around £0.7 billion a year, mainly because of the costs of the job-creation scheme.[8] It could also cut unemployment by at least 400,000. A new régime for unemployed people could make a real contribution to reducing the long tail of wasted human capacity in our economy.

Recommendation: An effort should be made to prevent people remaining unemployed for more than a year by using the money saved by not paying their benefits to subsidise job opportunities. A back-up scheme should provide part-time work at a local level for the long-term unemployed.

Jobs for the Unskilled

As well as attempting to reconnect the long-term unemployed to the labour market, there is a strong case for directing policies towards the unskilled. Nickell and Bell (1995) document the changing labour-market fortunes of different educational groups across the OECD. They find that in all countries the increase in unemployment from the early 1970s to the 1980s was markedly greater among the unskilled than among the more highly skilled. In the United Kingdom alone, Nickell estimates that around one-fifth of the increase in total unemployment was due to a shift in demand away from the unskilled. Moreover, in the UK and the USA there was an even more marked increase in non-employment (i.e. inactivity plus unemployment) among the unskilled compared with the skilled than elsewhere (see Table 7.3 for the UK data).

Given the scale of this problem, it must be tackled in a number of different ways. The primary long-term focus should be on converting potentially unskilled workers to skilled ones through education and training. In the short run, however, we need also

Table 7.3: UK Male Unemployment and Non-Employment Rates by Education Level, 1971–92

	1971–4	1975–8	1979–82	1983–6	1987–90	1991	1992
Unemployment							
Total	2.7	3.8	6.9	9.6	7.0	9.0	10.3
High education	0.8	1.6	2.9	3.6	3.1	4.7	5.8
Low education	3.6	5.0	9.8	15.4	12.1	15.2	15.7
Non-employment							
Total	7.9	9.7	14.8	19.9	18.3	20.9	22.6
High education	4.0	5.1	6.8	9.1	8.7	11.5	13.4
Low education	9.8	12.6	20.3	29.7	29.5	32.7	34.7

Source: Nickell and Bell (1995), Table 6.

to find ways to reintegrate currently inactive workers into the labour force.

One reason why nearly one-quarter of prime-age males are inactive is because the wages on offer to them in the labour market are simply too low to make it worth their while to come off social security, especially if they have families and mortgages (Shaw and Walker, 1996). One means of counteracting this inactivity trap would be to allow these people to retain a larger proportion of their benefit when entering work; in other words, through in-work benefits. This would ensure that working actually provides an increase in income, thus making work a more attractive prospect. This approach is being followed by the present government, which provides family credit for the low-paid with children and is currently piloting an extension of this benefit to the childless. There seems to be little alternative to this approach, and to reduce long-term unemployment it is probably necessary to increase in-work benefits and to reduce the rate at which they are withdrawn as income rises.

There is, however, an inherent danger in this policy. Some employers will use the opportunity offered by benefits to reduce already low wages in the knowledge that these wages will be topped up by benefits. If in-work benefits increase labour supply, low wages could get pushed even lower. Tax-payers would pick up the tab of ensuring that everyone in work could make a living. This is a classic case of welfare payments creating adverse incentives (in this case to employers) which result in the welfare bill becoming self-inflating. The state is pouring water into a bucket with no bottom. The much-discussed minimum wage for adult workers would be one means of preventing benefit abuse and one can therefore think of the minimum wage as putting the bottom back in the bucket of in-work benefits.

The national minimum wage has become a subject of intense controversy in Britain and, unfortunately, has become politicised. We have adopted a pragmatic approach to this issue. It is worth remembering that only four years ago the United Kingdom had a fairly uncontroversial system of minimum wages in the form of the wages councils, which covered 2.5 million workers. Now the UK is the only country in the EU to have neither a statutory minimum wage nor one fixed by collective agreement. Even the United States, despite the general absence of labour-market regulation, has a minimum wage. Nevertheless, many business leaders do fear that a minimum wage would damage competitiveness and destroy jobs.

There is a clear case for a minimum wage in combination with benefit reform, as outlined above, but it must be balanced against the risk that such a measure could cost jobs in low-paid sectors if set too high. It would also be wrong to insist that trainees (employed under our mandatory traineeship scheme proposed in Chapter 6) should be paid the adult minimum wage. When determining the level of a minimum wage, therefore, policy-makers need to weigh up these elements carefully. Consultation with representatives of employers, employees and the unemployed should facilitate this process.

Recommendation: The government should extend in-work benefits for low-income workers to combat the unemployment-benefit trap, but a minimum wage should be introduced to prevent this being exploited by unscrupulous employers at the taxpayers' expense. The minimum wage should not be set too high since it could destroy jobs in some sectors.

The Social Chapter

Most employers are hostile to the Social Chapter, which they believe will import into the UK the high non-wage labour costs found in a number of continental countries. The discussion of the Social Chapter is characterised by widespread ignorance, however, and there is further confusion over EU social policy in general. For example, given that the United Kingdom has opted out of the Social Chapter, why has there been so much controversy at European level over the Working Time Directive? The answer is because a large part of the argument has revolved around which social-policy issues are covered by the Social Chapter and which are not; the Working Time Directive is only one example. In an attempt to reduce confusion, we have set out in the Appendix (p. 198) how EU social-policy-making currently works and how it will work in the future.

Some have argued that the Social Chapter will encourage better employee relations through its consultation measures and, by closing the route to a low-wage, low-skill economy, force the United Kingdom to compete through raising skills and the quality of output. Any policy of raising costs is dangerous and can be easily overdone. We must, however, consider the costs and benefits in a broader political context, and our approach here will parallel that suggested in Chapter 10 when considering EMU.

There is some risk that the United Kingdom's continued opt-out from the Social Chapter will undermine our position in the Single Market, which requires certain minimum agreed standards if it is to operate properly. If we want the benefits of the Single Market, then we may have to accept consensus-based decisions on agreed standards in certain areas. To take a hypothetical example, UK chemical companies would complain if another member country unilaterally opted out of EU environmental legislation in order to protect dirty domestic producers. We must expect a similar European reaction to 'social dumping'.

To be sure, social protection in a number of European countries goes further than many in the UK consider reasonable or desirable. This is the result of national, not EU, legislation, but there is a risk that in future the Social Chapter could be used to increase employment costs throughout the Union. Does incompatibility among countries on social issues mean the Single Market is doomed? We are not so pessimistic. There is increasing recognition in the Commission and in other member states that some aspects of EU social regulation may be damaging competitiveness. It is more likely that national measures will be scaled back rather than extended through the EU. The United Kingdom is not able to take part in these debates at policy level since it is excluded from Social Chapter discussions. If we were at the table, our voice would reinforce those arguing for liberalisation. We judge it improbable, therefore, that the Social Chapter would ultimately impose continental costs on the UK. Certainly at present it would not, since those costs are the result of purely national legislation or taxation.

There is some justification for arguing that the current provisions of the Social Chapter, such as the European Works Council Directive, are desirable since they promote employee involvement. It is also true, however, that most businesses would prefer to have the freedom to determine their own structures for such involvement and other employment issues. On balance, though, the benefits of the Single Market far outweigh any current or probable costs of the Social Chapter. The decision about whether to end the opt-out is predominantly a political one. There is no need to rush the fence, but, if opting in is the only way to preserve the Single Market and Britain's influence in its construction, we would advocate signing up.

Recommendation: In order to preserve the EU Single Market and to influence the future development of European social policy, the UK should opt in to the Social Chapter.

Conclusion

Unemployment, especially long-term unemployment, is not just a social problem. It has important knock-on effects for business. Higher growth alone will not solve the problem of unemployment. Long-term unemployment must therefore be tackled on two fronts: the short-term unemployed should be prevented from becoming long-term unemployed, and the long-term unemployed need to be reconnected to the labour force. With this in mind the government should act to prevent people entering long-term unemployment by using the savings on benefits as a means to stimulate job opportunities. There should be two parallel approaches. Any employer hiring someone unemployed for over twelve months would receive a financial rebate for the first six months of the job, and there would be socially useful job-creation projects which employ people part-time for at least one year to help them become more attractive to regular employers. Although the long-term focus must be on converting unskilled workers into skilled workers through training, in the short term it is also important to find ways of sustaining their income in work, especially if we wish to reintegrate those who are currently inactive. In-work benefits are probably the best option, though they can result in lower wages. A minimum wage is necessary to prevent wage subsidies being exploited by unscrupulous employers, but if set too high it could destroy jobs in some sectors. A government committed to introducing a minimum wage must consult with business to avoid any damage to competitiveness. Informed discussion is needed on the issue of the Social Chapter and if opting in is the only way that Britain can influence developments in EU labour-market regulation, and to maintain our position in the Single Market, we should do so.

APPENDIX

Rough Guide to EU Social Policy

1 The Single European Act (SEA) of 1987 provided a legislative framework for the Single Market, and included various treaty articles attempting to harmonise minimum social standards across the market. All twelve member countries agreed at this time that a single market required some level playing field in social arrangements.

2 These standards were to be introduced by qualified majority voting (QMV) if concerned with health and safety issues, but by unanimity on other areas of employment (or social) policy. Under the SEA, a number of different directives have been brought forward, including ones on working time, part-time and temporary work, maternity rights and European Works Councils (EWCs). Some of these have been ratified by the Council of Ministers, but others have not, often because of a British veto.

3 After reviewing progress under the SEA, the draft Treaty of the European Union (or Maastricht Treaty) contained a chapter to widen the ambit of QMV on social policy. The UK government blocked this chapter, however, and so instead the Treaty

contains an annex, the 'Protocol on Social Policy', which has become known as the Social Chapter.

4 Although it is rather more complicated in reality, in simple terms the Protocol allows the other eleven (now fourteen) member states to adopt common social regulations by QMV on health and safety, working conditions, information for and consultation of workers, gender equality and the integration of persons excluded from the labour market. On other issues unanimity of the fourteen is required: these include employee representation, social security and protection against dismissal. Certain aspects of social legislation, such as pay and the right to strike, are excluded from EU competence altogether.

5 The Maastricht Treaty now sets out a dual approach to EU social policy. If the Commission wants to bring forward a new directive in the social policy area, it can first try to obtain unanimity under the old SEA provisions (or by QMV if a health and safety issue). If this route fails, it can then bring the directive forward under the Social Chapter for the other fourteen member states to vote by QMV. Given the UK government's current reluctance to go along with social legislation, most directives can only go through the Social Chapter route.

6 The Working Time Directive has been passed under the first track by QMV as a health and safety issue and therefore applies to the UK, whereas the EWC directive has been passed under the Social Chapter and therefore does not apply here.

NOTES

1 *Financial Times* (30 April 1996).

2 Although some of the recommendations, such as those on education and training, by increasing labour productivity will probably increase the sustainable growth rate without job creation.

3 For details see Layard and Philpott (1991), chapter 4. For evidence that this policy reduced unemployment by at least 2 percentage points see Jackman *et al.* (1996).

4 See OECD (1990:8), Schwanse (1995) and Government of Australia (1994). Commission of the European Communities (1993:18–19) also provides strong support for the approach.

5 The costings given later assume £75 a week (or £60 if under 25).

6 See Atkinson and Meager (1994). The Employment Committee (1996b) expressed strong support for Workstart; see for example p. li.

7 For a detailed analysis of this approach see Holtham and Mayhew (1996).

8 See Layard (1996) which analyses and costs this proposal (allowing also for a guaranteed offer for those under 25 once unemployed for over 6 months rather than a year). A scheme that relied exclusively on job-creation is estimated by Holtham and Mayhew (1996) to cost £1.3 billion a year.

PART THREE

FRAMEWORK

8

STRENGTHENING SCIENCE, TRANSPORT AND PUBLIC PROCUREMENT

The science base, transport and public procurement represent direct ways in which government sets the framework for business. An adequate science base is an essential foundation for innovation. Transport infrastructure is important to competitiveness, and a far-sighted approach to public procurement can promote innovation and quality. We pick out these aspects from other governmental responsibilities because we believe they have unexploited potential to improve national competitiveness if the government acts for the long term in parallel with our proposals for far-sighted companies.

In areas like taxation and infrastructure, the government sets the national framework within which business operates. In Chapters 9 and 10 we look at the effects of taxation and the macroeconomic environment on business performance; in this chapter we consider three specific areas where government can do more to promote business competitiveness. We concentrate on basic science research, transport and procurement policies, where there is room for improvement. Other forms of infrastructure are also important responsibilities of government, but we have no wish to fix what is not broken. While there are certainly live issues in the regulation of telecommunications and energy provision, for example, we judge that in these areas the United Kingdom is relatively well served.

The Science Base

One of the most frequently identified constraints on the competitive performance of the United Kingdom as a whole is its relatively poor record of innovation. There are two aspects to the problem. First, the UK's record of invention has been creditable, but now there is concern that underfunding of the science base may curtail it. Second, there have always been deficiencies in the commercial exploitation of British inventions by British business. Other OECD countries, such as Japan, Germany and the United States, have been more successful.

The relationship between the science base and commercial exploitation is an intricate one. We do not subscribe to the simple, linear view of innovation, in which science spending leads directly to invention and then on to commercial exploitation. On the contrary, many inventions are 'user-led' – the result of demand by consumers and business customers for new products or services – and occur within a commercial setting. We can begin to examine the nature of this complex relationship between the science base and competitiveness by looking at the comparative picture.

Innovation, in the sense of the development and exploitation of new products and new processes, is generally measured by proxy through R&D spending by firms. Innovation is, of course, much more than this narrow measure and can involve all a company's operations from marketing to design. But other aspects of innovation are hard to measure, whereas we can compare inter-country performance in R&D relatively easily. In terms of total R&D spending as a proportion of GDP, the UK ranked fifth out of the G7 countries in 1993 (OECD, 1995b). This compares unfavourably with 1981, when the UK was a close third behind the United States and (West) Germany. Moreover, of all the G7 countries, only the United Kingdom has seen a trend decline in the percentage of GDP spent on R&D over this period.

Although the government has a variety of instruments for influencing innovation, support for the science base is one of the most direct. Public scientific research, whether carried out by universities or government institutions, is referred to as either 'basic' (without any particular direct application, though possibly leading to innovations at a later date) or 'applied' (for a general or specific application or innovation). Many of the government's recent policy initiatives have focused, rightly, on increasing the interaction of higher education and firms and on identifying wealth-creating research. But this shift in priorities has resulted in reduced support for basic research. This, in turn, has had a dramatic effect on one, albeit highly partial and imperfect, measure of research excellence: Nobel prizes. Figure 8.1 shows how Britain's former success has fallen away. Not included in the chart is the 1996 Nobel Prize for Chemistry shared by Sir Harold Kroto of the University of Sussex. Hours before hearing of his award, his application for public funding – for research in the same area as the prize – was turned down. With mixed feelings, he commented in the *Independent*, 'Fundamental science in this country is now below its survival threshold. It used to be 14 per cent of funding . . . now it's more like 5 per cent.'

Figure 8.1: Britain's Nobel Prizes, 1946–95

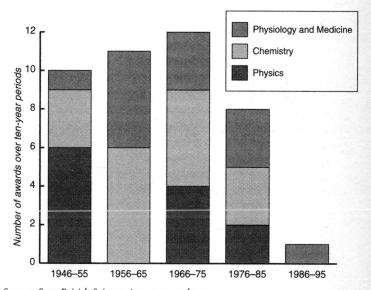

Source: Save British Science, in correspondence.

Why the science base is important

Open-ended research without a commercial goal is a vital source of future innovative ideas and new industries. Examples include the discovery of the double helix, which led to the biotechnology industry, and the research in solid-state physics, which underpins microelectronics. Because of the risks involved and the long lead times before possible commercial exploitation, pure scientific research is precisely the type most likely to be under-resourced if it is solely dependent upon commercial funds. That is why government finance is essential, and equally why government should not succumb to short-termism in its own research policies.

One counter-argument is that the United Kingdom can import science and concentrate on the application of others' research. We reject this. The reasons for maintaining a broad span of national basic science research are compelling:

- Innovations draw increasingly on multi-disciplinary science. It is therefore important to maintain a science base in a diversity of disciplines, not only for firms to draw upon but also to facilitate multi-disciplinary research.

- The benefits of basic research are contained to some extent within national boundaries. The knowledge produced by basic research is often tacit and non-codifiable. A diverse science base provides access to and ability to use international findings.

- New technologies can alter markets or create completely new industries.

- Basic research provides trained scientists and researchers for industry, together with new tools and techniques which can be used to solve complex problems.

Technology Foresight has been useful in bringing together a variety of players to analyse future potential developments, but this should not deteriorate into a policy of picking winners in basic research (where the exercise is even harder than forecasting market trends). Setting up future research orientations by this method is useful for focusing the attention of business and providing collaborative links between academics and business people, but it should not be used to direct all basic funding, so detracting from a wide knowledge base.

Getting the balance right

In supporting innovation, government has a twofold role. First, it should ensure that public science is properly funded so as to maintain and enhance the science base. Second, it needs to ensure that funding is divided in an appropriate manner between basic and applied research.

Funding for the science base covers research carried out in higher education and government research institutes. There are no direct statistics for such spending which are comparable across countries and none which distinguish between pure and applied, but two indicators illustrate the trends particularly well. The

Figure 8.2: Public Funding of Higher Education R&D, 1993

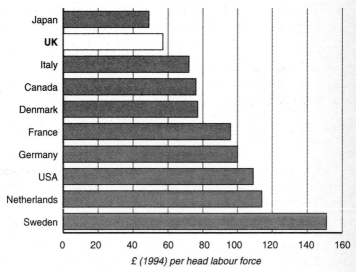

£ (1994) per head labour force

Source: Save British Science, in correspondence.
Note: Data for Sweden refer to 1991.

public funding of higher education R&D covers both pure and applied research. Figure 8.2 shows that the United Kingdom spends less per head of the labour force on higher education R&D than all of our significant competitors except Japan. With pressure from business, Japan has recently made a commitment to double its government spending on R&D (Save British Science, 1996) which will leave the UK languishing at the bottom of this league.

Government civil (non-military) R&D covers both higher education and government research. The trend over time (Figure 8.3) shows that the UK's spending has steadily decreased as a percentage of GDP between 1981 and 1993, and has risen only a little in absolute terms. Public funding of higher education research would now have to increase by over 40 per cent of its current total to reach the average percentage of GDP for the United States, Germany, Italy or Holland (Save British Science, 1996).

There has been a marked reorientation of spending away from pure research towards applied work aimed specifically at product market developments. This is illustrated particularly by Tech-

Figure 8.3: Government Civil R&D Spending as a Percentage of GDP, 1981–93

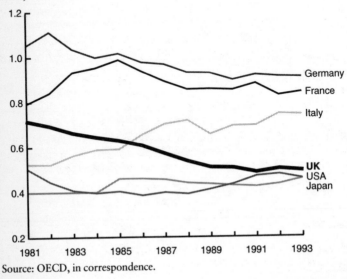

Source: OECD, in correspondence.

nology Foresight, which brings together industrialists, scientists, engineers and civil servants 'to identify opportunities in markets and technologies likely to emerge during the next 10–20 years, and the actions which will be needed to exploit them' (Office of Science and Technology [OST], 1995: I). This initiative follows a market-driven approach, aiming first to identify future markets and then to identify the technologies and related scientific research which should underpin them. Fifteen panels investigated different sectors and made recommendations for government support to business, basic research priorities and action by business itself. Another example of the emphasis on applied science funding is that of the Ropas research grants, which are available only to those who have received funding from business; these accounted for £15 million of the £150 million of research council money targeted to new work in 1996 (Save British Science, 1996). While we welcome this focus on applied research and believe that these initiatives should be used to influence business R&D strategy and lead to collaborative ventures between firms and higher education, we also believe that the government should not reduce its commitment to basic research.

In 1993 support for the public funding of higher education R&D was 0.25 per cent of GDP, whereas the average for the rest of the G7 countries was 0.32 per cent (Save British Science, 1996). We propose that UK government spending should increase over the next few years to reach and maintain the average for our competitors. This would currently require a spending increase of about £500 million per annum in current prices.

We are of course calling for an increase in public expenditure at a time when fiscal retrenchment is generally required, but this spending on the science base is a priority. Adequate resources are necessary to keep our most talented scientists in the country, and their work and presence can serve as the base for much other scientific and technical activity.

Recommendation: The government should increase spending on the public science base to the average of the UK's main competitors.

Transport

Whether it be London traffic moving little faster than in the days of the horse and cart, or the often-remarked contrast between the French TGV to Calais and the quaint British rail link from Folkestone to London, there is no shortage of examples of the inadequacy of UK transport. These problems are currently an irritant; they must not grow to threaten British competitiveness.

Improvements in transport infrastructure would help to increase the attractiveness of the United Kingdom as a place to do business, and would improve the efficiency of distribution and services. The key problem to be tackled is urban congestion, which creates difficulties for many companies. The solution must involve action both to improve the management of the supply of transport services, and to regulate demand for travel.

Since congestion is a worldwide problem, there are opportunities here for a forward-looking government and the private sector to develop solutions which will have international application and commercial value (OST, 1995). The correct balance between competition and co-operation in transport provision is vital. The deregulation and privatisation of transport services is potentially beneficial where competition can provide choice, reduce costs and improve focus on consumer needs, but without some public co-ordination of these services there is real potential for damaging market failure.

We believe that the government should tackle the causes of congestion by a combination of a more coherent transport strategy, urban road pricing and improved integration between different forms of transport. As well as providing direct benefits for many British companies, our recommendations will provide a boost to innovation in the transport, information and communication industries. Innovative solutions developed in this country could become valuable earners in export markets.

Transport and business

In arguing for changes in transport policy, it is important not to exaggerate the importance of transport to business. Transport accounts on average for only about 5–7 per cent of a company's total costs, and even large one-off increases in fuel prices, for example, are unlikely significantly to affect the performance of more than a small proportion of companies (CBI, 1995b). Most companies are small, and 50 per cent of all goods move less than 30 miles (80 per cent move less than 100 miles) (Lee, 1995). In some industries, however, transport can account for as much as 50 per cent of costs, and there is a variety of indirect costs associated with congestion and pollution.

The ever-increasing transport congestion in Britain, particularly in London and the south-east, has become a major focus of concern. Most commentators and policy-makers now recognise that increases in road traffic congestion are a real threat to both business performance and the attractiveness of the United Kingdom as a place to invest. Congestion affects business performance by reducing the reliability of the delivery of goods and services, both nationally and internationally. One of the consequences is that companies must then carry higher levels of stock than necessary as insurance against unreliability. This problem is particularly acute at a time when more and more businesses are employing just-in-time production methods. Congestion also makes commuting by employees more difficult, and detracts from the quality of the environment where the business is located. The CBI has estimated that congestion costs British business around £15 billion a year (CBI, 1995b).

The main cause of congestion involves the movement of people rather than freight. In the last half-century there has been a threefold increase in passenger traffic, but only a doubling in freight traffic. Figure 8.4 shows recent trends in the growth of freight and passenger traffic relative to GDP. On present trends, road traffic could nearly double by 2025 according to the Royal Commission on Environmental Pollution (RCEP, 1994).

The trends show that the demand for and use of cars increases as people become more affluent. In the United Kingdom, even more than our neighbours in the rest of Europe, we have become dependent on private cars. Car mileage per person in the UK is higher than in any other EU country, despite a lower level of car ownership (RCEP, 1994). In addition, 60 per cent of car journeys

Figure 8.4: Growth in Passenger and Freight Traffic and GDP in the UK, 1952–94

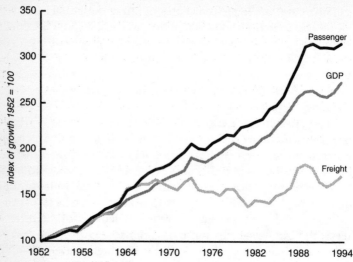

Source: CBI (1995b), Exhibit 7.

in the UK are under five miles in length. There are several reasons for this high level of car usage, including commuting, which is increasing as people move out of town centres; the inflexibility of public transport routes and their perceived lack of safety; and the 'school run'.

Congestion is also the result of substantial underinvestment in transport infrastructure. The level of this underinvestment is clearly visible when we look at our major competitors. For example, between 1985 and 1993 the United Kingdom invested 60 per cent less than Germany and 25 per cent less than France in transport infrastructure (CBI, 1995b). In order for the UK to catch up, the CBI suggests that a further investment of £2 billion per year is required across all transport modes. It also argues that the balance of investment should shift away from roads towards core rail links, urban rail, inter-modal links, airports, seaports and transport research and development.

One of the most significant shortfalls has been in investment in rail infrastructure, and it remains to be seen whether rail privatisation will help to rectify this deficiency. More generally, under-investment has meant that our transport infrastructure has failed to reflect changes in economic geography and the requirements of industries wishing to export. Specific problems include deficiencies in links between the west and the east coast ports, and the failure to connect Heathrow airport to the intercity rail network.

The solution to these problems requires certain limited additions to Britain's road infrastructure, along with substantial investment in other transport modes. There is no good case for increasing investment in the road infrastructure to try to match the projected increase in road traffic; the experience of the M25 has convinced many that simply building more roads does not solve traffic problems. Expanding supply merely causes demand to rise even faster than it otherwise would (SACTRA, 1994).

The recent White Paper, *Transport: The Way Forward* (Department of Transport, 1996) indicated a significant shift in policy. Whereas Mrs Thatcher had famously championed roads and private cars as the only real future for transport in Britain, the current government is taking a very different view. The White Paper proposed various measures to improve the planning of infrastructure, reduce the environmental impact of transport by cutting car dependency, improve interchanges between transport modes, use pricing signals where possible as the basis of efficient choice, and switch some spending from roads to public transport. We applaud this change in policy, but much remains to be done to ensure that the new approach is effectively translated into practice.

One of the key areas for investment in the UK must be the creation of an integrated transport system where each type of transport, for both passengers and freight, links well with others. Many other European countries seem to have achieved a better pattern of efficient inter-modal links. Britain's failings in this area are the result of a piecemeal approach to policy and unco-ordinated privatisation plans. We set out below a view of how this might be rectified, with three key recommendations for change in transport policy, and urge that these become a corner-stone of any future transport strategy.

Transport strategy

A long-term national transport strategy would provide a more reliable framework for all businesses to invest and plan for the future. It would encourage investment in new transport infrastructure, and would provide clear incentives for some companies to commit resources to research and development. Examples could include telematics and smart card technology to help manage both supply and demand for transport, and new mass transit vehicles and clean engine technologies to respond to changes in taxation or regulation. A national transport strategy should include the following elements:

- *Outcome targets*. There should be a range of targets, at both national and local levels, for the usage of different modes of transport and pollution levels. We believe that indicators should be developed which measure reliability of journey time, as this is particularly important for business and would provide a measure of how successful the government has been in tackling road congestion.

- *Investment plans*. The government should state its plans for transport investment, both to set the framework for private sector investment (perhaps through a Private Finance Investment-style arrangement) and to achieve its specified targets. Given evidence of recent underinvestment in transport infrastructure, we would like to see a commitment to a significant real increase in transport investment over a period of years. Such plans should also take into account strategic transport needs, with a particular focus on improving access to export markets. This would require limited extensions and improvements to the road and rail networks in order to improve connections with ports, airports and European rail terminals, along with more effective regional airports. We would also like to see a shift in investment away from roads (other than for maintenance and limited additions to the network) and towards improvements in other forms of transport infrastructure.

- *Plans for transport integration*. The government should set out its strategy to integrate the physical transport system, using

214

rail stations as the major transit points. This will also require the co-ordination of information collection and provision across transport modes in order to provide complete travel services and through-ticketing. Our proposals in this area are set out more fully below.

- *Plans for fiscal and pricing structures.* In order to allow businesses to plan ahead, the government should set out in advance its plans for fiscal and pricing structures associated with changes in transport policy. For example, the government should announce in advance any plans for urban road pricing (which we favour) so that companies are given sufficient time to reconsider their own transport arrangements.

- *Local implementation plans.* The government should be clear about the level – national, regional or local – at which transport is planned and implemented. We favour legislative changes to allow increased powers for either Passenger Transport Associations or local authorities to use a range of instruments such as road pricing and parking restrictions to achieve outcome targets. There should also be a wide range of community interests involved, including those of business, in transport decision-making.

> **Recommendation:** The government should set out a coherent statement of the principles and targets of its transport strategy.

Road pricing

We looked at a variety of methods of reducing urban congestion and concluded that, in some urban centres, road pricing should be used as one method to manage demand. Road pricing would make costs reflect the actual use of roads, which fixed costs such as road tax or vehicle excise duty do not do. Costs would then better reflect the social and environmental impact of road use and remove the bias against other transport modes which have fewer externalities.

The ultimate objective should be a system where vehicles are electronically tagged, and charges are then made according to such factors as the time of day, distance travelled and geographical area. Given the technical difficulties of achieving this, however, there is a strong case for local trials using supplementary road licences. For example, those wishing to operate a car in central London would have to pay for and display a second tax disk on their windscreen. Drivers wanting to bring their vehicles into the controlled area for a short period of time would be able to buy a disk from garages and shops. These disks could easily be valid for hours, days, weeks or months.

The main disadvantage of supplementary licences over electronic charging is that they provide no discouragement to repeat journeys once someone has purchased a licence; in other words, they become another fixed cost. Also, where these have been implemented (for example in Singapore), there has been a high incidence of fraud and great difficulties in policing the system (British Road Federation, 1995).

A recent comprehensive assessment of the effects of electronic road pricing in London found that there would be significant economic savings from both reduced journey times and increased reliability of travel time (MVA Consultancy, 1995). The study also projected increased bus usage, and overcrowding on trains unless capacity was increased. The impact of road pricing obviously depends on the level of charges. For example, if there was a simple £4 daily charge, traffic volumes in central London would decline by 15 per cent, traffic speeds would increase by 20 per cent and harmful vehicle emissions would drop by 35 per cent. The revenue gains would be substantial. For example, a cordon around central London would yield £270 million per annum while an extension to cover inner London could yield £460 million (MVA Consultancy, 1995).

As with any radical reform, road pricing would be unpopular at first, and a vigorous and positive information programme would be required. Much of the opposition to road pricing is on the grounds that those living nearest to a charge barrier would be hardest hit and the system could be regressive. However, the negative impact could be offset by giving a ration of 'free' use and by tailoring charges to car engine size. The benefits of road pricing lie largely in the impact on car use and road congestion, but the revenue collected could also be used to improve the transport system. In order to minimise effects on the competitiveness of London and the impact on users, there is a strong case for using the collected road licence fees to improve public transport and improve road quality.

> **Recommendation:** The management of demand for road use in some urban areas should involve road pricing.

Integrated transport network

In order to make public transport more attractive and to encourage the use of a variety of transport modes for freight, Britain needs significantly better inter-modal linkages. These linkages require not only an adequate physical infrastructure, but also a system whereby the traveller or user can access information about an entire journey from start to destination and then buy a through ticket. Inter-modal linkages are as much about the co-ordination of information about transport services as about direct links between the services themselves. There are examples of effective inter-modal links in Britain, such as the rail link between Gatwick airport and Victoria Station with connections to both the London Underground system and inter-city coach services; but even this case suffers from the lack of combined tickets and information. Elsewhere there are such significant gaps in the physical transport system that inter-modal linkages are impossible. There needs to be much greater emphasis on co-ordination, both between modes and between the public and private sector, in realising target outcomes.

As well as co-ordination between transport modes, there also needs to be greater co-ordination within modes. For example, the privatisation of Britain's bus services seems to have resulted in a poor and unco-ordinated network. This could have been averted if there had been some attempt to ensure a reasonably ordered structure of bus-service provision across local areas, and a requirement for bus companies to submit information on services to a central organisation in order to ensure co-ordinated travel information schemes. The experience of bus privatisation is clearly of concern as rail privatisation progresses, and it suggests that there should be a requirement for private train operators to guarantee through-ticketing and to provide real-time information on services.

The way in which such co-ordination happens could be the product of agreement between companies, but generally the local authority or Passenger Transport Authority is pivotal in ensuring such co-operation and all the more so where different transport modes are being linked. Whether or not these developments occur via regulation (which may be difficult given the differences between, say, urban and rural transport requirements), in all cases there is the need for a constructive public-private partnership. One example is the Confederation of Passenger Transport UK's idea of Quality Partnerships, which are 'formalised agreements between bus operators and local authorities to raise the quality of the nation's bus services' (Confederation of Passenger Transport, 1996). In exchange for bus operators agreeing to certain standards, information provision and through-ticketing, for example, local authorities would provide, say, inter-modal infrastructure or bus priority lanes.

In order to achieve a rationalised system in which an individual has access to information on all transport services and can choose on the basis of timely information (including delays and interchange times), information from all modes would have to be co-ordinated centrally or by regional bodies. The ultimate objective for policy in this area should be that envisaged by the Technology Foresight panel on transport: 'integrated travel information, ticketing, booking and payment facilities seamlessly across all passenger transport modes, updated in real time to reflect the actual state of services (on bus, rail, air etc.)' (OST, 1995:4).

For passenger services, the government has already set in place an initiative for managing national train information. This system needs to be expanded, and must involve regulation to guarantee the provision of such information from rail and other transport service providers. Ideally, rail and bus franchises should have a common IT framework to enable easier information management. In addition, a central Travel Authority may be required to co-ordinate the collection of such data and ensure through-ticketing.

For freight services, there is a need to identify major freight routes and inter-modal links across all transport modes, especially road to rail and sea. For example, alongside maintenance and limited additions to the main trunk network, there are several ways in which full utilisation of rail for freight could be realised. Examples are the development of multi-modal facilities and freight depots with the use of continental-style rail wagons or 'piggybacks' capable of moving loads from trailers to rail with great ease.

The value of improved inter-modal links lies not only in reducing congestion and increasing speed and efficiency of delivery for business, but also in opportunities for companies involved in helping to develop such links. The Technology Foresight panel argued that the development of technology for inter-modal linkages, environmentally friendly vehicles, new urban freight distribution systems and rapid transit systems would have huge export potential (OST, 1995). Examples of specific technologies include automatic vehicle location equipment, network management and control technologies (e.g. sensors, incident detection), smart cards, and information terminals and displays.

Recommendation: There should be increased emphasis on inter-modal linkages for freight and passenger transport.

Public Procurement

In 1993 £74 billion (15 per cent of GDP) was spent by local and central government on purchasing goods and services from the private sector (DTI, 1994:154). There are reasons to believe that public procurement could be better used to stimulate innovation and improve the quality of products in British companies. But changes in this area must be part of a general strategy for reducing costs and increasing the quality of government services through good procurement.

Procurement and innovation

This chapter has already emphasised the importance of the science base in promoting innovation in firms – the supply of innovative

219

ideas – and the importance of the transport system, where government intervention could stimulate a market for new products and techniques. This example can be generalised because the government can support innovation by raising the quality of its own demand in other areas. But this would involve changes to public procurement practices.

The great majority of innovations are 'user-led' in that they result from high-quality demand from customers and their ideas for products and processes. Michael Porter's investigation of what makes some countries more competitive than others reveals the importance of sophisticated demand – in other words, a clear specification of needs and requirements by customers – in promoting new and improved products and processes (Porter, 1990). Regarding government policy, if a healthy science base pushes innovation from behind, high-quality procurement can help to pull it in the direction of the market.

Paul Geroski of London Business School claims that public procurement can have greater beneficial effects on stimulating the production of innovatory products than R&D subsidies. It can be used 'to create a demand for new products or processes, or at least to make latent consumer demands more manifest' (Geroski, 1990:182). He argues that beneficial effects come from a variety of sources: the provision of an early testing ground for new products and processes; the specification of demand beyond current capabilities; the articulation of clear user needs; and the development of rigorous and high-level standards. Several international studies back up Geroski's conclusions. One examined government involvement in fifty clusters of innovations and showed procurement to have had a significant effect on the emergence of half, with subsidies only influencing four out of the total. Examples of industries affected were electronics, synthetic materials and new chemicals; procurement had less effect in mechanical, electrical and instrument engineering and basic materials (Lichtenberg, 1988).

An important example of the impact which government can have on a sector can be found in IT and communication technologies, where government itself is the largest single buyer. The decisions of government buyers can have a significant effect on the promotion of common standards and can influence the number of users through government's own interaction with business and the public. These are important factors in the development of critical mass in the use of multimedia products, for example, and underpin our proposal in Chapter 6 for the government to promote the market in educational services through an open learning agency. A more enterprising approach has also the potential to cut government's own costs. A study of the G7 countries calculated that implementing new information technologies could lead to savings of 10–15 per cent in government costs. The government of Singapore, which has for some time concentrated on the re-engineering of government processes and potential gains in efficiency and productivity, estimates a return of $2.71 on every dollar it has spent on IT (House of Lords, 1996).

Just how strongly and successfully government can affect an innovating industry through procurement can be seen in the case of the US semiconductor industry, which developed in response to the high standard of military requirements. The history of UK procurement, however, has been replete with expensive failures through the attempted promotion of 'big science'. A number of the great public expenditure disasters, from the fast-breeder reactor to Concorde, were justified by the assertion of enormous gains from stimulating markets and a false belief in the value of their technological spin-offs. It may now be that, as a reaction to this history, civil servants are programmed to seek least-cost solutions and not to explore the potential benefits of innovative solutions to government needs.

Porter (1990) spelt out the main reasons for the failure of procurement as being a guaranteed market, the exclusion of foreign suppliers and a propensity to buy products solely from national suppliers. In order to promote innovation and competition and hence products that can compete internationally, foreign companies should not be excluded from tenders. Recent international and EU legislation prohibits such discrimination and the UK government should strongly monitor its effectiveness for our own suppliers trying to enter foreign markets.

Current policy

On the face of it, the government recently moved in the direction we propose with significant policy initiatives aimed at increasing the training of procurement officials and focusing on the promotion of supplier competitiveness (Treasury, 1995a). Procurement has been described as a chance to 'improve quality, assist innovation, reduce costs, set standards, and provide a shop window for world sales' (Treasury, 1994). Recent policy changes include the development of a Central Unit on Procurement, which aims to improve departmental performance through an interdepartmental procurement strategy and training for procurement officials leading to a Certificate of Competence. In addition, the Treasury has recently acknowledged the importance of whole-life-cost analysis of potential government investments in order to promote savings over the lifetime of a service or product rather than focusing only on initial cost and its impact on the current balance sheet. However, this practice is not widespread and, in the view of a variety of experts, decisions are made primarily on lowest cost and through an adversarial approach to suppliers. Hence, despite the advertised policy changes, which specify innovation as a goal, we do not believe that there has been much change in practice.

We are not alone in our concerns. The CBI has argued that a large gap between rhetoric and reality has resulted in many companies being unwilling to risk providing innovative solutions, or indeed to enter the tendering process at all:

> It has proved impossible to track down case studies of Departments taking up innovative ideas, despite the many proposals which have been presented to Government departments. This speaks for itself. Companies whose innovative ideas have not been pursued view part of the problem as Departments' insistence on carrying out 'apples with apples' bid comparisons, perhaps because that most safely demonstrates compliance with procurement legislation (CBI, 1995c:4).

One aspect of innovation is design, and a recent paper by the Social Market Foundation highlighted, first, the importance of design to streamline production processes, cut run-on costs and improve profitability and, second, the lack of such considerations in most public procurement decisions in the United Kingdom. The report's authors, Raymond and Shaw (1996:2), conclude that 'despite efforts to influence the private sector, it is clear that the government is not taking its own use of design and design practice seriously'.

Changing the focus of procurement

We believe that there are several ways in which procurement could be made more open to innovative solutions, both to promote new markets and, eventually, to cut government spending on goods and services. There should be incremental improvement in existing products or services – through good design or applications of new techniques – rather than huge leaps forward in technology.

The focus of procurement policy must be shifted away from purely short-term considerations towards innovative solutions capable of achieving long-term cost savings and promoting the competitiveness of British business. Such a change in behaviour will inevitably involve an element of risk for the government, and will require better training for procurement staff.

Just as for far-sighted companies, a far-sighted government should keep the correct balance between co-operation and competition and hence adopt best practice customer-supplier relations. For example, Porter (1990) cites the case of Danish medical products, which are highly innovative partly because the national health service provides free clinical testing of some new products and collects carefully categorised data on patients for use in research and development.

The aim of procurement, therefore, should be to achieve value for money and quality public services while bearing in mind the potential impact on supplier competitiveness. The new approach should include the following five measures:

- *Improve staff training.* Both the design and the evaluation of innovation and new technologies should become part of the training requirements for key procurers, with greater use of secondees between the private and public sectors.

- *Change bid specifications.* At present, bid requirements are generally focused on inputs and strict specifications rather than on achieving specific outcomes by the best possible means. Procurers need to become better at articulating their own needs and at gaining awareness of market possibilities. If they can design bids based on these criteria, procurers should be able to attract innovative solutions which combine both high quality and long-term cost savings. In order to develop trust relations with suppliers, confidentiality and intellectual property rights will have to be carefully protected.

- *Develop appropriate appraisal criteria.* One of the main barriers to the acceptance of innovative bids is the difficulty experienced by procurement staff in evaluating competing ideas that are very different from previous norms. This is partly a matter of training, but also requires the development of improved appraisal criteria. Several methods of best practice have been developed in business and should be considered by the Central Unit on Procurement.

- *Achieve a balance between co-operation and competition.* There needs to be a balance between competitive tendering and partnership sourcing. There is clearly a danger of excessive 'cosiness' and thus a need for strict monitoring of progress against agreed criteria. Before a bid is put out to tender and the competitive process begun, as much information as possible about future needs should be made available to the market in order to initiate joint discussions between companies and government about possible solutions and to encourage collaboration and consortia, particularly involving SMEs.

- *Encourage electronic networking.* Electronic networking should be used to distribute tenders, gain information about potential suppliers and inform them about future developments. The use of such customer-supplier networks should reflect best practice in business and so help promote partnership and co-operation in the development of innovative products.

There is a danger that such changes to the civil service in their approach to procurement may result in too great a swing away from value for money. There is always the possibility that when the objectives of key decision-makers are altered, people will overreact to the new requirements. In government the usual preventive course is to establish a watchdog with the specific job of making certain that decision-makers do not neglect their objectives. In this area, the government could charge the National Audit Office with keeping an eye on innovation-friendly purchasers to ensure that they are not neglecting the value-for-money objective.

Recommendation: The government should implement a new approach to public procurement which promotes innovation and best practice in the private sector without forsaking long-term value for money.

Conclusion

In this chapter we have assessed three different aspects of 'getting the framework right', where government has a clear and direct role and where policy changes could promote innovation and business competitiveness. Perhaps the main failing in all three areas has been the government's short-term perspective. We have therefore recommended longer-term approaches to science funding, transport planning and investment, and procurement strategies. To summarise, our major recommendations are that the government should increase spending on pure science to the average of our main competitors while maintaining its support for applied science. The government should also set out a clear and coherent statement of the principles and targets of its transport strategy. The management of demand for road use in some urban areas should involve road pricing. There should be an increased emphasis on inter-modal linkages for freight and passenger transport and the government should implement an innovation-friendly approach to public procurement and promote best-practice relationships with suppliers.

9

EVEN-HANDED
BUSINESS TAXATION

The UK's corporate tax system is not onerous by international standards. It is, however, less favourable to investment than those of our competitors, it is more complicated than it need be, and it contains certain biases. In particular it gives a tax incentive to some institutional shareholders to take dividends rather than look to capital gains from retained earnings and investment. The system should be made more neutral. One promising way of doing this would be to allow companies to deduct a normal cost of capital on shareholders' equity from their taxable profits. The Allowance for Corporate Equity (ACE) would reduce the cost of capital by one to two percentage points and could significantly increase investment. Any change should be phased in slowly to reduce initial revenue costs and allow the increase in investment to make it revenue-neutral.

Our attention is directed to the tax system by the phenomenon of underinvestment in research and physical capital. As we saw in Chapter 1, Britain would generally be better off with more investment than companies are inclined to undertake. We investigate whether the tax system contributes to the phenomenon and has a role in the solution. Our initial bias, however, is against unnecessary change or *ad hoc* 'fixes' to treat symptoms rather than root causes of uncompetitiveness. We start, therefore, with some general reflections on the design of the tax system. What would we like to see?

Businesses, like individuals, would prefer to pay as little tax as possible. Beyond that statement of the obvious, there are two other highly desirable features of any system of business taxation:

stability and simplicity. Business planning is facilitated by a stable tax system that makes liabilities predictable. It is also one thing to pay taxes and another to have to spend a great deal of time and money calculating tax liability and ensuring that various operations are in accordance with tax law.

These practical considerations are too easily underrated in academic work on taxation, which tends to focus on various externalities and produce intellectually pleasing proposals for achieving optimal resource allocation via taxation. Seldom, however, do the theoretical models emphasise the costs of information or management's inevitably limited scope of attention; nor do they take adequate account of administrative, transaction and compliance costs. Simple and serviceable is better than sophisticated and unmanageable.

The other traditional canons of taxation – that the system should be as neutral as possible in its impact on resource allocation, which generally implies as broad a base and as low a rate as possible, and that it should conform to current social notions of fairness – are certainly relevant. Even these considerations, however, should be weighed in the light of the need for stability and simplicity. We have a prejudice against proposing any change to the tax system except to relieve clear and substantial problems with the *status quo*, and we have an aversion to 'fine tuning' the tax system to try to promote a large number of objectives since this will inevitably lead to a complicated tax code.

The argument for stability also makes us very sceptical of 'temporary' measures such as temporary increases in investment allowances, which have been suggested from time to time. If investment allowances are set at the wrong level, they should be changed; if not, they should be left alone. There is some argument for trying to bring forward investment if the economy is in a deep slump, but that is not the case at present and we see no advantage in trying to fine tune the level of demand in that particular way.

Business Tax Levels

We do not believe that underinvestment in the United Kingdom can reasonably be blamed on the general level of business taxation. International comparisons suggest that at present the UK business-tax system is relatively favourable. Rates of corporate profits tax levied by central government range in the OECD area from 25 to 56 per cent (two relatively small countries, Ireland and Switzerland, have much lower rates). But most countries also have regional or local profits taxes as well. When these are taken into account, the marginal tax rate ranges from 35 to 56 per cent, putting the United Kingdom at the bottom of the range.

Taxes on corporate income as a percentage of GDP show a less favourable picture. Corporate tax receipts are sensitive to the cycle, so we consider average receipts over the period 1989–93 (the last year that data are available internationally). During that period, taxes on corporate income in the United Kingdom netted 3.3 per cent of GDP, compared with 2.8 per cent for the European Union as a whole, 2.3 per cent in the United States and 2.7 per cent for the OECD as a whole (simple averages).[1] This reflects differences in profit share, but also the fact that many countries allow greater deductions for provisions or depreciation than does the UK.

However, taxes on corporate income do not tell the whole story. Countries differ widely in their approach to the taxation of dividends. Many countries, such as the United States, 'double tax' dividends and do not have the UK's imputation system, whereby payment of corporation tax results in a tax credit to receivers of dividends. Taxes on income and profits combined are a slightly lower proportion of GDP in the United Kingdom than in the EU as a whole. Moreover, in most countries there are additional taxes on business not related to profits. A net wealth tax is levied on business assets in a number of countries, including Germany and Switzerland, and there are also taxes that relate neither to income nor wealth; the most important examples are the German *Gewerbesteuer* and the French *Taxe professionelle*. In the UK there are business rates.

A more detailed comparison of overall business taxation and accounting in the UK, France and Germany for the Foundation for Manufacturing and Industry (1995) concluded that, 'the evidence points to UK companies being likely to have higher profits for tax purposes than their French or German colleagues but to be subject to fewer taxes, lower tax rates and less stringent payment times'. The study did note, however, that:

> UK companies do, though, have fewer incentives to invest, either in fixed assets or research and development or in human resources. There may very well be a case for reviewing depreciation rates for tax purposes and providing incentives such as additional tax weighting for special expenditure such as that on research and development or training.

Taxation and Investment Incentives

Expenditures on research and development and training are treated as expenses for tax purposes and are fully allowable against tax. It is true that in some countries these expenditures are actually subsidised in some way. In general, however, we are sceptical of subsidies. These can be expensive since there is the deadweight loss involved in subsidising activities which would have occurred anyway. There is extensive scope for relabelling marginal activities so that they qualify for tax relief, so the effectiveness of a subsidy in generating genuinely productive expenditures is doubtful.

The UK business-tax system does have anti-investment characteristics, however, which derive partly from the major reform of 1984. That reform deliberately reduced possible deductions as a *quid pro quo* for reducing the marginal rate of corporation tax. The idea was to pursue tax neutrality. It is possible to question whether this is the right approach in an open economy when other countries are privileging or encouraging investment. Without an offsetting 'distortion' in this country, location decisions could be affected. If neutrality had really been achieved, however, perhaps this reform would have been acceptable.

Table 9.1 shows the effect of the tax reform on the marginal tax rates on corporate investment. Investment is disaggregated by type of asset and by type of finance. The old system imposed rather arbitrary differences in the treatment of different types of asset and of finance: plant and machinery were privileged relative to other types of investment and debt finance was privileged relative to equity. These distortions have been reduced, though not

Table 9.1: Effective Marginal Tax Rates on Corporate Investment

	1983/4	1988/9
Type of asset		
Plant and machinery	-35.6	25.5
Buildings	24.2	66.3
Stocks	41.7	53.8
Method of finance		
Debt	-61.1	31.6
New share issues	-0.8	29.0
Retentions	15.2	48.9
Overall	-0.1	44.7

Source: Kay and King (1990), Table 11.1.

eliminated, under the current system, but the upshot has been a rise in the rate of taxation from zero to over 40 per cent.

Even this might be tolerable in itself, but it is combined with another factor: the system of tax imputation on dividends. In the United Kingdom, the company pays corporation tax and dividends received by shareholders are considered to have been paid net of tax at 20 per cent. Tax-exempt institutions receive a rebate for the tax paid at that rate, which means the total tax on profits paid out to such institutions is some 13 per cent compared with 33 per cent on retained earnings. Since investment has lost its tax advantages, that means there is a bias against retention for tax-exempt institutions, whether it be for reserves or for investment, and in favour of pay-out. Moreover, because higher-rate individual tax-payers pay tax on profits at an effective rate of some 48 per cent, when both corporation tax and personal income tax are considered, the tax system has contributed, along with other non-tax factors, to a large and increasing proportion of shares being held by tax-exempt institutions. Their increasing importance has in turn increased the tax advantage of pay-out to the average company. These linked phenomena have interacted to boost dividend pay-outs. Since the 1984 reform, the proportion of profits paid out in dividends has risen considerably and now stands at much higher rates than in any comparable country (see Chapter 4).

Since retained earnings are, rightly or wrongly, the finance source of choice for most firms, the pressure to pay out competes directly with the option of investment. Academic work by Bond and Meghir (1994) points clearly to many firms preferring retained earnings – presumably because of some real or perceived credit constraint – despite the relatively unfavourable tax treatment of such earnings. They conclude that 'the increase in the effective average tax rate on companies associated with the reform of corporation tax in 1984 and the favourable tax treatment of dividends, under the imputation system introduced in 1973, may both have had adverse implications for the level of UK company investment'.

Further work by Bond, Devereux and Gammie (1995) estimates that the 1984 reforms left the cost of capital to companies higher by 1 to 2 percentage points and this could depress the preferred level of the capital stock, and hence the long-term level of company investment, by up to 5 per cent. The shorter-run impact on investment could be higher. Even the lower figure would be approaching 1 per cent of GDP and is therefore an appreciable effect. If that number seems high, note the conspicuous failure of investment to pick up in the current recovery (Figure 9.1). This is not simply a reaction to the construction boom of the late 1980s, since even investment in plant and machinery is growing only slowly. The UK's relative investment levels, always on the low side, appear to be falling rather than rising. So, even given our bias to stability, an examination of the tax system is warranted. The objectives are relatively clear, but there are a number of possible options for meeting them.

Recommendation: The government should aim to restructure the system of corporate taxation to achieve neutrality and, in particular, to remove biases which favour distribution rather than retention of profits. Any reform should be self-financing.

Figure 9.1: Investment Performance in Three UK Business
Cycles, 1973–96 *(Peak quarter = 100; Quarters from GDP peak)*

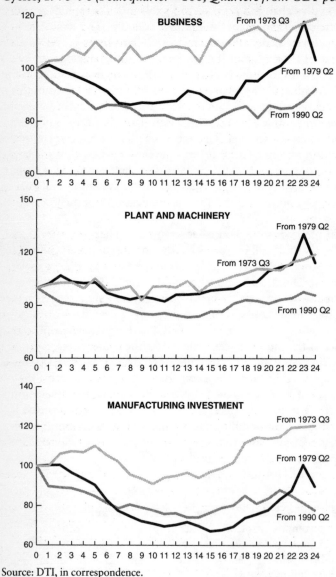

Source: DTI, in correspondence.

Alternative Reforms to Favour Investment

Two sorts of change have been proposed to make the tax system more neutral and more investment friendly. The first would increase investment allowances by enabling firms to write off investment more quickly. Small changes in allowances would be likely to have a negligible effect, so large changes would be necessary (Bond *et al.*, 1993; Young, 1995). The logical limit of this approach is to move to a cash-flow tax. Such a tax treats all expenditure, capital or current, as a deductible expense in the year that it is made. The second possibility is to allow a tax deduction for the cost of equity, in the same way that interest payments are currently deductible – the so-called Allowance for Corporate Equity (ACE) approach. This would reduce the overall cost of capital and improve cash flow, so it should favour investment.

Both of these methods are favoured by theorists, since both can be set up so that they equate to a tax on the 'pure profits' of a firm; that is, the profits it receives over and above a 'normal' return to capital. Taxing pure profits should have no effect on resource allocation and is therefore wholly neutral. In particular, it does not bias the investment decisions of firms.

The cash-flow tax would entail deducting all expenditures from the tax base in the year they are incurred but making no deductions of payments to suppliers of finance. The imputation system would therefore be abolished. There are at least two drawbacks to this reform. The first is the mere fact that it would be a very big change, not least to investors. The second is that it moves the system of UK corporate taxation away from those in other countries, making future harmonisation (particularly in a European context) more problematic.

The ACE approach, developed by researchers at the Institute for Fiscal Studies, has more potential since it involves greater continuity with the present system because it would tax profits net of depreciation, as currently calculated. It is preferable to the cash-flow tax on those grounds. However, it shares other drawbacks with the cash-flow tax. Notably, there would be a very large up-front revenue cost to the state from a full implementation of ACE.

This could possibly be avoided, however, by a gradual implementation of the system. Such a reform would reduce the marginal cost of capital for new investment immediately and phase in the allowance for pre-existing capital over a long period of time. The ending of tax imputation on dividends would equally be phased out slowly so as not to increase the tax burden on other important groups such as tax-exempt investors. Any up-front revenue cost should be modest and later, potentially larger, costs could be met by the enhanced revenue effects of higher investment coming through. Given that the ACE proposal is among the most innovative of the suggestions we received we believe it should be given serious consideration.

How ACE Would Work

First, we describe how the ACE system works when it is fully up and running. However, it must be introduced gradually to avoid excessive budgetary costs so, second, we discuss transition arrangements. Third, we face up to some possible snags or pitfalls.

A stock of shareholders' funds would be calculated for each firm, as the cumulation of previous injections of equity and post-tax profit retentions; this would be multiplied by the rate of interest on medium-term government bonds, that being the opportunity cost of investing those funds safely for a longish time. The capital cost so calculated would be deductible against corporation tax. The deduction would reduce the post-tax cost of capital. It would, incidentally, also restore neutrality between the tax treatment of equity and debt, although this is not an important consequence since companies already prefer equity to debt finance in the United Kingdom, despite the more favourable tax treatment of debt.[2] For convenience we can call the tax-exempt part of profits, that covered by ACE, normal profits; the taxable part of profits is 'extra' profits.

It would be logical to combine ACE with reducing or ending the tax imputation for dividends since these could be deemed to be paid, entirely or in part, out of 'normal' profits that have already been exempt from tax. This would have the effect of abolishing tax credits to institutional investors. Other dividend recipients would become liable to tax on their dividends. It would, however, be administratively very expensive to try to collect tax on dividends from small shareholders, particularly those paying only basic rate tax. To avoid this, there would be an allowance for dividend income high enough to let all or almost all basic-rate tax-payers out of paying any tax. The allowance would also reduce the effective rate of tax on higher-rate tax-payers below the full 40 per cent rate, which would operate at the margin. Current calculations are that even with additional net revenue from abolishing tax imputation on dividends, however, ACE could currently cost the Exchequer around £4 billion a year.

Revenue neutrality could be restored by raising the marginal rate of corporation tax to over 40 per cent. A 40 per cent rate would have the advantage of equalising corporation tax and higher rate income tax, which would remove the incentive for many small businesses inappropriately to incorporate themselves as a tax-sheltering device. Such a rate would still leave the marginal rate in the United Kingdom slightly lower than that in most other OECD countries. But, despite the overall revenue neutrality, raising the marginal corporation tax rate could send the wrong signal to business. Many business people are suspicious of politics and politicians and would probably regard the higher rate as somehow more certain and durable than the larger deductions.

In order to reduce the revenue cost of ACE it could be applied only to new investment; and its application to existing capital could be phased in only very slowly. New equity issues and retentions would be admissible together with a small proportion of pre-existing shareholder funds. Since investment is a fraction of the capital stock, the cost of such a change would initially be rather small. The allowance would build up to be equivalent to a full ACE, but that could take a decade or so. The effect of a marginal ACE on investment is uncertain, but it could be big enough to generate additional revenue for the government so that the tax reform would eventually be self-financing.

Ending the imputation system would be a substantial change for institutional investors, and this could arouse opposition within the pensions industry. We certainly accept that a design criterion for any tax change must be that it should not penalise tax-exempt institutions. Social policy currently involves encouraging people to make arrangements for private pensions to supplement the state pension, so it is inconsistent to withdraw the tax advantages of the pension funds. However, an ACE system need not do so. It would leave their tax advantages over other investors or investments quite undisturbed. Moreover, it need not lead to any increase in tax on profits received from companies in which they invest. We have seen that distributed earnings are taxed at a 13 per cent rate in the hands of pension funds (corporation tax at 33 per cent less an imputation of 20 per cent). Retained earnings are taxed at 33 per cent. With ACE, corporation tax at 33 per cent would be levied only on profits over and above a normal return on equity; if normal profits were, for example, half the total, the average rate of corporation tax at 16.5 per cent would be slightly more than the rate institutions are paying now on distributed profits and much less than they pay implicitly on retained earnings. ACE would amount to a substantial reduction in tax on retained earnings and in general companies would be able to compensate shareholders for any cash-flow effect of the marginal increase in tax on dividends with higher payouts.

While ACE would not raise the overall tax rate on pension funds' profits, it does end the tax bias in favour of their taking dividends. To the extent that it encourages retention, this has implications for cash flow. These can be handled easily enough by professional fund managers. Greater retention, if it occurs, should swell investment and future profits. Since that should have beneficial effects on economic growth and share prices, pension funds should be better off in the long run. Shorter-term liquidity problems can be accommodated by holding a different mix of assets: more debentures, for example, with higher yields than ordinary shares.

There may be a further problem, stemming from the actuaries' rules for the valuation of pension funds. These are not valued according to the current market value of financial assets since the stock market is considered too volatile to provide a sound measure. Instead, valuation is done by capitalising average income flows. If dividends grow more slowly and more of funds' earnings in future take the form of capital gains, present valuation methods may fail to reflect that and result in undervaluation of pension funds. That could have knock-on effects on premiums. This is not, however, a reason to abandon tax reform but a reason to ask the actuaries to devise a superior valuation method, which acknowledges the reality that capital appreciation is an important part of the return to equity investment.

Transitional issues

Another potential difficulty with ACE is that by distinguishing the tax treatment of new and old equity capital, it would mean a further departure from neutrality and a new opportunity for tax arbitrage. There would be an incentive for companies to present old capital as new. This issue is considered further in the Appendix to this chapte (p.241).

Assuming that ACE was introduced slowly over a long period and applied fully only to new investment, for the immediate future, firms would continue to pay corporation tax on profits with only a very partial allowance for the cost of equity they employ. By the same token, it would be wrong to eliminate dividend tax imputation all at once. A phased reduction, over say ten years, of the current ACT (advance corporation tax) payments and dividend imputation would be more appropriate. That would also give pension fund managers ample time to deal with liquidity issues that arise. When firms arrived at the point where all their equity attracts an allowance, dividend imputation payments would have fallen to zero.

Final cost of ACE

Consistent with our own strictures on taking a longer view, it is important to ask whether the government would in the end face a revenue deficit if and when ACE became fully operational. Would the cost of ACE simply be postponed? The answer is no, at least not if things went according to plan. ACE would involve the government making an admittedly risky investment; but if the change were associated with the sort of increase in investment projected by its advocates, there should not be a financing problem.

The ACE would reduce the cost of capital by between 1 and 2 per cent. Analysis suggests that could raise gross investment by as much as 10 per cent for several years, which implies that the increment to the business sector's gross capital stock would go up by half a percentage point a year. In other words, the business capital stock might grow by 3 per cent a year at constant prices rather than 2.5 per cent or so. In ten years' time, the company sector's gross capital stock would be some 5 per cent higher than it would have been in the absence of the change (Bond *et al.*, 1995). With more capital stock, the country could produce more output. Even without any additional employment, business output could be up by a couple of percentage points after ten years; with more employment, the increase could be still greater. Output up by 2 per cent, relative to where it would have been without the tax change, implies tax receipts up by a similar or greater percentage amount. A level increase in GDP of 2 per cent, even if there is no permanent effect on the growth rate, would be expected to generate tax revenues of at least £5 billion a year at 1996 prices.

This would be sufficient to finance the reform, which is estimated to cost roughly £4 billion a year when fully implemented at 1996 prices. On the best estimates we have of the investment response – and these are of course uncertain – this tax reform should result not only in a bigger economy but one sufficiently larger that its extra tax payments will finance the reform. The reform seems at least to be worth serious consideration and it should therefore be at the top of a list of possibilities in a much-needed review of corporate taxation in Britain.

Other Reforms

Meanwhile there is another change of particular benefit to smaller companies, that could be made. At present the Inland Revenue allows full deduction of classical interest payments, but any more complicated or conditional payments as part of a loan contract are likely to be assimilated to equity payments and disallowed for deduction. The bias should be the other way around.

Ordinary shares with voting rights should be classified as equity, but other instruments should generally be regarded as debt and payments deducted for tax purposes. Bank or other loans, for example, indexed to the cost of living or with a bonus element related to the company's performance should be allowable, as should the dividends on preference shares. This still leaves the system with a bias against equity but draws the boundary in a different place which is more favourable to investment.

As stated above, this could be of particular benefit to smaller companies. Lending to such companies, at least when not fully collateralised, has an element of equity anyway, since repayment may well depend on the success of the company. Banks and others should have maximum flexibility to negotiate loan contracts with a conditional or profit-related element. That gives the lender a bonus if the company does well, so compensating for the greater risk and reducing the need for high fixed-interest rates. Similarly, the companies themselves may wish to pledge part of their profits without the loss of control that ordinary equity issuance implies. There is no good reason why tax legislation or practice should penalise this greater flexibility.

> **Recommendation:** The Inland Revenue should relax rules about the types of business loans on which interest payments are tax deductible.

There are several other areas, one general and the others specific, where tax law and practice should be changed. The general area relates to the philosophy of tax law in this country. The current philosophy is that tax legislation is to be treated like a text and taken quite literally. Practices which do not break the letter of the law are permissible; if they go against the spirit of the legislation, new legislation or amendments are required. There is now a groundswell of opinion towards a more 'purposive' approach, whereby the legislation has a preamble that states the motives and intentions of the legislation. Of course, tax-payers and authorities would still disagree over some practices and systems of arbitration, and legal recourse would be required as at present. The task of the judiciary would, however, be made easier by a statement of intention, which could lead to the simplification of tax legislation and introduce more certainty into fiscal matters.

> **Recommendation:** Tax legislation should include a preamble indicating the purpose of the legislation in order to assist the courts' interpretation in disputes.

A specific change relates to small company taxation. At present, there is a lower rate of corporation tax of 24 per cent, payable on profits below £300,000. It is unsatisfactory to make eligibility for this rate depend on one year's profits. A small company which is highly successful in one year can be penalised. Eligibility for lower rate tax should be based on company results, or perhaps turnover, averaged over three years.

> **Recommendation:** Eligibility for the lower rate of small company taxation should be based on company results, or perhaps turnover, averaged over three years.

Another much canvassed change is variable rates of capital gains tax (CGT), with the rate falling with the duration of the holding period. This is meant to discourage speculation and encourage committed investors. We have doubts about the equation of the holding period with the social benefits of an investment in the first place; but the main objection to such a change is that it would be a standing invitation to financiers to invent derivative instruments which enabled investors to limit or terminate their exposure to an investment without actually realising a gain. The scope for avoidance, and the diversion of resources into inventing instruments of avoidance, is very great.

Capital gains tax itself is unpopular with many business people, especially those running smaller companies. It is an expensive tax to administer and one that collects relatively little revenue. Its preservation at the same rate as income tax is almost certainly necessary, however, to limit further growth of the tax avoidance industry and to protect the revenue yield from income taxes. In our view, rate reductions should only be contemplated for assets that have been held a very long time indeed, that is for at least ten years.

Thereafter the rate could fall until capital gains tax was eliminated on assets held for, say, twenty years. A small business director who has spent half a working lifetime building up a firm could then be allowed to sell without incurring capital gains. A ten-year period before CGT rates fall would make avoidance more difficult since financial markets do not support many private sector securities of more than ten years' duration. Capital gains taxation can, however, give rise to considerable complexities and it would be necessary to consult widely before introducing this change.

> **Recommendation:** After consultation about the change, the government should introduce a new, lower rate of capital gains tax for assets held for the very long term, meaning at least ten years.

Conclusion

We have reviewed a number of proposals aimed at removing biases in the current tax system which operate against investment. We have not sought special or extraordinary biases in favour of investment or other expenditures on training and research and development. Moreover, the principal change we identified as deserving particular consideration, ACE, would involve only a very gradual shift in the system of company taxation over a long period, perhaps a decade. In view of the data on UK investment and dividend payments over the past decade, these changes would be a very measured response to strong evidence that biases in the current system are having marked effects.

APPENDIX

Cost of ACE and Dealing with Tax Avoidance Issues

In this appendix we provide more detail on the operation of ACE and consider one or two tax avoidance issues it raises. We draw heavily on the work of ACE's inventors and particularly on the final report of the IFS Capital Taxes Group (IFS, 1994).

Calculating ACE

For ACE to operate, each firm would need to calculate a Shareholders' Fund Account (SFA) composed of retained post-tax profits and amounts subscribed for new share capital, calculated on a cash basis. This should equate to the book value of the firm's assets minus debt or other liabilities. Note that it thus bears no necessary relation to the market value of the firm's shares, which reflect expectations about future earnings as well as existing capital. The SFA is adjusted each period as shown in Table A9.1 below.

The proposed transition arrangement we think is worth considering would work as follows. Increments to the SFA each year from the date of the system's introduction would attract the full ACE allowance. The allowance would also increase by a pro-

Table A9.1: Guide to the Shareholders' Funds Account

The closing balance of the SFA in the previous period
+ the ACE allowance for the previous period
= the opening balance for the period

Additions during a period include:

+ Profits on which tax is paid during the period
+ Proceeds of new equity issues
+ Dividends received from other companies
+ Amounts received on the disposal of shares in other companies
+ Tax repaid during the period on an adjustment of taxable profits

Reductions during the period include:

− Tax paid during the period on taxable profits
− Dividends paid and other distributions made
− Capital repaid or shares repurchased
− Amounts invested in shares of other companies
− Profits in respect of which tax is repaid during the period

---

Source: IFS (1994).

portion of the initial value of the SFA at the time the new system was introduced. A ten-year transition would mean that one-tenth of the initial SFA would become eligible for the ACE allowance each year in addition to that year's increase in SFA. IFS estimates that the cost in corporation tax of introducing a full SFA immediately would be about £12 billion, which implies that the tax cost of a phased introduction would be £1.2 billion in the first year building up to the full amount. In 1995 the addition to SFA from retained profits and net share issues was probably around £40 to £50 billion, implying an incremental tax loss of about £1 billion a year because of the growth of SFAs.

Against that, the gain in tax receipts from phasing out dividend-tax imputation would be £8 billion if done all at once. This gain would increase over time, of course, with the growth of the economy and of dividend payments. A phasing out would net £0.8 billion a year plus a further amount due to economic growth and inflation.

The net cost of full SFA would be about £4 billion, which could be met if tax receipts were higher by about 1.5 per cent; that is, if the economy were 1.5 per cent bigger. As set out in the body of the chapter, it does not seem unreasonable to suppose the economy could be that much bigger after ten years relative to where it would have been anyway. The reform would then be self-financing. Of course, the actual figures for the net cost of ACE and the necessary compensating extra revenue flows will also be bigger in ten years' time, again due to the growth of the economy and of the price level in the meantime.

Avoidance issues

A main concern with the ACE proposal is that companies should not be able to inflate the eligible part of their SFAs by purely financial transactions. Obviously, the Inland Revenue would have to keep a close eye on the developing situation. In principle, however, a company could not inflate its SFA by taking over another company. If it issued shares to purchase another company, that new issue would increase SFA, as shown in Table A9.1 above, but the purchase of the other company's shares would reduce the SFA by the same amount. For ACE purposes, the purchase of one set of shares with another implies the shares were of equivalent value. A purchase of shares using cash reduces the SFA of the acquiring company but does not affect the SFA of the company being bought. But the cash payments to its former shareholders increase their SFAs if they are companies.

The clearest source of potential tax avoidance would be through investment companies. Individuals could take shares in such companies (increasing their SFAs), which could invest the proceeds in bank deposits. The ACE allowance would then reduce the tax paid on the accruing interest. There are a number of ways of dealing with this possibility, including denying a deduction for the ACE allowance to the extent that it related to shareholders' funds invested in cash deposits or similar instruments, but we do not explore these complexities further.

Notes

1 The source is the OECD Directorate of Financial Fiscal and Enterprise Affairs (1996).

2 Over the period 1970–94, UK firms financed over 80 per cent of their investment from retentions with bank finance, the next most important source of finance, accounting for 10–15 per cent (see Jenkinson and Corbett, 1996).

10

MACROECONOMIC STABILITY

Probably the most important aspect of the economic framework for most companies is the level and variability of demand in the economy as a whole. The role of the government in influencing the macroeconomy is often overlooked in an assessment of why individual countries are more competitive than others. This chapter demonstrates how macroeconomic policy in the past has too often aggravated an already unstable environment and sets out a policy framework involving co-ordination of fiscal and monetary policy, a change in policy targets and an enhanced role for the Bank of England. We also address the desirability or otherwise of the single currency.

There has been a tendency in recent years to downplay the role of macroeconomic policy and to insist that supply-side measures are more important. That ignores, however, the importance of stability in the business environment. Relatively unstable inflation and a more pronounced business cycle have been important elements detracting from British competitiveness in recent decades, as Chapter 1 explained. Macroeconomic policy errors must take a large part of the blame for that.

In the quest for consistency and steadiness in government policy, this chapter looks at macroeconomic policy and its two arms: fiscal and monetary policy. Macroeconomic policy measures work by influencing the level of demand in the economy; put simply, they make people want to spend more or less. These changes in demand can have one or both of two possible effects: they can stimulate changes in the level of economic activity (the amount of goods and services provided at a given set of prices), or they can cause the aggregate price level to shift, affecting the rate of inflation.

The purpose of macroeconomic policy is to keep demand growing steadily, so as to permit the economy to grow as evenly as possible with low inflation. It cannot make an economy grow fast indefinitely or increase its competitiveness; these are indeed supply-side matters. What it can do is provide a stable framework that helps business do its job. It is argued here that over the past several decades, macroeconomic policy errors have not only failed generally to provide stability, they have also often aggravated instability.

A successful macroeconomic policy requires the co-ordination of both fiscal and monetary policy in such a way that economic disturbances are reduced or eliminated. Stability is the critical goal. How those goals are set, and how institutions (such as the Bank of England) are used to implement them, will be a critical factor in the UK's future economic success. Of course, any discussion of macroeconomic policy is overshadowed by the possibility that the UK will join a European monetary union. In this chapter we consider first of all the principles that we think should govern monetary and fiscal policy, and then how those principles might be implemented either before entry into EMU or in the event that the United Kingdom does not join. Finally, we consider the implications of EMU and the issues at stake.

Policy Errors and Instability

The instability of the British economy over the past thirty years has been a serious impediment to business in the UK. Inflation peaked at over 20 per cent in the 1970s, fell to around 3 per cent in the mid-1980s, and rose again to high rates at the end of the decade before falling to current low rates of below 3 per cent. There have been three large recessions during that period; the longest saw GDP decline for three years in succession. Many of the practices for which British business is criticised – short-termism, high hurdle rates, a reluctance to borrow – stem from operating in that sort of climate. The prime requirement of macroeconomic policy must be that it should, as far as possible, work against that kind of instability. It should certainly not contribute to it.

It would be wrong to blame British macroeconomic policy for all the ills that have befallen the economy, which has clearly been subject to global shocks. High inflation, for example, was a global phenomenon in the 1970s. The British recessions occurred at a time of recession in other countries. Unfortunately, however, policy in this country has sometimes exacerbated rather than damped the effect of those shocks. We can see a pattern in that failure, which is particularly evident in monetary policy.

Let us begin with the mid-1970s oil shock. This raised inflation and unemployment simultaneously all around the world, introducing the concept of 'stagflation'. The countries which emerged least scathed from that experience were those which followed tight monetary policies and forced the economy to adjust without too much inflation. The UK was not among those countries. Only after the infamous IMF visit of 1977 did the United Kingdom tighten monetary policy sufficiently. When the second oil shock hit in 1980, however, it seemed that the UK had learned the lesson rather too well. The attempt to target a particular monetary aggregate, ignoring other indicators such as the exchange rate, led to a rapid appreciation of the pound, the deepest British recession since the 1930s, and the worst recession in the Western world at that time. Industrial production fell by 25 per cent and one-fifth of the capacity of the manufacturing sector was eliminated. That policy did succeed, of course, in bringing inflation down; it fell in all countries, but fastest in the United Kingdom.

Then came the late 1980s, a period of global boom; but again in the UK the boom was more heated than elsewhere, with GDP growing at over 4 per cent a year for four years and inflation back fleetingly to double-digit rates. Financial deregulation was of course partly responsible for the boom, but it was reinforced by excessively easy monetary policy, with low interest rates, and tax cuts. Interest rates were too low initially because the Chancellor tried to prevent the pound appreciating against the deutschmark. Again the lessons of the previous period, this time the early 1980s, had been learned not wisely but too well.

The credit-fuelled boom was bound to end in tears. As the government forced up interest rates to master inflation, the credit crunch came: borrowing costs rose and the over-exposed had to cut back severely on spending. One consequence was a collapse of asset prices, which reduced wealth and spending further in a vicious spiral of debt-induced deflation. The strains were felt both in the business sector and among householders, many of whom were left with negative equity. The ultimate result was Britain's longest post-war recession.

When this process was under way, the wish to reinforce the disinflation led the government to lock the pound into the European Exchange Rate Mechanism (ERM) at a high rate. That policy then had to be abandoned when German reunification led to a boom in Germany and monetary policy became inappropriate for recession-bound Britain. The UK's inflation record compared with our major competitors is shown in Table 10.1. It demonstrates that not only has the level of UK inflation been one of the highest among these countries, but nearly as importantly it has consistently been among the most volatile.

Contrary to mythology, the history of monetary policy has not been one of consistent laxity resulting in inflation. Rather, it has been one of swings of fashion, sometimes targeting money

Table 10.1: Inflation Record of Six OECD Countries, 1980–95

Country			*1980–1987*	
	Mean		*Variance*	
	Value	*Rank*	*Value*	*Rank*
UK	7.78	4th	0.64	6th
USA	5.46	3rd	0.48	4th
Germany	3.26	2nd	0.34	1st
France	8.20	5th	0.38	2nd
Japan	2.14	1st	0.62	5th
Italy	13.23	6th	0.38	3rd

Source: *OECD Economic Outlook*, Table 14.

supply, sometimes targeting the exchange rate, often fighting the previous war. As has been rightly said, most policy errors have been an overreaction to the previous policy error (Stephens, 1996).

Fiscal policy has not been so obviously responsible for instability, although it responds to an electoral cycle more clearly than does monetary policy. The most recent case was the very rapid growth in public spending before the election of 1992, resulting in a Public Sector Borrowing Requirement (PSBR) above 7 per cent of GDP. At present, after two years of rising taxes, we now see taxes falling in response to the prospect of the next election. That cannot be right. Either it is not appropriate to cut taxes now or, if it is, then clearly taxes should not have been raised so much in the first place. Large moves in opposite directions within the space of a year are evidence of overactive policy-making (see Figure 10.1).

It is imperative, in our view, for macroeconomic policy – both fiscal and monetary – to become more conducive to stability. Keeping inflation low is an essential part of stability, and we applaud the present universal agreement on this issue. There is, however, a little nervousness in our applause in case the requisite determination should become a monomania that ignores all other risks. We must find a less neurotic and fashion-ridden

1988–95				*1980–95*			
Mean		*Variance*		*Mean*		*Variance*	
Value	*Rank*	*Value*	*Rank*	*Value*	*Rank*	*Value*	*Rank*
4.75	5th	0.40	5th	6.27	5th	0.65	4th
3.20	4th	0.30	3rd	4.33	3rd	0.53	2nd
3.09	3rd	0.40	4th	3.18	2nd	0.37	1st
2.53	2nd	0.24	1st	5.36	4th	0.67	5th
1.08	1st	0.83	6th	1.61	1st	0.78	6th
5.60	6th	0.27	2nd	9.41	6th	0.57	3rd

Figure 10.1: Cyclical and Structural Elements of the UK Deficit as a Percentage of GDP, 1979–95

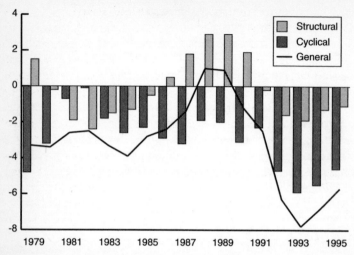

Source: *OECD Economic Outlook*, Annex, Tables 30 and 31.

approach to policy than that which has characterised the past.

It is also clear that a key element of macro policy must be simply to avoid policy mistakes which will themselves create instability. It does not necessarily follow that the economy is stabilised by keeping policy instruments (such as tax rates and interest rates) stable, but we do believe there should be a bias towards instrument stability. That means renouncing 'big bang' attacks on unemployment or inflation, and refraining from trying to 'fine-tune' the level of activity in the economy. Trying to eliminate policy-induced fluctuations will tend to imply a stickiness in the use of policy instruments; they will not be moved so much.

There is another reason for supporting this approach. The response of economic agents to changes in key variables such as interest rates, the exchange rate or even the level of demand itself, as reflected in firms' order books, will depend on the degree to which they expect the change to last. To take exchange rates as an example, exporters faced with a depreciated exchange rate that they expect to persist may invest in order to increase their foreign market share. If they expect the depreciation to be of only short duration, however, they will do no such thing; instead, they may increase their sterling prices to take advantage of the temporary depreciation.[1] Furthermore, given the general uncertainty about how the economy actually works, people's expectations about the persistence of any change are founded less upon fancy theories than upon practical experience of how long-lasting such changes have been in the past. Past experience of instability breeds expectations of further instability in the future.

It follows that policy instruments are not like muscles; they do not become stronger the more they are used. On the contrary, the more sparingly they are used, the more efficacious they will tend to be. This conclusion is necessarily a general one, but there would seem to be a strong case for modesty in the use of 'demand management' instruments. We now turn to the question of how, given this principle, demand can be managed and fiscal and monetary policy co-ordinated.

Co-ordinating Policy

If the government is concerned with maintaining the stability of aggregate demand, then it must consider both fiscal and monetary policy. It is important to understand that the presence of these two instruments does not allow us to target independently both growth (full employment) and price stability, because the two instruments themselves are not fully independent. Both operate via the level of demand. As Nobel Laureate James Tobin has put it, 'the consequences of a given volume of aggregate demand ... are independent of the sources and composition of that volume of demand ... The output/price or unemployment/inflation trade-off is inexorable; that is to say it cannot be eliminated or mitigated by altering the fiscal/monetary mix' (Tobin, 1993). The key thing is to deliver the right amount of aggregate demand; how we divide that demand is of secondary importance.

Tobin does allow one exception to this rule. In an open economy with floating exchange rates and free currency movement, 'an easy fiscal/tight money policy mix means higher interest rates are associated with any given real GNP'. This lifts the exchange rate, putting downward pressure on prices at least in the short run. This particular policy combination may therefore seem to offer a better mix of output and inflation response, and is thus a standing temptation to policy-makers. Pushing up the exchange rate, however, leads to the 'twin deficit' problem – a fiscal deficit accompanied by an external deficit – and thus is not sustainable in the long run. This situation tends to penalise the traded goods sector – firms producing for international markets – and favour suppliers of services to the government; it can thereby aggravate de-industrialisation or the 'hollowing out' of the economic structure.

Government must be concerned with more than merely the level of aggregate demand. It must also be concerned with the composition of demand, with distortions in demand, and in particular with the rate at which the economy is accumulating foreign debts or assets through its current-account balance. Tobin also acknowledges that in the longer run the policy mix does matter because it affects the composition of national output in terms of consumption and investment (though not the breakdown into output and inflation).

All this means that monetary and fiscal policy must be compatible, and this in turn suggests that we should avoid having these policies set by different people with different objectives in mind. This obvious point, emphasised by distinguished economists such as James Meade (1994), has been forgotten in recent years owing to the preoccupation with the 'credibility' of policy, especially monetary policy. As is now evident in some European countries, where the policy arms are too rigidly separated and unco-ordinated, monetary policy tends to be too tight while fiscal policy is far too loose and problems with government debt then arise.

This point is particularly relevant when we look at the question of whether the monetary authority should be independent of government. Certainly it is possible that the implementation of monetary policy could be devolved to some body acting as an agent of government; but the objective or target of the devolved policy must be set by the government itself, in the interests of co-ordinating the activities of the two arms. If not, then clashes –

such as the monetary authority putting up interest rates to counteract tax breaks for investment, so negating the point of the exercise – may occur. The government must be in a position not only to prevent this kind of clash but also to co-ordinate policy. If the monetary authority tightens policy in response to an inflationary shock, then the fiscal authority must also show restraint if all the adjustment burden is not to fall on the exchange rate and the traded goods sector.

Case for Policy Targets

Fiscal and monetary policy co-ordination is vital if aggregate demand is to be controlled without adverse effects on the composition of demand and the national savings–investment balance. We believe that the best means to achieve co-ordination in practice is to set public targets for macro policies and to make clear that both arms of policy have some responsibility for both targets. Often the argument for public targets rests on an idea of credibility: the government should seek to reassure citizens and financial markets by putting its cards on the table.[2] That is important but it is not, in our view, the main reason for having public targets; rather, targets have an intrinsic value in themselves.

As an example, let us look at inflation. Small upward changes in inflation do no harm. Yet this fact is what makes inflation dangerous, because there is no obvious limit to the upward drift. The government must set some fairly arbitrary target to stop it creeping upwards, and should announce this target clearly so that the private sector, and the political opposition, can monitor its actions. Of course setting a target will not by itself ensure that the target will be achieved, and measures will still need to be taken. By publicising the target, however, the government in effect declares that it will have failed if the target is missed, and the potential for political embarrassment becomes a force against inflation in its own right. By giving such a hostage to fortune, the government creates a political disincentive to any excessive relaxation of policy in the future. Helpful expectations may indeed be set by this process, but these are of secondary importance.

Credibility does matter, but credibility cannot be achieved by declarations or an institutional fix. Only the long-term accumulation of a good reputation will suffice, and to achieve this, the government needs to have targets and to meet them consistently.

Fiscal Framework

How should we then assess the stance of fiscal policy? What should the indicators and targets of policy be? Traditionally the focus has been on the Public Sector Borrowing Requirement. PSBR is a purely 'cash' measure of public-sector financing needs in a given year, ignoring the effect of contemporary transactions on future government revenue or expenditure. For example, revenue generated by privatisation reduces the PSBR for a year, but no allowance is made for the loss of public assets and future revenue flows.

If the government leases rather than buys a capital good, it will spend less in year one and therefore there will be less impact on the current PSBR – even if the terms of the lease are very disadvantageous and outright acquisition would be better in the long run (Corry, 1995; Stella, 1993). A switch – as proposed in a recent Treasury paper (1995b) – to resource-based accounting with a balance sheet is essential if the government is to run its affairs properly. Proper accruals accounting would include any liability (promise to make future payments) at the time that liability was incurred. Thus the promises of future payment represented by a leasing contract, for example, would be included and their present value could then be compared with the cost of outright acquisition of the capital good. Similarly, the loss of future revenues from the sale of a profitable public enterprise would be counted.[3]

> **Recommendation:** Fiscal policy should be supported by a proper system of accounts on an accruals basis.

We believe the move to proper accruals accounting is particularly important given the introduction of the Private Finance Initiative and public-private partnerships. At its worst, the PFI is a way of getting capital spending off the government's books; under present accounting systems, the government's contractual liabilities created by PFI may not show up anywhere. This threatens to undermine public expenditure control. It is therefore urgent for the government to move rapidly to accrual accounting, and to publish and target a proper balance-sheet measure, such as public-sector net worth. It is also vitally important that such measures be audited by an independent, statutory body.

Even within a cash-accounting framework, the PSBR has a grave drawback: it fails to distinguish borrowing that will eventually have to be paid for by the tax-payer[4] from borrowing used to acquire an asset that itself produces an income stream. We believe the two should be distinguished. Borrowing which will definitely be serviced out of general taxation is clearly different from commercial-style borrowing that is expected to service itself, and it is nonsense to treat all such borrowing as a potential charge on the tax-payer in the same way as general government borrowing. In practice, the impact of the PSBR is to hamper infrastructure investment by bodies such as the Post Office or the Civil Aviation Authority that may be beneficial to their own business and to business at large.

The government should move towards a new measure as its principal cash-based fiscal indicator, one that excludes self-financing borrowing apart from a risk or insurance premium. An approximation to such a concept is given by the General Government Financial Deficit (GGFD), which excludes the borrowing of public corporations. Figure 10.2 shows that the GGFD is on the whole more stable than the PSBR. Since most commercial-style public borrowing is done by such corporations, GGFD is a reasonable target. Further, given that the Maastricht Treaty specifies that countries be judged on GGFD rather than PSBR, there is no reason not to target it.[5] Meanwhile, public corporations could issue their own debt, as they do in other countries. If these corporations receive a government guarantee on their debt, then they should pay a fee for this guarantee to the government. There would be no effect on the government's deficit, the GGFD, since the fee revenue would balance the government's contingent liability.

Figure 10.2: UK GGFD and PSBR as a Percentage of GDP, 1966–95

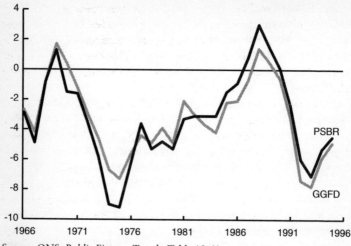

Source: ONS, *Public Finance Trends*, Table 10.61.

What should the target for GGFD be? A budget balanced over the cycle is one frequently favoured target, but this is unnecessarily restrictive. It is normal in a growing economy that the stock of publicly owned assets – schools, bridges, police equipment, etc – should grow as well. It is equally normal that borrowing to finance those assets should grow proportionately. When the government publishes proper balance-sheet accounts, then it will be possible to assess government borrowing by its impact on public-sector net worth. Meanwhile, a reasonable rule of thumb might be that government assets and debts should generally grow at the same rate as GDP, or at least not faster. Since debts can grow at that rate without increasing the tax burden, this rule would permit a limited amount of net public borrowing on a continuous basis.

The above argument suggests a policy of stabilising the debt burden. The Maastricht Treaty sets a limit to the general government debt ratio of 60 per cent; currently the UK government's debt is around 50 per cent of GDP. The value at which the ratio is stabilised is essentially arbitrary – there is no satisfactory theory or evidence about the optimal debt ratio, though increasing debt

256

to finance government consumption will generally lower growth – but the above numbers suggest stabilisation at current levels would be reasonable. That would permit an average deficit of about 2 per cent of GDP over the cycle, or some £13.5 billion at current prices. It follows that current government borrowing, at over 4 per cent of GDP, is too high, especially since it is financing consumption. Public investment is smaller than borrowing (PSBR) and has been for several years.

If debt is to be stabilised, discretionary changes in fiscal policy in order to influence aggregate demand should be a weapon of last resort. The automatic stabilisers, whereby in recession government revenues tend to fall and expenditures tend to rise, should generally be fiscal policy's contribution to cyclical stabilisation. Note that the greater the effect of fiscal stabilisers, the less is required of monetary policy and hence the less is the impact on the traded goods sector. It stands repeating that the two policy arms should be co-ordinated in the interests of not distorting the pattern of demand. Public-sector debt targets may be amended, for example, if the current account of the balance of payments seems seriously out of balance.

> **Recommendation:** The government should adopt a new, tighter framework for fiscal policy but one which would also allow more investment by self-financing public corporations.

Monetary Policy

The present procedures for monetary policy involve the targeting of the inflation rate. This has the merit of being simple and understandable. The drawback, however, is that no one believes that inflation is the government's sole concern. Targeting inflation alone implies that the level of activity or real growth is not influenced by monetary policy, that the government does not care about it, or that the government has some other means of stabilising it, if necessary, in the short to medium term. None of those propositions is true.

Having such a narrow target also makes it difficult to devolve power to the Bank of England, since it creates the risk that the

Bank would behave in ways that would make policy co-ordination difficult and lead to the kind of policy imbalances seen in some other countries. Monetary policy determines the growth of monetary demand, not primarily how that demand is met (in other words, how nominal GDP growth splits into increased output and increased inflation). But the Bank of England, charged with worrying only about inflation, would have a very strong incentive to raise interest rates whenever it saw the possibility of inflation rising at all, whatever the effect on the economy.

Let us go back to the basic objective, which is to establish appropriate and stable conditions of monetary demand. Stable inflation will follow from that objective. Surely, then, there is a case for targeting the whole objective directly rather than inflation alone. Nominal GDP targeting would get closer to this. Nominal GDP is a combination of real output growth and inflation: it measures total cash expenditure in the economy (in most circumstances that is close to aggregate demand). As mentioned earlier, monetary and fiscal policy are really only capable of targeting aggregate demand; how much of nominal GDP growth turns up in prices and how much in increased production, is determined by supply-side factors. So we are setting a target that our instruments are well suited to hit.[6]

Some have argued that there should be a growth target as well as, and separate from, an inflation target. Certainly the nominal GDP target must be made up of notionally distinguishable targets for growth and inflation, and for some purposes the two can be thought of separately. In setting macro policies, however, the growth and inflation targets must be combined. Since monetary and fiscal policy are not truly independent in manipulating aggregate demand the government really has only one instrument. It is inappropriate to announce two separate targets. The markets would, quite reasonably, want to know which target 'wins' if and when there is a conflict between them. A nominal GDP target avoids most of these problems.

A key advantage of nominal GDP targeting is that it would tend to reduce inappropriate policy activism. A stagflationary shock, for example, lowers output and raises inflation at the same time, but a recession will tend to reduce inflation once the original shock passes through. With inflation targets alone, as soon as any event pushes inflation above the target the government has to choose between sacrificing credibility by missing or changing the target, or exacerbating the recession, which will have real effects on real people. In contrast, nominal income targeting might suggest no change of interest rates in response to a small stagflationary shock (although a massive stagflationary shock which pushed up inflation to dangerous rates, as in 1974 for example, would not be accommodated).

A more normal cycle typically starts with quick growth and subdued inflation. Growth peaks but inflation continues to rise, only to peak in its turn when growth is well on the way down once more. The fact that real growth and inflation tend to be out of phase means that nominal GDP growth will have a smaller variance than inflation (see Figure 10.3). The variation in inflation between 1971 and 1993 was 40 per cent greater than the variation in nominal GDP growth. Targeting nominal GDP growth will therefore generally lead to less adjustment of mone-

Figure 10.3: UK Annual Inflation and Annual Percentage Change in Nominal GDP, 1970–95

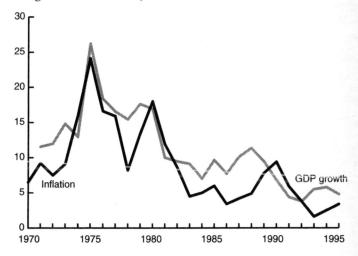

Source: *OECD Economic Outlook*, Annex, Tables 2 and 16.

tary instruments, and consequently a lower risk of aggravating instability. In 1995, for example, it became obvious that growth was slowing at the same time as inflation was nudging up. With a nominal GDP target, the Governor of the Bank of England would not have been under pressure to propose higher interest rates. At the same time, nominal GDP will send an earlier warning than will inflation of future problems. Had Nigel Lawson looked at nominal GDP, he would not have slackened policy to such an extent in 1987–8. Even using the unrevised figures then available, nominal GDP was growing at an annual rate of 10 per cent when Lawson cut income tax.

Operation of Monetary Policy and the Role of the Bank of England

Whatever target we give monetary policy, there remains the question of how it is implemented. In recent years there has been a considerable groundswell of opinion in favour of making the Bank of England independent in some sense.[7] But there is also a case for monetary policy not being determined by a body independent of government. This is partly because decisions on monetary policy have persistent real consequences and are thus appropriately matters of political accountability in a democracy, and also because of the co-ordination issues we have already emphasised.

The issue of who pulls the trigger is actually less important for democracy than the question of who sets the target and what it is. There are advantages in an independent bank being given the job of implementing monetary policy, as long as the policy framework has been set by politicians. A system in which the bank sets its own targets – as with the Bundesbank – is not optimal. Academic literature, which once provided support for the fashion of independent central banks, has now begun to favour a situation where the bank is an independent agent of government policy, and may have to take account of more complex objectives than inflation alone.[8]

We are against the idea of 'target independence' for the Bank of England, but favour 'instrument independence' so long as the Bank is given a target that adequately reflects what the government wants it to achieve: low inflation but with a minimum of fluctuations in real output. The government could annually select rolling nominal GDP growth targets, obtain the assent of Parliament and then hand these targets to the Bank to achieve. With the assent of Parliament, the government would have the right to override or change the target in the event of a clear shock or emergency. The Governor of the Bank could be obliged to answer for his stewardship to a parliamentary select committee on a regular basis, perhaps twice a year, as happens in the United States. The US example could also be followed in making the Bank of England more accountable and its policy discussions more transparent and germane to the real economy, through the introduction of a Monetary Policy Committee.

Such an approach has advantages over the current system in the United Kingdom. At present, the Governor's opinion is made public and is influential but the Chancellor still has final responsibility for interest-rate decisions. Public disagreement is then a possible source of market instability. A degree of instrument independence for the Bank of England, as described above, could be useful in avoiding market repercussions should the Governor and a future Chancellor (particularly one from the political centre-left) disagree.

Recommendation: The government should set a nominal GDP growth target and give independence to the Bank of England to achieve the target through control of interest rates.

Macroeconomic Policy and EMU

The macroeconomic landscape may be changed if Britain enters the European Monetary Union. To some, this is the answer to the problem of poor policy-making. In EMU, they believe, the UK would not have an independent monetary policy and therefore could not make mistakes. Interest rates in the common currency would be set by a European Central Bank, which would be independent of any government and therefore not tempted to excessive ease for electoral reasons. Moreover, given the current fiscal position and the so-called Maastricht conditions on government borrowing, it would be a very long time before the United Kingdom would have any room for fiscal manoeuvre within EMU (at least so long as it played by the rules). But entry into EMU carries with it the risk that the UK might move out of cyclical phase with much of continental Europe, and would then be stuck with inappropriate policies that it could not change. Were this to happen, while the policies themselves might be stable, the effect on the economy would not be stabilising and a painful recession (or exaggerated boom) could result. From a narrowly macroeconomic point of view, therefore, both options – entering EMU and remaining outside it – carry risks. Ultimately, the decision about whether and when to join must be made in a much broader context.

For business it is vitally important that Britain is part of an open, free-trading, single European market. Not only is this the right competitive environment for British companies, it is also the basis of much of the foreign investment currently taking place in this country. It is also important that the UK retains enough standing with its European partners to be powerful in their counsels in arguing for a liberal European order, with free trade and competition extended into areas now inhibited by government policies. We do not know for certain whether these objectives can be secured without entering EMU, but it seems doubtful that they can be achieved if EMU becomes an inclusive system with the great majority of EU states as members but with the United Kingdom remaining outside. Given this likelihood, it seems on balance that the greatest advantage for British business lies in EMU entry.

Let us suppose for argument's sake, however, that it is possible for the United Kingdom to be a full member of the single market and an influential partner in the EU without joining EMU, perhaps because many other states are also outside the system. The question of whether to enter or not then becomes much less important for business. The reduced transactions and forward cover costs from a single currency are worthwhile but not particularly important, and must be balanced against the increased risk of policies being locked inappropriately. Entry in this case is not a first-order decision; businesses can cope equally well whether the United Kingdom is in or out.

The prime question is therefore political, and it is obvious that the sooner the politicians are able to clarify the situation the better. If the country can continue to enjoy the benefits of the single market and a constructive political role only by joining, then we should join and accept the risk involved. If events enable us to enjoy those advantages without joining, then the issue becomes much less critical; indeed, there is no unanimity in this Commission about the balance of advantages in that case. The British government should make an early assessment of the central question in the light of how many countries are likely to join the first wave of EMU, and remove the current uncertainty as soon as possible.

Another consideration must be the conditions prevailing at the time of joining. EMU will entail an entirely undemocratic structure for monetary policy, which will not always be tailored to specifically British circumstances. Fiscal policy might then have to play a more active stabilisation role than that we have outlined above. It is particularly important that the United Kingdom should have maximum room for fiscal manoeuvre, which means it must more than meet the Maastricht conditions. The deficit on GGFD must be well below 3 per cent, preferably around zero; then the government can expand fiscal policy substantially should the need arise. The mix of policy in the next few years, therefore, should be towards tight fiscal policy with monetary policy sufficiently accommodating to allow adequate growth in nominal GDP.

Whether the UK joins EMU or not, its genesis will have enormous implications for the UK economy. Yet apart from the technical preparations by the Bank of England, important questions about how to ensure that the British economy is fully prepared for the new environment have been largely ignored. In or out, the key to our position will be the extent to which the UK can compete. We therefore believe that the government should work with leading economic actors to examine the implications of EMU and to promote greater understanding of the steps that need to be taken to prepare the UK for the changed environment.

> **Recommendation:** The government should decide about EMU on the basis of a political judgement. If a substantial majority of EU economies choose to enter in the first wave, then the UK should join them.

Conclusion

Macroeconomic policy should be oriented towards stability. This means that fiscal and monetary policy must be co-ordinated and used with caution to eliminate policy-induced disturbances. Fiscal policy should be supported by a proper system of accounts on an accruals basis, including a public-sector balance sheet as currently proposed. These should be independently audited and the government should set long-term goals for public-sector net worth. This should entail stabilising the ratio of government debt to GDP which, since current borrowing is too high, will require tighter fiscal policy than we have had in recent years. A new framework for fiscal policy would permit more productive investment by public corporations with marketed output. An inflation target is too narrow and threatens policy co-ordination if more autonomy is given to the Bank of England. Monetary policy should have a target that ensures inflation control but also builds in the legitimate task of real-economy stabilisation. That implies a move to targets for nominal GDP growth. These should permit real growth at the trend rate or slightly faster while aiming to keep inflation at or below the current rate. With such a target, there would be operational advantages in giving more autonomy to the Bank of England to control interest rates. The government should reduce uncertainty about the UK's entry into EMU at the earliest possible opportunity. If most of the important EU economies join in the first wave, then we should join them.

NOTES

1 The point is made in Krugman (1990), Chapter 2. It is what seems to have happened in Britain after the 1992 devaluation.

2 For classic expositions of this theory, see Barro and Gordon (1983) and Kydland and Prescott (1977).

3 This approach is not without problems; see Blejer and Cheasty (1993) for a discussion of these.

4 This can include investments that will lead to higher growth and hence higher tax receipts. Although in some sense such investment is self-funding (at least in expectation), the finance comes through taxes. It should still be distinguished from investment which leads to a revenue stream as a result of voluntary purchases of traded goods or services.

5 Hawksworth and Wilcox (1995) make a similar case. While we agree with their arguments in general, the sector which they were considering (low-cost housing) is not the best candidate for de-control of borrowing, since the government ultimately pays for the debt of providers of low-cost rental housing through housing benefit and other subsidies to tenants.

6 Strictly speaking, total nominal demand in an economy is best measured by total final expenditure, which is equal to GDP plus imports in nominal terms. But we do not explore this refinement further. Nominal GDP targets are favoured by economists of almost every ideological persuasion. Weale *et al.* (1989) give one of the fullest justifications; Judd and Motley (1993) argue that a nominal GDP target can be useful as a feedback rule, helping to secure stable inflation while retaining some flexibility over policy for short-run cyclical reasons. Other advocates include James Meade, Samuel Brittan and Charles Bean.

7 If the UK should join EMU, it will have to accept an independent central bank. The issues here are rather different, however, and are not discussed further in this paper.

8 See Canzoneri *et al.* (1995), Currie *et al.* (1996) and Walsh (1995) for the debate.

POSTSCRIPT

Our business agenda for Britain calls for action in eight areas of public policy and lists over forty recommendations. These extend from wide-ranging proposals such as the overhaul of competition policy and reforming the framework of monetary policy, to more detailed proposals such as the launch of a Financial Management Certificate for SME owner-managers. To implement some of these proposals would incur financial costs. Our aim is not to provide a mere wish-list of uncosted policies. In developing our recommendations, we have taken account of the fiscal implications of our combined proposals.

Fiscal Implications

Many of our recommendations would have little or no impact on the public purse. A change in directors' duties (as defined in the Companies Act), a shift to nominal GDP targeting, and a more independent Bank of England are examples of changes with no cash cost. Some would require small amounts of funding, such as the seedcorn finance for mutual guarantee schemes. Others – for example, the provision of nursery school places for all three- and four-year-olds – carry substantial spending implications. We make the reasonable assumption that proposals requiring small amounts of funding can be implemented via reallocation of funds in spending departments. Therefore we concentrate here on the recommendations that involve substantial spending, which occur in Chapters 6, 7 and 8. In Chapter 6 – on education – we identify opportunities for savings, which could help pay for the other proposals. Table P.1 draws up a rough account and shows that we are left with a shortfall of some £2.8 billion.

One proposal, made in Chapter 8, which will raise revenue is the recommended introduction of urban road pricing. This has not been included in the costing table for two reasons. First, estimates of the sums it would yield differ enormously. Second, and more important, we do not see road pricing primarily as a revenue-raising measure. Much of the money raised should be used to fund improvements in transport infrastructure such as new or updated urban public transport systems. Another potential source of net revenue is more effective public procurement: according to CBI estimates, this could save up to £2 billion annually. Although that would finance the bulk of the net expenditure in our programme, we exclude it in the interests of prudence.

Table P.1: Net Spending Account (£ *million*)

Spending implications		Savings	
Chapter 6 (Improving skills)			
Schools	1,000	Higher education fees	200
Pre-school	860	Student loans	2,000
Class sizes	100		
Traineeships	800		
Education for adults	1,000		
Total	**3,760**		
Chapter 7 (An Effective Labour Market)			
Long-term unemployment programme	700		
Chapter 8 (Strengthening Science, Transport and Public Procurement)			
Science base	500		
Total	4,960	Total	2,200

Similarly if our recommended reform of corporation tax took the form of the ACE proposal as outlined in Chapter 9 and it had the impact on investment that its architects project, it would yield substantial extra tax receipts. However, any such contribution to the fiscal shortfall would come well into the future and has been omitted from the account.

The priorities in our programme are as follows. We rank the recommendations on education and training in Chapter 6 above those on long-term unemployment in Chapter 7, and the latter above the increased science funding proposed in Chapter 8. Within Chapter 6, we see funding for schools and pre-school education as having greater priority than subsidised traineeships and reduced fees for adult education.

Attaining the Vision

Let us suppose – since we are optimists – that the UK government decided that our business agenda for Britain had hit the policy nail right on the head and decided to implement all of our proposals. How do we picture the UK economy in, say, ten years' time?

Already the keener competition induced by the continued development of the European Single Market and a more stringent competition policy has toned up companies and shortened the long tail of underperforming firms. After some initial cynicism, ten years of company reporting on customer, employee and supplier relations have helped to promote a shift in management focus. Managers take pride in the healthy state of these relationships, and what they imply about the long-term health of their company. Investors have grown knowledgeable about them; this is particularly important because managers are more concerned than ever about investor opinion. Being listed by the powerful Council of Institutional Investors is regarded as a radical sanction – one that intervenes earlier, when a firm is just beginning to stagnate, than the old hostile takeover ever could. Takeovers still happen, of course, but they are less frequent. The pages of the *Financial Times* reflect this new longer-term orientation of British companies. In place of pages of stories about real or rumoured merger deals, the gossip of a nervous marketplace, there are stories about new product development, new marketing campaigns, and new export orders won.

Small companies continue to be created in greater numbers than in other countries, but the failure rate is lower, owing to better management training, more flexible finance, and growing habits of co-operation. The expanding population of small firms has galvanised employment. Unemployment is around 4 per cent, with long-term unemployment eliminated by the special programmes we outlined in Chapter 7. Crime has fallen.

GCSE and GNVQ results stand on the threshold of a startling improvement as the first generation of children to benefit from reforms and extra resources for nursery and primary schools begins to sit these exams. A culture of lifelong learning is taking root as adults call on open learning agency schemes to update their skills at home or at work. The tail of underachieving people remains, but it is shrinking, not least because of compulsory traineeships for those who leave school early. Although the full repercussions of educational investment have yet to be felt, the British workforce is already perceptibly better trained, and its productivity is rising.

Public procurement of new, innovative public transport systems, financed by road pricing, has boosted important sectors of the engineering industry. Ultra-safe, economical, zero-emission vehicles will soon be entering service and promise to capture markets abroad. The present government's programmes to forge a link between business and those working on new technologies are paying off, and in addition, after a fallow interval, British science is reviving and expanding in the light of increased budgets. The *Financial Times* carries stories about exiled professors returning home from the United States – the counter-brain-drain.

Inflation is low throughout Europe, and the United Kingdom is no exception. Interest rates are low too, since inflation expectations have finally adjusted to fifteen years of near price stability. Few recall the days when inflation regularly exceeded 3 per cent. Investment has risen in response, fuelled by more favourable tax treatment. While the UK is already a more prosperous place in 2007 than it was ten years ago, there are firm grounds for expecting even better performance in the years ahead, as improved education and higher investment begin to affect the growth rate. With the prospect of outcompeting the other G7 countries, the United Kingdom is set to make dramatic strides up the international league tables.

Of course, anyone can dream. But we believe that all of these outcomes are achievable, as the vigour and enterprise of the private sector interact with the intelligent commitment of public policy. Once they are achieved, we can create not only a more prosperous but also a more inclusive society, with a higher quality of life for all its citizens.

BIBLIOGRAPHY

Aaronson, R. (1992), 'Do Companies Take Any Notice of Competition Policy?', *Consumer Policy Review*, 2.3, pp.140–5.

Aaronson, R. (1996), *The Future of UK Competition Policy* (London: IPPR).

Advisory Council on Science and Technology (1990), *The Enterprise Challenge: Overcoming Barriers to Growth in Small Firms* (London: HMSO).

Albert, M. (1993), *Capitalism Against Capitalism* (London: Whurr Publishers).

Allen, D., (1992), 'Target Payout Ratios and Dividend Policy', *Managerial Finance*, 18.1, pp.9–21.

Andersen Consulting (1994), *The Second Lean Enterprise Report* (London: Andersen Consulting).

Ashton, D., and Green, F. (1996), *Education, Training and the Global Economy* (Cheltenham: Edward Elgar).

Aston, B., and Williams, M. (1996), *Playing to Win: the Success of UK Motorsport Engineering* (London: IPPR).

Aston Business School (1991), *Constraints on the Growth of Small Firms* (London: HMSO).

Atkinson, J., and Meager, N. (1994), *Evaluation of Workstart Pilots*, Institute for Employment Studies, Report 279.

Audit Commission (1996), *Counting to Five: Education of Children Under Five,* National Report (London: HMSO).

Ball, C. (1994), *Start Right: the Importance of Early Learning* (London: RSA).

Bank of England (1995), 'The Provision of Bank Finance for Small Businesses in Germany', August, mimeo.

Bank of England (1996), *Finance for Small Firms: a Third Report*, January.

Bannock, G., and Peacock, A. (1989), *Government and Small Businesses* (London: Paul Chapman Publishing).

Barro, R., and Gordon, D. (1983), 'Rules, Discretion and Reputation in a Model of Monetary Policy', *Journal of Monetary Economics*, 12, pp.101–126.

Barro, R., and Sala-i-Martin, X. (1995), *Economic Growth* (Washington: McGraw-Hill).

Beecroft, A. (1994), 'The Role of the Venture Capital Industry in the UK', in Dimsdale and Prevezer (1994).

Bennett, R. (1995), *Meeting Business Needs in Britain* (London: British Chambers of Commerce [BCC]).

Birley, S., Cromie, S., and Myers, A. (1991), 'Entrepreneurial Networks: Their Emergence in Ireland and Overseas', *International Small Business Journal*, 9.

Blair, M. (1995), *Ownership and Control: Rethinking Corporate Governance for the Twenty-First Century* (Washington: The Brookings Institution).

Blejer, M., and Cheasty, A. (eds.) (1993a), *How to Measure the Fiscal Deficit* (Washington: IMF).

Blejer, M., and Cheasty, A. (1993b), 'The Deficit as an Indicator of Government Solvency: Changes in Public Sector Net Worth', in Blejer and Cheasty (1993a).

Blundell, R., Dearden, L., and Meghir, C. (1996), *The Determinants and Effects of Work Related Training in Britain* (London: IFS).

Body Shop (1995), *The Body Shop Social Statement*.

Bond, S., Chennelis, L., and Devereux, M. (1995), 'Company Dividends and Taxes in the UK', *Fiscal Studies*, 16.3, pp.1–18.

Bond, S., Denny, D., and Devereux, M. (1993), 'Capital Allowances and the Impact of Corporation Tax on Investment in the UK', *Fiscal Studies*, 14.2, pp.1–14.

Bond, S., Devereux, M., and Gammie, M. (1995), 'Tax Reform to Promote Investment', Institute of Fiscal Studies, December, mimeo.

Bond, S., and Jenkinson, T. (1996), 'The Assessment: Investment Performance and Policy', *Oxford Review of Economic Policy*, 12.2, pp.1–29.

Bond, S., and Meghir, C. (1994), 'Financial Constraints and Company Investment', *Fiscal Studies*, 15.2, pp.1–18.

Booth, A., and Snower, D. (eds.) (1996), *Acquiring Skills: Market Failures, Their Symptoms and Policy Responses* (Cambridge: Cambridge University Press).

British Chambers of Commerce (1996), 'Internationalisation', *Small Firms Survey*, no. 10 (London: BCC).

British Road Federation (1995), Submission to the Transport Select Committee on Urban Congestion Charging, Third Report, *Urban Road Pricing*, vol. III, Appendices (London: HMSO).

Brusco, S. (1992), 'Small Firms and the Provision of Real Services', in *Industrial Districts and Inter-Firm Co-operation*, ed. F. Pyke and W. Sengenberger (Geneva: International Institute for Labour Studies).

Burrough, B., and Helyar, J. (1990), *Barbarians at the Gate* (London: Arrow).

Cabinet Office (1996a), *Competitiveness: Creating the Enterprise Centre of Europe*, CM 3300, June (London: HMSO).

Cabinet Office (1996b), *The UK's Investment Performance: Fact and Fallacy*, Occasional Paper, June (London: HMSO).

Cabinet Office (1996c), *Helping Business to Win: Consultation on New Approach to Business Support* (London: HMSO).

Cadbury Committee (1992), *Report of the Committee on the Financial Aspects of Corporate Governance* (London: GEE).

Canzoneri, M., Nolan, C., and Yates, A. (1995), 'Mechanisms for Achieving Monetary Stability: Inflation Targeting Versus the ERM', Bank of England, mimeo.

Cave, M. (1996), Discussant's comment in Aaronson.

Caves, R. (ed.) (1968), *Britain's Economic Prospects* (London: Allen & Unwin).

Centre for Exploitation of Science and Technology (CEST) (1995), *Bridging the Innovation Gap* (London: CEST).

Charles, D. (1996), 'Technology Support for SMEs', Centre for Urban and Regional Development Studies, University of Newcastle, mimeo.

Clark, A., and Oswald, A. (1994), 'Unhappiness and Unemployment', *Economic Journal*, 104, pp.648–59.

Commission of the European Communities (1993), *Growth, Competitiveness, Employment: the Challenges and Ways Forward into the 21st Century*, COM(93) 700, December (Brussels: CEC).

Confederation of British Industry (CBI) (1993), *Finance for Growth: Meeting the Financing Needs of Small and Medium Enterprises*, report of CBI Smaller Firms Council, August.

CBI (1995a), *Loosening the Strait-Jacket*, May.

CBI (1995b), *Moving Forward: a Business Strategy for Transport*, December.

CBI (1995c), *Competing for Quality: the Way Ahead*, Memorandum to the Competing for Quality Review.

CBI (1996a), *Realising the Vision: a Skills Passport*, January.

CBI (1996b), *Reform of UK Competition Law*, May.

Confederation of Passenger Transport UK (1996), *Quality Partnerships: Bus Services for the Next Millennium*, Briefing Paper.

Coopers and Lybrand (1994), *Made in the UK: The Middle Market Survey*.

Coopers and Lybrand (1995), *Made in the UK: Hypergrowth Companies*.

Corry, D. (1995), 'Public and Private Partnerships', *Renewal*, 3.2, pp.41–8.

Cosh, A. (1996), 'Where Do SMEs Get Funding?', in Milner (1996).

Cosh, A., and Hughes, A. (ed.) (1996), *The Changing State of British Enterprise* (ESRC Centre for Business Research, University of Cambridge).

Cosh, A., Hughes, A., and Rowthorn, R. (1993), 'The Competitive Role of UK Manufacturing Industry: 1979–2003', in *The Future of UK Competitiveness and the Role of Industrial Policy*, ed. K. Hughes (London: Policy Studies Institute).

Cosh, A., Hughes, A., and Wood, E. (1996a), 'Innovation: Scale, Objectives and Constraints', in Cosh and Hughes (1996).

Cosh, A., Hughes, A., and Wood, E. (1996b), 'Financing Innovation', in Cosh and Hughes (1996).

Crafts, N. (1996a), 'Reversing Relative Economic Decline? The 1980s in Historical Perspective', in *Readings in Macroeconomics*, ed. T. Jenkinson (Oxford: Oxford University Press).

Crafts, N. (1996b), 'Post-Neoclassical Endogenous Growth Theory: What Are Its Policy Implications?', *Oxford Review of Economic Policy*, 12.2, pp.30–47.

Curran, J., Blackburn, R., Kitching, J., and North, J. (1996), *Establishing Small Firms' Training Practices, Needs, Difficulties and the Use of Industry Training Organisations*, DfEE, Research Studies, RS17 (London: HMSO).

Currie, D., Levine, P., and Pearlman, J. (1996), 'The Choice of Conservative Bankers in the Open Economy: Monetary Régime Options for Europe', *Economic Journal*, 106, pp.345–58.

Deakin, S., and Slinger, G. (1996), 'Legal and Institutional Aspects of the Stakeholder Model', Cambridge University, mimeo.

Deakins, D., and Philpott, T. (1994), 'Comparative European Practices in the Finance of New Technology Entrepreneurs: UK, Germany and Holland', in *New Technology Based Firms in the 1990s*, ed. R. Oakey (London: Paul Chapman).

Dearing, R. (1996), *Review of Qualifications for 16–19 Year Olds* (London: HMSO).

Department for Education (1994), 'Statistics of Schools in England', *Statistical Bulletin*, August (London: HMSO).

Department for Education and Employment (DfEE) (1996), *The Skills Audit: a Report from an Interdepartmental Group* (London: HMSO).

Department of Education and Science (1988), *Top-Up Loans for Students* (London: HMSO).

Department of Trade and Industry (DTI) (1989), *Opening Markets: New Policy on Restrictive Trade Practices*, Cm 727, July (London: HMSO).

DTI (1992), *Abuse of Market Power*, Cm 2100, November (London: HMSO).

DTI (1993), *Abuse of Market Power: Summary of Responses*, April (London: HMSO).

DTI (1994), *Competitiveness: Helping Business to Win*, Cm 2563, May (London: HMSO).

DTI (1995), *Competitiveness: Forging Ahead*, Cm 2867, May (London: HMSO).

DTI (1996a), *Tackling Cartels and the Abuse of Market Power*, Consultation Document, March (London: HMSO).

DTI (1996b), *Small Firms in Britain*, URN 96/15, July (London: HMSO).

DTI (1996c), *Forward Look of Government-Funded Science, Engineering and Technology*, Cm 3257-1 (London: HMSO).

Department of Transport (1996), *Transport: the Way Forward, the Government's Response to the Transport Debate*, CM 3234 (London: HMSO).

Dimsdale, N., and Prevezer, M. (eds.) (1994), *Capital Markets and Corporate Governance* (Oxford: Clarendon Press).

Employment Committee (1996a), *The Work of TECs*, HC99 (London: HMSO).

Employment Committee (1996b), *The Right to Work/Workfare*, HC82 (London: HMSO).

Employment Department (1994), *The Competitive Edge: Employee Involvement in Britain* (London: Employment Department Group).

Fairtlough, G. (1996), 'Focusing the DTI on Networks', *Demos*, 8, pp.49–51.

Fay, R. (1995), 'Enhancing the Effectiveness of Active Labour Market Policies: the Role of – and Evidence from – Programme Evaluations in OECD Countries', OECD, mimeo.

Foundation for Manufacturing and Industry (1995), *Accounting Rules, Taxation and the Medium-sized Business in the United Kingdom, France and Germany* (London: FM&I).

Fukuyama, F. (1995), *Trust: the Social Virtues and the Creation of Prosperity* (London: Hamish Hamilton).

Gaved, M. (1996), 'The Rise of the Institutional Investor', in Westall (1996).

Geroski P. (1990), 'Procurement Policy as a Tool of Industrial Policy', *International Review of Applied Economics*, 4.2, pp.182–98.

Goldstein, H., and Sammons, P. (1994), *The Influence of Secondary and Junior Schools on 16-year Examination Performance: a Cross-Classified Multi-level Analysis* (London: Institute of Education).

Government of Australia (1994), *Working Nation.*

Greenhalgh, C. (1990), 'Innovation and Trade Performance', *Economic Journal*, 100, pp.105–18.

Guinet, J. (1995), 'Financing Innovation', *OECD Observer*, 194, pp.10–16.

Hawksworth, J., and Wilcox, J. (1995), *Challenging the Convention: Public Borrowing Rules and Housing Investment* (Chartered Institute of Housing/Coopers and Lybrand).

Hay, D. (1993), 'The Assessment: Competition Policy', *Oxford Review of Economic Policy*, 9.2, pp.1–26.

Higson, C., and Elliott, J. (1994), *The Performance of UK Takeovers*, Institute of Finance and Accounting, London Business School Working Paper, no. 181.

Hillman, J. (1996a), 'Education and Training', in *Options for Britain: a Strategic Policy Review*, ed. D. Halpern, S. Wood, S. White and G. Cameron (Aldershot: Dartmouth).

Hillman, J. (1996b), *University for Industry: Creating a National Learning Network* (London: IPPR).

Hirst, P., and Thomson, G. (1996), *Globalization in Question* (Cambridge: Polity Press).

Holland, J. (1995), *The Corporate Governance Role of Financial Institutions in Their Investee Companies*, Chartered Association of Certified Accountants, Research Report 46.

Holtham, G., and Mayhew, K. (1996), *Tackling Long-Term Unemployment* (London: IPPR).

House of Lords (1996), *Information Society: Agenda for Action in the UK*, Fifth Report, HL 77, July (London: HMSO).

Hughes, A. (1994), 'The "Problems" of Finance for Smaller Businesses', in Dimsdale and Prevezer (1994).

Humphries, C. (1995), 'Territorialisation of Industrial Policies: the Role of Public Governance and Funding', TEC National Council, September, mimeo.

Hutton, W. (1995), *The State We're In*, (London: Jonathan Cape).

Institute for Fiscal Studies (IFS) (1994), *Setting Savings Free: Proposals for the Taxation of Savings and Profits* (London: IFS).

Institute of Directors (1996a), *Business Link*, IoD Research Paper.

Institute of Directors (1996b), *Education: a Business Opinion Survey.*

Jackman, R., Layard, R., and Nickell, S. (1996), 'Combating Unemployment: Is Flexibility Enough?', paper presented to the OECD conference on 'Interactions Between Structural Reform, Macroeconomic Policies and Economic Performance', Paris, January.

Jameson, J. (1995), *Convergence and the New Media: a Roadmap* (London: IPPR).

Jarousse, J. P., Mingat, A., and Marc, R. (1995), 'Nursery Education for Two-Year-Olds: Social and Education Effects', in *Education Reform in France: the Mitterrand Years 1981–95*, eds. B. Moon and A. Corbett (London: Routledge).

Jenkinson, T., and Corbett, J. (1996), 'The Financing of Industry: an International Comparison', Centre for Economic Policy Research, May, mimeo.

Judd, J., and Motley, B. (1993), 'Using a Nominal GDP Target to Guide Discretionary Monetary Policy', *Federal Reserve Bank of San Francisco Economic Review*.

Kaplan, R., and Norton, D. (1993), 'Putting the Balanced Scorecard to Work', *Harvard Business Review*, Sept–Oct, pp.134–47.

Kay, J. (1993), *Foundations of Corporate Success* (Oxford: Oxford University Press).

Kay, J., and King, M. (1990), *The British Tax System*, 5th edn (Oxford: Oxford University Press).

Kay, J., and Silberston, A. (1995), 'Corporate Governance', *National Institute Economic Review*, 153, pp.84–97.

Keeble, D. (1996), 'SMEs and Inter-Firm Networks in Britain', ESRC Centre for Business Research, University of Cambridge, mimeo.

Kenworthy, L. (1995), *In Search of National Economic Success: Balancing Competition and Cooperation* (Thousand Oaks: Sage Publications).

Kester, W. (1992), 'Industrial Groups as Systems of Contractual Governance', *Oxford Review of Economic Policy*, 8.3, pp.24–44.

Kitson, M., and Wilkinson, F. (1996), 'Markets and Competition', in Cosh and Hughes (1996).

Krugman, P. (1990), *Exchange Rate Instability* (Boston: MIT Press).

Krugman, P. (1995), 'Growing World Trade: Causes and Consequences', *Brookings Papers on Economic Activity: Microeconomics*, 1, 25th Anniversary Issue, pp.327–77.

Kydland, F., and Prescott, E. (1977), 'Rules Rather than Discretion: the Inconsistency of Optimal Plans', *Journal of Economic Policy*, 85, pp.473–91.

Latter, D., and Garnsey, E. (1995), *Venture Capital and High Technology Enterprise*, University of Cambridge, Research Papers in Management Studies, no. 24, October.

Lavarack, D. (1996), 'British Banks Have Changed', in Milner (1996).

Layard, R. (1996), *Briefing Paper on Long-Term Unemployment* (London: Employment Institute).

Layard, R., and Philpott, J. (1991), *Stopping Unemployment,* (London: Employment Institute).

Layard, R., Steedman, H., and Robinson, P. (1995), 'Lifelong Learning', Centre for Economic Performance, LSE, mimeo.

Lee, P. (1995), 'Transport, the Economy and Employment', Road Haulage Association, mimeo.

Leuven, E., and Tuijnman, A. (1996), 'Life-Long Learning: Who Pays?', *OECD Observer*, 199, pp.10–14.

Lichtenberg, F. (1988), 'The Private R&D Investment Response to Federal Design and Technical Competitions', *American Economic Review,* 78, pp.550–9.

Lichtenstein, G. (1993), *Types and Aspects of Interfirm Cooperation: a Strategic Typology of Network Approaches*, presented at Conference on Co-operation and Competitiveness, Interfirm Co-operation – a Means Towards SME Competitiveness, Lisbon, Portugal, October.

Lindey, G. (1996), 'The Myners Report and Greenbury', in Westall (1996).

Lissenburgh, S., and Bryson, A. (1996), *The Returns to Graduation*, Department for Education and Employment, Research Studies, no. 15 (London: HMSO).

Machin, S., and Wilkinson, D. (1995), *Employee Training: Unequal Access and Economic Performance* (London: IPPR).

Maddison, A. (1991), *Dynamic Forces in Capitalist Development* (Oxford: Oxford University Press).

Marsh, P. (1993), *Short-Termism on Trial* (London: Institutional Fund Managers' Association).

Marshall, M. (1990), 'Regional Alternatives to Economic Decline in Britain's Industrial Heartland: Industrial Restructuring and Local Economic Intervention in the West Midlands Conurbations', in *Global Challenge and Local Response*, ed. W. Stöhr (London: United Nations University).

Mason, C., and Harrison, R. (1995), 'Final Review and Evaluation of Five Informal Investment Demonstration Projects', Department of Trade and Industry, November (London: HMSO).

Mason, G., van Ark, B., and Wagner, K. (1994), 'Productivity, Product Quality and Workforce Skills: Food Processing in Four European Countries', *National Institute Economic Review*, 147, pp.62–83.

Mason, G., and Finegold, D. (1995), 'Productivity, Machinery and Skills in the United States and Western Europe: Precision Engineering', National Institute of Economic and Social Research, Discussion Paper, no. 89, December.

Mayer, C. (1994), 'Stock-Markets, Financial Institutions and Corporate Performance', in Dimsdale and Prevezer (1994).

Mayer, C. (1996), 'Corporate Governance and Performance: The Evidence', in Westall (1996).

Mayer, C., and Alexander, I. (1991), 'Stock Markets and Corporate Performance: a Comparison of Quoted and Unquoted Companies', Centre for Economic Policy Research Discussion Paper.

Meade, J. (1994), *Full Employment Without Inflation* (London: Employment Policy Institute).

Meadows, P. (ed.) (1996), *Work Out – or Work In?* (York: Joseph Rowntree Foundation).

Melville-Ross, T. (1996), 'Two-Tier Boards and Non-Executive Directors', paper delivered to Institute of Chartered Secretaries and Administrators Conference, March.

Middleton, M., Cowling, M., Samuels, J., and Sugden, R. (1994), 'Small Firms and Clearing Banks', in Dimsdale and Prevezer (1994).

Midland Bank (1994), *The Mittelstand, the German Model and the UK*, September.

Miles, D. (1993), 'Testing for Short-Termism in the UK Stock Market', *Economic Journal*, 103, pp.1079–96.

Miles, D. (1996), 'Asking the Right Questions', in Milner (1996).

Miliband, D. (1990), *Technology Transfer Policies for Innovation*, Industrial Policy Paper, no. 2 (London: IPPR).

Millward, N. (1994), *The New Industrial Relations?* (London: Policy Studies Institute).

Milner, S. (ed.) (1996), *Could Finance Do More for British Business?* (London: IPPR).

Moore, B. (1994), 'Financial Constraints to the Growth and Development for Small High-Technology Firms', in *Finance and the Small Firm*, eds. A. Hughes and D. Storey (London: Routledge).

Mortimore, P. (1995), *Effective Schools: Current Impact and Future Potential* (London: Institute of Education).

Murray, G. (1994), 'The European Union's Support for New Technology Based Firms: an Assessment of the First Three Years of the European Seed Capital Fund Scheme', *European Planning Studies*, 2.4, pp.435–61.

Murray, G., and Lott, J. (1995), 'Have UK Venture Capital Firms a Bias Against Investment in New Technology-Based Firms?', *Research Policy*, 24, pp.283–99.

MVA Consultancy (1995), *The London Congestion Charging Research Programme: Principal Findings* (London: HMSO).

Myners Report (1995), *Developing a Winning Partnership: How Companies and Institutional Investors Are Working Together*.

National Association of Pension Funds (1995), *The Powerful Vote: Voting in the Context of Good Corporate Governance*, Investment Committee Briefing, November.

National Commission on Education (NCE) (1993), *Learning to Succeed* (London: Heinemann).

National Consumer Council (1995), *Competition and Consumers: Policy and Practice in the United Kingdom* (London: National Consumer Council).

Nickell, S., and Bell, B. (1995), 'The Collapse in Demand for the Unskilled and Unemployment Across the OECD', *Oxford Review of Economic Policy*, 11.1, pp.40–62.

Oakey, R. (1984), *High Technology Small Firms* (London: Francis Pinter).

The Observer (1996), *The Observer Blueprint for a National Travel Plan to Take Britain's Transport System into the 21st Century*.

OECD (Organisation for Economic Co-operation and Development) (1990), *Labour Market Policies for the 1990s* (Paris: OECD).

OECD (1993), *Employment Outlook* (Paris: OECD).

OECD (1995a), *United Kingdom* (Paris: OECD Economic Surveys).

OECD (1995b), *Industry and Technology: Scoreboard of Indicators*, (Paris: OECD).

OECD (1996), *Globalisation: What Challenges and Opportunities for Government?* (Paris: OECD).

Opler, T., and Sokobin, J. (1995), 'Does Co-ordinated Institutional Activism Work? An Analysis of the Activities of the Council of Institutional Investors', Ohio State University, mimeo.

Orts, E. (1992), 'Beyond Shareholders: Interpreting Corporate Constituency Statutes', *George Washington Law Review*, 61.14.

OST (Office of Science and Technology) (1995), *Technology Foresight: Progress Through Partnership, Transport* (London: HMSO).

Oulton, N. (1995), 'Supply Side Reform and UK Economic Growth: What Happened to the Miracle?', *National Institute Economic Review*, 154.4, pp.53–70.

Oulton, N. (1996), 'Competition and the Dispersion of Labour Productivity Amongst UK Companies', National Institute of Economic and Social Research, September, mimeo.

Payne, J. (1990), *Adults' Off-the-job Skills Training: an Evaluation Study* (Sheffield: Policy Studies Institute).

Pendleton, A., McDonald, J., Robinson, A., and Wilson, N. (1995), 'Patterns of Employee Participation and Industrial Democracy in UK Employee Share Ownership Plans', Centre for Economic Performance, LSE, Discussion Paper, no. 249.

Pezzini, M. (1996), 'Entrepreneurial Towns', *OECD Observer*, 197, pp.9–11.

Philpott, J. (1996), 'The Cost of Unemployment and Reflections on Employment Programmes', in Meadows (1996).

Porter, M. (1990), *The Competitive Advantage of Nations* (London: Macmillan).

Prais, S. (1993), 'Economic Performance and Education: the Nature of Britain's Deficiencies', *Proceedings of the British Academy*, 84, pp.151–207.

Prais, S., Jarvis, V., and Wagner, K. (1989), 'Productivity and Vocational Skills in Services in Britain and Germany: Hotels', *National Institute Economic Review*, 130, pp.52–74.

Putnam, R. (1993), *Making Democracy Work: Civic Traditions in Modern Italy* (Princeton: Princeton University Press).

Pyke, F. (1992), *Industrial Development Through Small-Firm Co-operation*, (Geneva: ILO).

Raymond, K., and Shaw, M. (1996), *Better Government by Design: Improving the Effectiveness of Public Purchasing*, Social Market Foundation Memorandum, no. 21.

Reich, R. (1992), *The Work of Nations* (New York: Vintage).

Robinson, P. (1995a), 'Qualifications and the Labour Market: Do the National Education and Training Targets Make Sense?', Centre for Economic Performance, LSE, Working Paper, no. 736, July.

Robinson, P. (1995b), 'The British Disease Overcome? Living Standards, Productivity and Educational Attainment, 1979–94', Centre for Economic Performance, LSE, Discussion Paper, no. 260, August.

Robinson, P. (1996), 'Rhetoric and Reality: the Take Up of the New Vocational Qualifications', Centre for Economic Performance/Gatsby Foundation, LSE, mimeo.

Robson, S. (1996), 'A View from the Treasury', in Milner (1996).

Rosewell, B. (1996), 'Small Firms and Their Finances', in Milner (1996).

Rough, D. (1996), 'In Defence of Institutional Investors', in Milner (1996).

Royal Commission on Environmental Pollution (RCEP) (1994) *Transport and the Environment*, Cm 2674 (London: HMSO).

Royal Society for the Encouragement of Arts, Manufactures and Commerce (RSA) (1995), *Tomorrow's Company: the Role of Business in a Changing World* (London: RSA).

Sako, M. (1992), *Prices, Quality and Trust: Inter-Firm Relations in Britain and Japan* (Cambridge: Cambridge University Press).

Sako, M. (1996), 'The Effects of Supplier Relationships and Worker Involvement on Corporate Performance', in Westall (1996).

Salter, W. (1966), *Productivity and Technical Change,* 2nd edn. (Cambridge: Cambridge University Press).

Sammons, P. (1994), *Continuity of School Effects* (London: Institute of Education).

Sammons, P., Hillman, J., and Mortimore, P. (1995), *Key Characteristics of Effective Schools: a Review of School Effectiveness Research* (London: OFSTED).

Save British Science (1996), *Policies for the Next Government, Science and Technology*, SBS Memorandum (Oxford: SBS).

Schuller, T., and Erdal, D. (1996), 'Whose Capital? Sustainable Employee Ownership', Bradford University Management Centre, mimeo.

Schwanse, P. (1995), 'The Effectiveness of Active Labour Market Policies: Some Lessons from the Experience of OECD Countries', paper presented to OECD technical workshop, Vienna, November.

Shaw, A. and Walker, R. (1996), 'Disjointed Interaction: the Labour Market and the Benefits System', in Meadows (1996).

Silberston, A. (1981), 'Industrial Policy in Britain 1960–80', in *Industrial Policy in Innovation*, ed. C. Carter (London: Heinemann).

Soskice, D. (1993), 'Social Skills from Mass Higher Education: Rethinking the Company-Based Initial Training Paradigm', *Oxford Review of Economic Policy*, 9.3, pp.101–13.

Standing Advisory Committee on Trunk Road Assessment (SACTRA) (1994), *Trunk Roads and the Generation of Traffic* (London: HMSO).

Steedman, H., and Wagner, K. (1989), 'Productivity, Machinery and Skills: Clothing Manufacture in Britain and Germany', *National Institute Economic Review*, 128, pp.40–57.

Stella, P. (1993), 'The Fiscal Impact of Public Enterprises', in Blejer and Cheasty (1993).

Stephens, P. (1996), *Politics and the Pound: the Conservatives' Struggle with Sterling* (London: Macmillan).

Storey, D. (1995), *Understanding the Small Business Sector* (London: Routledge).

Storey, D. (1996), 'Correcting Continuing Market Failures', in Milner (1996).

Sylva, K. (1994), 'The Impact of Early Learning on Children's Later Development', in *Start Right: the Importance of Early Learning*, ed. C. Ball (London: RSA).

Thurow, L. (1993), *Head to Head: the Coming Economic Battle among Japan, Europe and America* (London: Nicholas Brearley).

Thurow, L. (1996), *The Future of Capitalism* (London: Nicholas Brearley).

Tobin, J. (1993), 'On the Theory of Macroeconomic Policy', in *Tinbergen Lectures on Economic Policy*, ed. A. Knoester and A. Wellink (Amsterdam: North-Holland).

Tomlinson, J. (1994), *Government and the Enterprise since 1900* (Oxford: Clarendon Press).

Trade and Industry Committee (1995a), *UK Policy on Monopolies*, HC 249-I, May (London: HMSO).

Trade and Industry Committee (1995b), *The Small Business Sector*, HC 194, July (London: HMSO).

Trades Union Congress (1994), *Human Resource Management: a Trade Union Response* (London: TUC).

Treasury (1994), *Government Purchasing: Progress Report to the Prime Minister 1993–4* (London: HMSO).

Treasury (1995a), *Setting New Standards: a Strategy for Government Procurement*, Cm 2840 (London: HMSO).

Treasury (1995b), 'Public Finances and the Cycle', *Treasury Occasional Paper*, no. 4 (London: HMSO).

Voss, C., Blackmon, K., Hanson, P., and Oak, B. (1995), 'The Competitiveness of European Manufacturing – a Four Country Study', *Business Strategy Review*, 6.1, pp.1–25.

Walsh, C. (1995), 'Optimal Contracts for Central Bankers', *American Economic Review*, 85.1, pp. 150–67.

Weale, M., Blake, A., Christodoulakis, N., Meade, J., and Vines, D. (1989), *Macroeconomic Policy, Inflation, Wealth and the Exchange Rate* (London: Unwin Hyman).

Wes, M. (1996), *Globalisation: Winners and Losers* (London: IPPR).

Westall, A. (ed.) (1996), *Competitiveness and Corporate Governance* (London: IPPR).

White, L. (1993), 'Competition Policy in the United States: an Overview', *Oxford Review of Economic Policy*, 9.2, pp.133–53.

Wiener, M. (1981), *English Culture and the Decline of the Industrial Spirit, 1850–1980* (Cambridge: Cambridge University Press).

Williams, M. (1993), 'The Effectiveness of Competition Policy in the United Kingdom', *Oxford Review of Economic Policy*, 9.2, pp.94–112.

Young, G. (1995), 'The Economic Effects of Changes in Capital Allowances', NIESR, November, mimeo.

WRITTEN AND ORAL EVIDENCE

We are extremely grateful to all the people who helped the Commission, whether through submitting written papers, providing oral evidence, participating in working groups or generally answering queries and locating data. Those who submitted written evidence have been marked with an *.

Robin Aaronson, Coopers and Lybrand*
Graham Allen, National Association of Pension Funds
Elizabeth Amos, Foundation for Manufacturing and Industry
Stephen Atkins, Policy Studies Manager, London Transport Planning
Edward Balls, Office of Gordon Brown MP
Kate Barker, Chief Economist, Confederation of British Industry
Terry Barker, Chairman, Cambridge Econometrics
Chris Beauman, European Bank for Reconstruction and Development
Alison Beer, The Forum of Private Business
Bob Bennett, London School of Economics
John Boatman, Managing Director, Coldstream Distribution and
    Chairman, Institute of Logistics
Stephen Bond, Institute for Fiscal Studies*
Gordon Borrie, Chairman of Social Justice Commission and previously
    Director-General of Fair Trading*
Elizabeth Boyd-Adams, Commercial Director, The Association of
    British Chambers of Commerce
Bill Bradshaw, Wolfson College, Oxford University
Alison Brawn, Business Services Manager, Freightliner Ltd
Graham Broome, The Society of Motor Manufacturers and Traders
    Industry Forum*
Colin Brown, Deputy Director of Research, Consumers Association
Joan Brown, Accounting Standards Board*

Philip Burns, London Economics
Bill Callaghan, Trades Union Congress*
John Cantwell, Reading University*
Martin Cave, Brunel University*
Mike Chapman, Management Development Manager, Lucas Industries
Jonathan Charkham, author of *Keeping Good Company**
David Charles, Centre for Urban and Regional Development Studies,
    Newcastle University*
Penny Childs, Management and Development Manager,
    Legal & General
Judith Church MP
Bert Clough, Trades Union Congress
David Coates, Trades Union Congress
Stephen Coleclough, Head of Corporate Tax, Simmons & Simmons
Allan Cook, Accounting Standards Board*
Michael Coolican, Aerospace Division, DTI*
Mark Conaty, HM Treasury
Helen Conner, Institute for Employment Studies, Sussex University
Martin Conyon, Centre for Corporate Strategy and Change, Warwick
    Business School*
Tony Cornish, Senior Telecommunications Policy Advisor, Reuters
Dan Corry, Senior Economist, IPPR*
Willie Coupar, Involvement and Participation Association
Christopher Cowyn, DJ Freeman
John Cuckney, IT Director, Lucas Industries
Lord Currie, London Business School
Howard Davies, Director-General, CBI (now Bank of England)
Simon Deakin, ESRC Centre for Business Research, Cambridge
    University*
Nicholas Dee, ESRC Centre for Business Research, Cambridge
    University
Michael Devereux, Keele University*
Bob Dobbie, Competitiveness Division, Cabinet Office
Ron Dore, Centre for Economic Performance, London School of
    Economics
Eliza Dungworth, Association of Unit Trusts & Investment Flows
Tony Dye, Phillips and Drew Fund Management
Michael Elves, Glaxo Wellcome plc
Paul Everitt, Deputy Director, British Road Federation*
John Fallon, Powergen plc
Peter Fanning, Office of Andrew Smith MP

Robin Fears, SmithKline Beecham Pharmaceuticals
Manfred Fox, Innovation Marketing
Julian Franks, London Business School
Moira Fraser Steele, Director of Education and Training, the Design
　Council
Judith Freedman, London School of Economics
Harold Freeman, HM Treasury
Carol Galley, Mercury Asset Management
Malcom Gammie, Linklaters & Paines*
Nick Garnham, Centre for Communication and Information Studies,
　Westminster University*
Matthew Gaved, Institute of Management, LSE*
Paul George, Coopers and Lybrand
Paul Geroski, London Business School
Glasgow Development Agency
David Glazebrook, Touche Ross Management Consultants
Andrew Glyn, Oxford University
Douglas Godden, Confederation of British Industry
Mark Goyder, RSA*
David Grayson, Director of Business in the Community*
Paul Gregg, Centre for Economic Performance, LSE
Martin Harris, Brunel University
Chris Haskins, Chairman, Northern Foods plc*
Mark Hastings, Institute of Management
Richard Hawkins, Science Policy Research Unit, Sussex University
Chris Hayes, Prospect Centre
John Healey, Head of Communications, Trades Union Congress
John Heath, Yorkshire Electricity
Chris Hewett, IPPR
Patricia Hewitt, Head of Research, Andersen Consulting*
Martin Higginson, Confederation of Passenger Transport UK
Derek Higgs, SG Warburg
Chris Higson, London Business School*
Josh Hillman, IPPR*
John Holland, Glasgow University *
Jonathan Hopkins, Ian Greer Associates
Peter Horsman, Legal & General Group plc
Bernard Hughes, Tesco plc
Kirsty Hughes, Royal Institute for International Affairs
David Instone, Head of Transport Policy Unit, Department of
　Transport

Charles Jackson, Mercury Asset Management
Andrew James, Policy Research in Engineering, Science and Technology,
    Manchester University
Mark Johnson, Project Finance Unit, S J Berwin & Co
Neil Johnston, Centre for the Exploitation of Science and Technology
Bernard Jones, Freight Transport Association
Stephen Joseph, Transport 2000*
Andrew Joy, British Venture Capital Association*
David Keeble, ESRC Centre for Business Research, Cambridge
    University*
Peter Kenway, Reading University
Charles Latham, Confederation of British Industry
Patrick Law, British Gas
Clive Lawson, ESRC Centre for Business Research, Cambridge
    University*
Geoff Lindey, JP Morgan Investment Management *
W T Little, Unilever
James McCormick, Commission on Social Justice and IPPR
Amanda McIntyre, Confederation of British Industry*
Ewen Macpherson, Chief Executive, 3i plc*
Doug McWilliams, Centre for Economic and Business Research
Christine Mallin, Nottingham Business School, Nottingham Trent
    University*
Geoff Mason, National Institute for Economic and Social Research*
Nick Matthews, The Labour Party
Colin Mayer, School of Management, Oxford University*
David Mayes, National Institute for Economic and Social Research
Ken Mayhew, Pembroke College, Oxford University*
Tim Melville-Ross, Director-General, Institute of Directors*
John Moore, 3i plc
Derek Morris, Oriel College, Oxford University*
Neil Mullett, Manager of Facilities, British Aerospace
John Mulvey, Save British Science*
Cristina Murroni, IPPR
Chris Nash, Institute of Transport Studies, Leeds University*
James Nelson, British Venture Capital Association
Geoffrey Norris, Office of Tony Blair MP
Bill Nuttall, Department of Trade and Industry*
Kate Oakley, Policy Studies Institute*
Nick Oulton, National Institute for Economic and Social Research*
Geoffrey Owen, Centre for Economic Performance, LSE

James Owen, Competitiveness Division, Cabinet Office
John Parkinson, Law Department, Bristol University*
Keith Pavitt, Science Policy Research Unit, Sussex University*
Joan Payne, Policy Studies Institute
Sarah Perman, Trades Union Congress
Ian Peters, National Westminster Bank*
John Philpott, Director, Employment Policy Institute
Craig Pickering, HM Treasury
David Pitt-Watson, Braxton Associates*
Mark Pragnell, Centre for Economic and Business Research
Sig Prais, National Institute for Economic and Social Research*
Dan Prentice, Oxford University
Quentin Rappaport, British Telecommunications plc
James Redman, Forum of Private Business
Alec Reed, Reed Executive plc
John van Reenen, Institute for Fiscal Studies*
Richard Ritchie, BP Oil
Michael Roberts, Confederation of British Industry
Peter Robinson, Centre for Economic Performance, LSE*
Alex Roney, London Chamber of Commerce and Industry
Alistair Ross-Goobey, Hermes Asset Management
Paul Ryan, King's College, Cambridge University
Charles Sabel, MIT*
Mari Sako, London School of Economics*
Naomi Sargent, Independent Education Consultant
Richard Saunders, MAI
Chris Savage, Trades Union Congress*
John Shave, Prudential Corporation Ltd
Saleem Sheikh, London Guildhall University
Giles Slinger, ESRC Centre for Business Research, Cambridge
    University*
Martyn Sloman*
Ian Small, Bank of England
Stephen Smith, Deputy Director, Institute for Fiscal Studies
Dennis Snower, Birkbeck College, London University *
Mark Spelman, Andersen Consulting*
Hillary Steedman, Centre for Economic Performance, LSE*
Sigmund Sternberg
Bryan Steven, Involvement and Participation Association
Paul Stoneman, Warwick Business School
Charles Strutt, SmithKline Beecham Pharmaceuticals

Edward Swan
Julian Tapp, British Aerospace
Keith Telford, IBM
Kate Tillet, Merck, Sharpe and Dohme
Stephen Tindale, IPPR*
Adair Turner, Director-General, Confederation of British Industry
Tracy Turner, Trades Union Congress
Roberto Unger, Harvard Law School*
Ian Vance, Nortel Ltd
Anna Walker, Deputy Director-General, OFTEL
John Waller
Roy Warden, Inland Revenue
Jo Webb, IPPR
Marina Wes, Centre for Economic Performance, LSE*
Alick Whitfield, Railtrack
Andrew Whyte, News International plc
Frank Wilkinson, ESRC Centre for Business Research, Cambridge
    University
Janet Williamson, Trades Union Congress
Steven Woodcock, London School of Economics
Irving Yass, Director of Transport and Planning, London First
Ivan Yates, author of 'Innovation, Investment and Survival of the UK
    Economy' (Royal Academy of Engineering, 1992)
Simon Zadek, New Economics Foundation*

COMMISSION PUBLICATIONS

As part of the process of collecting evidence and stimulating debate, the Commission published six issue papers. These are available from the Institute for Public Policy Research, 30–32 Southampton St, London, WC2E 7RA. The complete set is available for £25.

Issue Paper 1
Employee Training: Unequal Access and Economic Performance, by Stephen Machin and David Wilkinson (Dec 1995), ISBN: I 86030 016 2, £3.95.
A comprehensive assessment of who receives training at work, what type of employer provides training and who gains from it.

Issue Paper 2
Could Finance Do More for British Business?, edited by Simon Milner (Feb 1996), ISBN I 86030 022 7, £5.50.
Is finance the cause of, accessory to or innocent bystander in the failings of British industry? Includes contributions from Will Hutton, Michael Stoddart and David Lavarack.

Issue Paper 3
Globalisation: Winners and Losers, by Marina Wes (Mar 1996), ISBN I 86030 029 4, £3.95.
A thorough examination of one of the central dilemmas of our age – globalisation – with particular emphasis on its implications for the UK.

Issue Paper 4
The Future of UK Competition Policy, by Robin Aaronson, Gordon Borrie, Martin Cave and David Pitt-Watson (Apr 1996), ISBN I 86030 033 2, £3.95.
Four authors debate the need for, and possible form of, competition policy reform in the United Kingdom including its interaction with European competition regulations.

Issue Paper 5

Competitiveness and Corporate Governance, edited by Andrea Westall (May 1996), ISBN I 86030 039 1, £5.50.

Various authors (including John Kay, John Monks, Tim Melville-Ross and Christopher Haskins) discuss the impact of different governance arrangements on corporate performance and the role of public policy in promoting 'good' governance.

Issue Paper 6

Small Firms On-Line, by Gillian Lauder and Andrea Westall (Jan 1997), ISBN I 86030 043 X, £5.50.

An investigation of new technology and its applications for the success of small firms. Policy implications stress partnerships between companies and public and private organisations.

Commission Conferences

The Commission held two participative conferences which attracted a wide variety of business people, academics and policy-makers:

Could Finance Do More for British Business?
Friday 20 October 1995

City-industry relations

Chair: Gerald Holtham, CPPBB Commissioner; Director, IPPR
Colin Mayer, Institute of Management, Oxford University
David Miles, Chief UK Economist, Merrill Lynch
Will Hutton, Assistant Editor, the *Guardian*
Stephen Nickell, Institute of Economics and Statistics, Oxford University

Finance for SMEs

Chair: Alan Hughes, CPPBB Commissioner and Director, ESRC Centre for Business Research, Cambridge University
Michael Stoddart, Chairman, Electra Investment Trust plc
David Storey, Director, The Centre for Small and Medium-Sized Enterprises at Warwick Business School, Warwick University
Ian Peters, Head of SME Unit, Confederation of British Industry
David Lavarack, Small Business Services Director, Barclays Bank plc
Bob Bischof, CPPBB Commissioner and Chairman, Boss Group
Bridget Rosewell, Director, Business Strategies
Andy Mullineux, Director of Money, Banking and Finance Programmes, Birmingham University

Competitiveness and Corporate Governance
Thursday 29 February 1996

Does governance affect competitiveness?

Chair: Professor George Bain, Chairman, CPPBB and Principal, London Business School

Jonathan Charkham, Member, Cadbury Committee; director of several companies including GUS plc

Mari Sako, Reader in Industrial Relations, LSE

David Grayson, Director, Business in the Community

Professor Colin Mayer, Deputy Director, School of Management, Oxford University

Where are we now?

Chair: Alan Hughes, CPPBB Commissioner and Director, ESRC Centre for Business Research, Cambridge University

Christopher Haskins, Chairman, Northern Foods plc; Member of Cadbury II

Geoff Lindey, Investment Manager, JP Morgan; Member of Myners Group

Mark Goyder, Director, RSA Inquiry, Tomorrow's Company

Matthew Gaved, Institute of Management, LSE; editor of *Governance*

Future policy forum

Chair: Gerald Holtham, CPPBB Commissioner; Director, IPPR

John Monks, General Secretary, TUC; Commissioner CPPBB

Tim Melville-Ross, Director-General, Institute of Directors

John Parkinson, Professor of Law, Bristol University

John Kay, Chairman, London Economics Ltd; Commissioner CPPBB

INDEX